The World Today

W. E. F. Ward has been able to observe many of the changes he examines in this book at first hand. His experience includes many years of teaching in West Africa, he has been Director of Education in Mauritius, and served as a member of the U.K. delegation to seven general conferences at UNESCO and many other international meetings on education.

His other books include

A History of Ghana
Emergent Africa
Government in West Africa
A History of Africa (3 vols)
The Royal Navy and the Slavers

The World Today

W. E. F. WARD
C.M.G., B.Litt., M.A.

London · George Allen & Unwin Ltd
Ruskin House · Museum Street

First published in 1974

ISBN 0 04 909007 0 hardback
ISBN 0 04 909008 9 paperback

Printed in Great Britain
in 10 point Times Roman type
by Clarke, Doble & Brendon, Ltd
Plymouth

Preface

There were two impulses that led me to write this book. One was that a friend, speaking about international affairs, remarked despairingly, 'I suppose that to you as a historian this modern world makes sense, but to me it seems quite unintelligible'. The other impulse was that I find myself so flooded with day-to-day information that it is hard to remember the background of today's events. Without looking it up I could not recall (for example) why Dr Sukarno had his 'confrontation' with Malaysia, or why the French pulled out of Indo-China and the Americans went in. I believe that no one can understand the nature of a difficulty, much less find the solution, unless he knows how the difficulty arose in the first place.

This book therefore is a sort of notebook on the background to some of the problems which have filled our newspapers during the last forty years or so. With such a beginning, the book cannot have an overall theme, such as the rise of nationalism, the collapse of imperialism, or the rise of the Third World. We have indeed witnessed the collapse of the Western colonial empires and the multiplication of new states in Asia and Africa as well as in Europe. It would however be misleading to suggest that international affairs today can be explained by any such simple formula. The pattern is more complicated; the development of communism and the strivings after some sort of world government are two examples which would not fit into any short formula. The matters discussed in this book are all questions of international affairs; they have all occupied much space in the newspapers; and most of them have aroused heated partisanship among people not directly involved.

In each chapter I have had to ask myself how far back in time I need to go. It depends: I can begin the Arab-Israeli chapter for example in 1917 with the Balfour Declaration, but to understand the burning question whether there should be two Vietnams or one Vietnam we have to go back three centuries; and when we deal with Irish affairs, Oliver Cromwell seems but as yesterday.

I am writing of matters which are acutely controversial, and I have of course tried to be dispassionate and factual. In these bitter disputes, each side usually has something of a case, even though the other side will not admit it. But ideas are facts, and the behaviour of governments and statesmen will sometimes be unintelligible until we examine the ideas by which they are guided. This is why I have given a good deal of space to a discussion of Marxism and its effect on the thinking and action of the governments which have adopted it as their creed.

I have found writing the book a useful exercise for myself. I hope the book may be useful also to other people: to general readers who are interested in these world problems, and to students whose examiners require them to show some knowledge of recent events and their causes.

W. E. F. WARD

Contents

Maps

1 Introduction

'Each age', says the poet, 'is a dream that is dying, or one that is coming to birth.' The third quarter of the twentieth century saw the death of two dreams: the British 'dominion over palm and pine', and the supremacy of Western Europe in world affairs. The fourth quarter of the century is watching the birth of a new dream, a dream that is strange, bewildering, and unfriendly. It is the dream of a world dominated by three suspicious world powers, with Africa and the lesser states of Asia playing the part which was played a century ago by the Balkan states; and with Western Europe reduced to comparative insignificance. What is happening to us, and why is it happening in this way?

Important as these political changes are, the world today has other features which many people consider more striking. It is a world troubled by the fear of over-population and hunger, and by pollution on a vast scale. Above all, it is a world of speedy communications. Newsworthy events can be seen instantaneously on television screens all over the world; and no pair of important towns anywhere on the globe are further apart in travel time than London and Bristol in the eighteenth century. To most people in Western Europe however, the world of televised news and jet air travel is familiar and welcome, and fears of over-population and hunger are remote; whereas the face of modern international politics – the super-powers, the cold war, the Afro-Asian block, the decline of Europe – is strange and alarming. In this book we shall try and answer their question, 'Why are these things happening?'

The future and the present are largely the result of the past. However radical or revolutionary we may be in some matters, much of our life is governed by a conservative instinct. As far as we can, we base ourselves on familiar foundations; we do not love change for its own sake. The tailor still puts buttons on my coat which are purposeless now, but represent buttons which had a purpose long ago. Twice in its history, in the Great Fire of 1666 and in Hitler's air raids, the City of London has had much of its area laid waste. But when the rubble has been cleared away, men have rebuilt on the old foundations. The narrow lanes and alleys of the medieval

City still run their old courses and keep their old names, though they run no longer between low houses and shops of mèdieval wattle-and-daub or Elizabethan half-timber, but between towering office blocks of steel and concrete.

Similarly, today's world is the world which we and our fathers have made in the past. The statesmen in the White House, the Kremlin, Downing Street and the Elysée cannot escape from their national myths and memories and ways of thinking. In some peculiarly sensitive regions there is a deliberate fostering of national myths and memories. The prentice boys of Derry, and King Billy on his white horse, arouse very different feelings on opposite sides of the Irish border; and the celebrations of Dingaan's Day are not viewed with the same eyes by white South Africans and black.

Britain's decline from her position as a first-class power, and the weakening in the status of Western Europe as a whole, are events of the first importance. Throughout the nineteenth century Britain's industrial and naval strength gave her immense reputation and authority in the world; and for nearly 500 years – since the voyages of Columbus and Vasco da Gama – the countries of Western Europe have been climbing to a position of dominance over the other continents. Australasia and the Americas they colonised, Asia and Africa they conquered and exploited. The decline of Western Europe and of Britain removes from the stage, at least for the time being, the actors who have dominated it for so long.

The second half of the fifteenth century was the great age of Portuguese exploration; the sixteenth century was the golden age of Spain. It was not until the second half of the seventeenth century that France became supreme in Europe, not only in war but in the arts of peace. There were times when it seemed possible that French troops might garrison England and enable the English King to get rid of his troublesome parliament.

French ambition was checked in Marlborough's war at the beginning of the eighteenth century. In this war Holland fought side by side in an equal partnership with England against the armies of France. But Holland was exhausted by her efforts; in the eighteenth century she ceased to be a first-class power, and England and France were left to fight it out together. In 1707 England and Scotland were united into one country of Great Britain, and Englishmen and Scotsmen together extended the British colonies in North America and began building an empire in India.

In the latter years of the eighteenth century the industrial revolution began in Britain. Hand industries were replaced by machine industries; cottages were replaced by factories. Britain became the workshop of the world, exporting her manufactures and importing food for the crowded factory workers in the grimy new industrial cities.

In 1773 a riotous group of American colonists emptied a ship-load of tea into Boston harbour; and ten years later the British government was compelled to admit defeat and recognise the independence of the United States. This American revolution was quickly followed by the French revolution; and the French revolution led to a war of more than twenty years which France (first under amateur revolutionary generals and then under Napoleon) fought against Britain and the rest of Europe. Thanks to her island situation and to her dominant navy, Britain was the only belligerent country which was never occupied by French troops. After Napoleon had been defeated and exiled, Britain was left in supreme command of the sea.

The Americans and the French had effectively taught the world the idea of self-determination: peoples ought in principle to be independent and self-governing, preferably under some sort of parliamentary system. During the nineteenth century this principle was gradually put into practice in Europe. Italy and Germany ceased to be mosaics of independent principalities, and developed into well organised nation-states. The Turkish empire, which in the seventeenth century had reached almost to the gates of Vienna, lost nearly all its European territory. By 1914 Europe had organised itself into a group of six Great Powers (Britain, France, Germany, Austria-Hungary, Russia and Italy) and twenty smaller or weaker states.

As British technology spread to other countries, the states of Europe began to compete with each other for markets and for raw materials. The unknown interior of Africa was as great a challenge to nineteenth-century explorers as the Poles or Everest were to their children, or the Moon to their grandchildren. By the 1870s the main features of African geography were known; in the 1880s the European colonisation of tropical Africa began; and by 1914 only Liberia and Ethiopia remained independent of European rule. South-East Asia too was colonised, and the European states made sundry attempts to peg out spheres of influence in China. International rivalry became so intense, whether for economic power or political prestige, that the six Great Powers broke apart into two hostile groups, and they began to drift towards war. The United States meanwhile was so fully occupied in settling its huge territory and organising its internal affairs that it took little part in the affairs of Europe.

The two World Wars of 1914–18 and 1939–45 destroyed the predominance of Europe. In the second war, Britain fought side by side with the United States in an equal partnership. But Britain was exhausted by her efforts, just as Holland had been exhausted 200 years earlier by fighting as an equal partner with England against the France of Louis XIV. After 1945 Britain could no longer compare with the United States in wealth or in power. The Royal Navy, which before 1914 had been maintained equal in strength to the combined forces of the next two strongest navies of the world, now saw itself greatly outnumbered by the immensely powerful American navy.

As a result of these two wars, the principle of self-determination was applied in Asia and Africa, and the European colonies gained their independence. The Turkish empire in Asia was broken up: Turkey herself formed a very solid nation-state in Asia Minor, while her former Arab subjects formed a sort of Balkan mosaic of jealous states, agreeing on very little except their detestation of the new state of Israel. The world was dominated now by two rival super-powers, the United States and Russia. One of them was the champion of free enterprise, the other of communism; each was armed with the atomic bomb; and the fear of nuclear warfare hung like a thunder-cloud over the rest of the world.

After the 1914–18 war the victorious allies, in an attempt to prevent future wars, set up a League of Nations. The League had fewer than sixty members; half of them were in Europe and most of the others in Latin America. The United States declined to join, and for some years Russia was excluded. After the second war, the League was replaced by a new body, the United Nations, with a much wider membership. Both Russia and the United States are members of the United Nations, and the organisation has twenty members from Asia and more than forty from Africa. The United Nations undertakes a wider range of tasks than the old League. Its successes are not much publicised, its failures make headlines. In particular, the United Nations organisation has so far failed to remove the fear of war and give ordinary people throughout the world a feeling of security. On the other hand, many of the successes achieved by the United Nations are of kinds which do not help to sell newspapers and cannot be shown in a short television news broadcast: international teams succeed in smothering an epidemic or an outbreak of locusts, in rehousing refugees, in rescuing works of art from destruction, in providing specialised training or expert advice in countries which cannot supply it from their own resources. All these tend to be forgotten; the world cries out for peace, and asks why the United Nations cannot ensure it.

2 The United Nations

When the victorious statesmen met in 1945 to establish the United Nations Organisation they had very much in their minds the old League of Nations, which had existed since 1919. The League had had successes, some of them very encouraging; but its successes had been overshadowed by its failure in the important task of preventing war. The biggest questions facing the statesmen of 1945 were: 'Why did the League fail in this task? and What could be done to prevent the new United Nations Organisation from failing again?'

A complete answer to these questions would be lengthy and complicated; but there were two facts about the League which together went a long way towards an answer. The first was that the League was small: it had only fifty-seven member states, twenty-nine of which were in Europe; Asia and Africa together had eight. The United States was never a member, and the Soviet Union did not join until 1934. The second fact was that although the members of the League were ready to use strong measures against small countries which disturbed the peace of the world, they were afraid to do so when faced with a strong and determined evil-doer. Thus, the League took no effective action when Japan invaded China in 1931 and Italy invaded Ethiopia in 1935, although all four countries were members of the League.

From these facts, the founders of the United Nations drew two conclusions. First: the United Nations must become as soon as possible representative of all the peoples of the world. Second: there must be in the United Nations an inner group of strong powers which could be relied on to act quickly together in any threat to world peace, and whose united strength would be so great that no single state would dare to defy it.

These two considerations led to the establishment of the General Assembly as the organisation's main deliberative body, and of the Security Council as its executive branch in matters of keeping the peace. All member states are represented in the General Assembly; each member has one vote, and only one. The Security Council, originally of eleven member states, now consists of fifteen: five permanent members (Britain, China, France, Russia and the United

B

States) and ten other members elected for a term of two years. Each member state on the Security Council has one vote.

The General Assembly is a deliberative body: it is to meet annually. It can discuss any question; but as originally planned, it could take no action when peace was threatened except to refer the matter with its recommendation to the Security Council. In recent years, as we shall see, the General Assembly has gone further than this. The Security Council is responsible for preventing or removing threats to world peace, for suppressing acts of aggression, and for seeing that international disputes are settled peacefully. The Charter lays down that the Security Council is to be 'so organised as to be able to function continuously'. It is an executive, not merely a deliberative body, and during the first ten years of the United Nations, the Security Council met 730 times, an average of one meeting every five days.

Matters to be decided by the Security Council may be matters of procedure, or they may be matters of substance. Decisions on procedure are taken by a vote of at least nine of the fifteen members, but the Charter declares that 'decisions of the Security Council on all other matters shall be made by an affirmative vote of nine members including the concurring votes of the permanent members'. Thus, if a single one of the five permanent members votes 'No', the motion is lost; though the Charter provides that a member state which is a member of the Security Council must abstain from voting if it is a party to a dispute before the Council. It has been agreed that it is merely a procedural question whether a particular matter is to be regarded as one of procedure, or of substance. Thus, it is not possible for a permanent member in a fit of bad temper to block all business in the Security Council by declaring everything to be a matter of substance, and then vetoing it.

This provision of the Charter that all action by the Security Council requires the concurrence of all five permanent members was laid down in the hope – possibly a naive hope – that the five powers which had fought a victorious war together would remain in harmony afterwards. But it was not merely naive. The provision seemed realistic in the light of what had happened to the League of Nations. The Covenant of the League provided that sanctions were to be applied to any state which was declared to be an aggressor. In 1935, fifty member states of the League, out of the total membership at that time of fifty-four, declared Italy to be committing aggression against Ethiopia; but they could not agree to run the risk of applying any serious sanctions against Italy for fear of provoking a major war. With this unhappy experience behind them, the founders of the United Nations thought that in practice, no effective action would be taken unless the five permanent members of the Security Council were in agreement; and if so, it would be better to draw up the Charter so as to recognise this fact.

Unfortunately, this hoped-for harmony between the five permanent members of the Security Council does not exist. Russia and America are on terms of hostile rivalry, the so-called 'cold war'. China has been devastated by civil war, and after mainland China came under communist rule, the Chinese seat in the UN was occupied for many years by the representative of a government whose authority was limited to the island of Taiwan or Formosa. This leaves France and Britain, both greatly weakened by their efforts and losses in the war. The Council's power of taking effective action has been destroyed by this weakness of some of the permanent members of the Security Council, and by the continuous disagreement between others.

A constitutional point of some importance has arisen over voting in the Security Council. The Charter makes it plain that on a matter of substance, a single negative vote by a permanent member wrecks the proposal before the Council. But what if a permanent member is absent, or is present but abstains from voting? On this, the Charter is not explicit. It might reasonably be held that the Charter requires five affirmative votes from the five permanent members, and if a proposal obtains only four such votes, it is lost, even though no permanent member votes against it. This is the interpretation which the Soviet Union puts upon the Charter, and as we shall see, such an interpretation can have far-reaching political implications.

During the first ten years of the United Nations, the Security Council was many times prevented from action by a negative vote from a permanent member, the so-called 'veto'. Most of these negative votes were cast by Russia: between 1949 and 1955 Russia vetoed all applications for admission to membership of the United Nations, and on various occasions when the Security Council proposed action which Russia disapproved of, the Soviet delegate vetoed the resolution. The Russian blockade of Berlin and the Russian occupation of Prague and Budapest are examples. But even without the veto, the United Nations would have been helpless in the Berlin, Prague and Budapest incidents, for the Russian troops could have been stopped only by a new war, the very thing which the UN was designed to prevent. Britain used the veto for the first time in 1956, when the Israeli army was invading Egypt, and the Security Council was voting on an American resolution calling on Israel to withdraw her troops. Britain vetoed this resolution, and went on to land her own troops in Egypt. The Security Council could do nothing, since presumably Britain would have vetoed any hostile resolution. But the General Assembly took the lead; a resolution requiring a cease-fire within twelve hours was carried in the Assembly by sixty-four votes against four, and Britain obeyed. This unfortunate affair showed that even if the Security Council cannot act, it is sometimes possible for the General Assembly to act in its stead. It is certainly a weakness of the Security Council that its action can be paralysed by the use of the veto; but this weakness cannot be cured simply by redrafting the constitution. It will disappear whenever the five permanent members of the Security Council are once more able to act in harmony.

The Korean War

The one occasion when the Security Council took decisive action was the Korean war of 1950. Korea, formerly a province of China, had been annexed by Japan in 1895, and had been in Japanese occupation ever since. The allied intention in the war against Japan was to restore to Korea the independence it had once had, long ago before being absorbed into the Chinese empire.

In the last days of the war, the Russian and American troops, advancing into Korea from opposite ends, met at the 38th parallel of latitude, and both armies stayed in the area they held, waiting until arrangements could be made to set up an independent Korean government. The United Nations set up a commission to try and unite the two halves of Korea and enable a united Korea to form a representative government. This it was unable to do, since the Russian and American ideas of representative government were very different. The UN commission did however succeed in holding elections in South Korea, and a government took office there and was recognised by the United Nations. The Russians at once set up a government in North Korea, and this government was recognised by all the communist countries. In 1949, on the suggestion of the United Nations, the American troops were withdrawn from South Korea. On 25 June 1950 the army of North Korea crossed the 38th parallel and invaded the South.

The UN commission in South Korea reported the invasion to the Secretary-General, and the matter was laid before the Security Council. It came there at a moment when the Soviet seat chanced to be vacant. At that time the Chinese nationalists under Chiang Kai-Shek were rapidly losing ground to the communists under Mao Tse-Tung, and the demand was made that the Chinese seat in the United Nations should be occupied by a communist instead of by a nationalist delegate. The Assembly rejected the demand, whereupon the Soviet Union declared that it would boycott UN meetings until the demand was accepted. It was during this Soviet boycott that the Korean affair came before the Security Council. In the absence of the Soviet delegate, the Security Council passed a resolution calling on the North Korean army to withdraw. Two days later, with fighting still continuing on South Korean soil, the Security Council passed a stronger resolution, calling on member states to help South Korea to resist this aggression. Only one vote, that of Yugoslavia, was cast against the resolution; but in the absence of the Soviet delegate, both resolutions obtained only four votes from the five permanent members. This constitutional point was noted by the communist countries.

The United States took the lead in complying with the Security Council's resolution. It announced that American naval and air forces would support South Korea; and after the Council's second and stronger resolution, the United States resolved to throw in ground troops as well. This American lead was quickly followed by other states, and the American General Douglas MacArthur eventually found himself in command of an army composed of fighting units from sixteen member states, with medical units from five more. There were at that time fifty-nine member states, so the UN forces in Korea represented more than one-third of the membership. The Soviet government did not abandon its boycott and return to the council chamber until August, though it never ceased to maintain that the Security Council's resolutions were unconstitutional and invalid without the concurrence of all five of the permanent members. On this constitutional point the great majority of the member governments held a contrary view. When the Soviet delegate returned to his place in August, the UN force was organised and in the field.

From the United Nations point of view, the Korean expedition was by no means a complete success. When the UN troops arrived, the North Koreans had already occupied the South Korean capital, and the UN and South Korean troops were at first confined to a small bridge-head on the coast. From this however they were able to break out, and they drove the invaders back over their own frontier. At that point the UN forces had a choice: either to halt and defend the frontier line, or to push on into the North and go for complete victory. Against the advice of India, which feared that a further advance might provoke the government of communist China, they decided to push on. India's fears came true: a large army of Chinese volunteers came to reinforce the North Koreans, and the UN forces were thrown back to the frontier on the 38th parallel. This became an armistice line. No peace treaty has ever been signed, and the line still has to be guarded by troops.

All these events made the General Assembly of the United Nations fear that the Security Council was likely to be often paralysed by the veto of one of the permanent members. To prevent any future peace-keeping efforts by the UN from being frustrated, the General Assembly in November 1950 passed a resolution which had the effect of enabling the Assembly to take action if world peace was threatened and the Security Council was prevented from acting by the veto. This resolution is commonly known as the Uniting For Peace resolution; it was sponsored by the United States, and was strongly opposed by the Soviet Union. The Soviet government has never ceased to regard the resolution as unconstitutional and invalid. Its reason for this is that under the resolution the General Assembly assumes powers which are not conferred upon it by the Charter. This amounts to altering the Charter; but the Charter is explicit in laying down the procedure to be followed if alterations are desired, and the prescribed procedure has not been followed. This again is a legal point; the Soviet argument appears reasonable, but the great majority of the member states have taken a different view.

How much of this is law, and how much politics? Article 12 of the Charter prohibits the General Assembly from duplicating the work of the Security Council in a given situation. But if the Security Council (whether because of the veto or for any other reason) is not 'exercising in respect of any dispute or situation the functions assigned to it by the present Charter', the General Assembly is empowered by Article 10 to 'discuss any questions or any matters within the scope of the present Charter' and to 'make recommendations to the Members of the United Nations or to the Security Council or to both'. Article 11 empowers the Assembly to 'discuss any questions relating to the maintenance of international peace and security brought before it'; and again it may make recommendations to anyone concerned. The Charter certainly gives greater powers to the Security Council. If necessary, the Council can 'call upon member states to sever economic and diplomatic relations with' an erring member: cutting all communications, blockading it, and in the last resort using armed force against it. The Security Council may call upon member states to take action, the General Assembly may only recommend them to do so. Between these two, the Soviet Union draws a sharp distinction: a nice point.

It was in accordance with this Uniting For Peace resolution that the United Nations established its expeditionary force to take over from French and British troops after the Suez affair of 1956. Similarly in 1960, a UN force was sent to the Congo to try and maintain peace there; UN forces have had similar peace-keeping tasks in Cyprus and on the frontier between Egypt and Israel. The Soviet Union, maintaining that the Suez and Congo operations were illegal because launched by the Assembly instead of by the Security Council, refuses to pay its share of the costs. The costs, it says, should not fall on all the members of the United Nations: they should be borne by the 'aggressors' who have involved the UN in all this trouble – Britain, France and Israel in the case of Suez, and Belgium in the case of the Congo.

The Assembly and the Secretary-General

The General Assembly today is very different from the original Assembly of 1945. The 52 members have increased to more than 120, and a third of them are former colonies that have become independent. The tone of the Assembly has changed; there is now a large group of members who do not feel much concerned with the fears and jealousies of Russia and America, and are disinclined to look to either for leadership. Nor do they wish to take a lead from the former colonial powers. On the other hand, the Assembly, like all committees, needs guidance; and receiving little guidance from the Security Council, it tends to look for it more to the secretary-general. Circumstances thus tend to impel the office of secretary-general to a more important position than the framers of the Charter foresaw. It becomes inevitable that the post should be filled by a man from one of the smaller and less partisan countries, not from any of the rival great powers. Trygve Lie was a Norwegian, Dag Hammarskjold a Swede, U Thant a Burmese; Kurt Waldheim is an Austrian. Dag Hammarskjold indeed, appointed in the first place, after various candidates had been rejected by one side or the other, as a quiet harmless man against whom nothing was known, was in the process of giving such strong leadership to the UN when he was killed in an air crash in the Congo, that he had already incurred the severe displeasure of the Soviet Union, and had been invited in blunt terms to resign.

The Specialised Agencies

Keeping the peace is one of the most important functions of the United Nations, and much disappointment has been caused by its weakness in this matter. But the UN carries out other tasks, which seldom receive newspaper publicity, but which are an extremely important means of making the wealth and the skills of the more developed nations of the world available for the assistance of countries that are less fortunate. The UN has taken over some of the old League's international organisations, such as the International Postal Union and the International Labour Office; and it has added to them a whole range of new ones. These are the United Nations Specialised Agencies: the World Health Organisation, the Food and Agricultural Organisation, the International Bank for Reconstruction and Development, the United Nations Educational, Scientific and Cultural Organisation, the International Atomic Energy Authority, and others. There is a wide range of UN activities carried on by various branches, such as the UN work for children and for refugees. And there are regional bodies such as the UN Economic Commission for Africa.

The problems which these United Nations agencies deal with are too big to be tackled by two or three nations alone. Individual charities like Christian Aid, Oxfam, and the Save the Children Fund do admirable work, but the needs of the world are far greater than they can cope with. Some sort of international organisation is needed.

The Educational, Scientific and Cultural Organisation (UNESCO) has carried out a great variety of tasks all over the world: adult literacy and community development projects, scholarship and training schemes, lecture tours, translations of Asian literature into European languages and vice versa, and the recording and preservation of works of art in danger of destruction, ranging from a set of frescoes by Masaccio to ancient Egyptian statuary and paintings about to be inundated by the damming of the Nile at Aswan.

But the FAO and the WHO offer perhaps the most striking examples of successful international co-operation organised through the United Nations. Agricultural pests and diseases ignore national frontiers. Locusts breed in the Middle East, and from there the swarms fly out to devastate the crops in Africa and Iran and India. Likewise, cholera and influenza will sweep the whole world if they are allowed to, and only quick international action can check them. In such matters as these, the UN organisations are able to act like a radar set which gives warning of an enemy air attack. They can spot the trouble in its early stage – perhaps in a country which is short of skilled staff – and can deal with it before it gets out of hand. Apart from this remedial work, they carry out a great deal of research in such matters as tropical medicine and the raising of pest-resistant and higher-yielding varieties of tropical crops.

A hundred years and more ago, when slavery still existed in the United States, Abraham Lincoln said, 'This Government cannot endure permanent half slave and half free'. The world today is as small as the United States was then, and though slavery as Lincoln knew it may exist no longer, other evils exist to which his dictum will apply. As a Russian statesman observed between the wars, peace is indivisible. It is easy for a local quarrel to flare up and involve other countries who have really nothing to do with its original cause. Other evils too are brought to the attention of the whole world: poverty, ignorance, famine, oppression, not to mention natural calamities like floods and earthquakes. A century ago it was possible for people in Victorian England to remain comfortably ignorant of what went on outside their own country. It is not possible today, when television brings pictures of fighting in Vietnam or floods in Bengal into our homes. In international conferences, the poorer countries now speak for themselves, and they will not allow us to be content with our prosperity and our high standards in the social services, while they are desperately short of doctors and engineers and qualified people of all kinds, and short too of the capital which they need to build roads and airfields, colleges and hospitals, dams and power stations.

This new confrontation of the 'haves' with the 'have-nots' leads the United Nations to a programme of technical assistance, in which the richer nations do what they can to help the poorer nations with money and with skilled staff. In colonial times, after 1945, Britain and France had legislation under which the governments gave assistance to their own colonies. Now that their colonies are independent, they continue to give assistance: partly direct, partly through the various organisations of the United Nations. From the recipients' point of view, the UN has the advantage of representing the whole world and of being free from any suspicion of colonial patronage or of neo-colonialist self-seeking.

The United Nations and Colonies

One important task which the United Nations has carried through almost to completion is the supervision of all colonial affairs. The League of Nations did not attempt such a large task; it limited itself to a small group of territories, the Arab provinces of Turkey and the former German colonies. By the peace treaty of 1919, Germany and Turkey were deprived of these lands; but there was a feeling that it would be wrong if the victorious allies simply annexed them. A compromise was adopted. The territories were handed over to the new League of Nations, which entrusted them 'on a mandate' to various allied countries: thus, Iraq and Palestine were entrusted to Britain, and Syria to France; various Pacific islands were entrusted to Japan; Tanganyika was divided between Britain and Belgium, and Germany's West African colonies between Britain and France. Although America was not a member of the League, Britain pressed her to accept the mandates for Palestine and Tanganyika, but America refused. The League set up a permanent Mandates Commission to supervise the work of the mandatory powers. The powers had to make regular written reports to the Commission and send representatives to meet the Commission and discuss them. The League hoped that the mandatory powers would prepare their mandated territories for independence, and several Arab countries did become independent before 1939.

As far as the mandated territories were concerned, this was a useful piece of work. But the League made no inquiry into the administration of colonies other than mandated territories, for this was regarded as a domestic matter for the colonial power concerned. The British Labour Party did indeed propose that all British colonies should be surrendered to the League and brought under the supervision of the Mandates Commission. But nothing came of the proposal.

When the UN replaced the League, it took over the League's concern for the mandated territories. It renamed them trust territories, and replaced the Mandates Commission by a Trusteeship Council. The temper of the United Nations was more opposed to colonial rule of any kind than that of the League, and the Trusteeship Council was more formidable than its predecessor. The United States, the Soviet Union and all communist countries were hostile to the idea of colonial rule, and from the very beginning they put pressure on the administering powers to hasten the grant of independence. The Mandates Commission of the League was composed of individuals who were not government representatives and were free to use their discretion; some of them were former colonial administrators of distinction, who knew from experience the problems facing the overseas governments. The members of the new Trusteeship Council were government representatives bound by government instructions. The representative of an administering power who attended the Trusteeship Council found himself facing a group of men less sympathetic to his difficulties and more openly advocating the interests of the people in his trust territory. The Trusteeship Council not merely received petitions from the inhabitants of the trust territories, but at regular intervals sent round international inspecting teams to see for themselves how the territories were being governed. No doubt members of the Council and its visiting teams were sometimes doctrinaire and unrealistic; but colonial officials were sometimes unadventurous and too much absorbed in the everyday administrative problems. The Council's supervision helped to speed up the progress of the trust territories towards independence.

The United Nations however did not limit its attention to the trust territories. The Charter gave it no powers to compel colonial powers to submit their colonial administration to UN supervision. But by a resolution of the Assembly, the secretary-general invited them to send him annual reports on the educational, social and economic progress of their colonies. Spain and Portugal refused, on the grounds that they had no colonies; they regarded their overseas territories as provinces of the mother-country. But Britain, France, Belgium and the other colonial powers felt it would be unwise to refuse. The UN drew up elaborate questionnaires, to which the colonial powers sent replies; and their replies were circulated by the secretary-general to all member states. The next step was that the Assembly set up a committee to discuss these reports; and on the analogy of the Trusteeship Council, the committee invited the administering powers to send representatives to attend the committee meetings and discuss their colonial administration. The UN did not receive petitions from colonies, as it did from trust territories; nor did it send out inspecting teams. But every detail of administration was discussed and criticised, and the representatives of the administering powers found themselves being invited to explain why progress in this or that matter was so slow.

Here again, the emphasis was laid on the speedy attainment of independence. The natural attitude of a colonial power was, 'We will try to govern this colony better'. The attitude of the committee was, 'How long will it be before this colony is fit to govern itself?' There is no doubt that this constant pressure of the UN for constitutional development and the grant of independence speeded up the end of the colonial empires.

Since 1947, when India and Pakistan became independent, nearly all colonies have joined the UN as full member states. The Trusteeship Council has finished its work, and the committee on colonialism is left with little more than a few small islands. But there remain as well a few intractable problem cases. The Portuguese territories in Africa have never been submitted to the United Nations. The white minority government of Rhodesia has declared itself independent, though its independence is recognised neither by Britain nor by the United Nations. South-West Africa, formerly German, was administered by South Africa under a mandate from the League, and when the UN invited South Africa to administer the country as a trust territory, she refused. The country has since been annexed to South Africa, which regards the mandate as extinguished and the UN as devoid of authority. The UN would like to see all these five African territories independent under

African governments. They present the UN with problems which will not easily be solved.

On the whole however, the UN may fairly claim to have helped to dispose of the colonial question. It is now faced with the far bigger task of curing world poverty and the evils that result from it. These do not vanish on the day that the British or French flag is hauled down and replaced by the independence flag; nor are they found only in former colonies. The United Nations programme of technical assistance is yet far from adequate to the desperate needs of the Third World, and many of the wealthier member states spend much more on armaments than on technical assistance.

The United Nations, like the League before it, was founded with high hopes, and nobody will claim that those hopes have been fully realised. In their disappointment, many people turn on the UN and criticise it as merely an expensive and ineffective talking-shop.

This is too superficial. It is true that the UN costs money; that not all the projects of the specialised agencies succeed; that UN meetings are the occasion for a great deal of useless oratory and of intrigue and lobbying. It is tempting to put the blame for this on the new member states, who are inexperienced in world affairs and cannot afford to send large delegations of specialist advisers, as some of the older and wealthier nations do. But we may reflect that these older and wealthier nations have brought about two world wars, and did not show great wisdom and courage in handling world affairs in the days of the League from 1919 to 1939. It ill becomes them to be too critical of the new member states.

The United Nations can be no better than its members allow it to be. Every government desires peace, but peace on its own terms. Similarly, every government believes in international co-operation, but tries to put as little as possible into the pool and to take as much as possible out. There is no room for arguing over the size of a member state's annual contribution, for that is determined by a fixed formula based on population and wealth. But there is room for differences in the warmth of a member's support of the UN and its purposes. A poor and youthful member state may have selfish reasons for supporting the UN: its subscription is small, and it hopes that membership will bring it material assistance as well as increased prestige. But some old and wealthy member states may have equally selfish reasons for giving the UN little active support. They feel that they receive no benefit from membership, and they find the Assembly critical of their policy and eager for them to increase their contribution to UN funds. A member state taking this attitude is in no position to blame a poor and youthful member state for trying to make the most of its new membership. Useful and encouraging as the work of the specialised agencies is, it is considerations such as these which prevent the agencies' programmes from being completely successful. There are too many member states clamouring for assistance, like the states in America, each wanting its share of Federal funds; or like local authorities in Britain, each hoping for government grants for its own pet schemes of roads or bridges or hospitals.

The UN General Assembly is sometimes spoken of as a world parliament. This is misleading, and leads to disappointment. The Assembly has not yet developed into a world parliament, though it may yet do so. Member states bring their fears and prejudices with them into the Assembly. It is true that in a large gathering, such as the House of Commons or the UN General Assembly, there may develop a corporate feeling which will respond to inspiring leadership. But this is for the great occasion. In the ordinary routine, there is a great difference between the UN Assembly and the House of Commons. Members of parliament have great discretion; subject to their party whip, they can speak and vote as they like. But UN delegates have no discretion. They are bound by instructions from their governments; and those instructions are issued by a cool-headed foreign minister, remote from the excitement of the debate, in accordance with what he and his colleagues consider to be the national interest. As long as this is so, we must expect to see wisdom and idealism (there is plenty of both in the UN building) sometimes frustrated by rather shabby playing at politics; by considerations of national prestige; by personal animosities; by political bargaining. Such things are to be expected while the United Nations is young. In fifty or a hundred years time the UN will have matured; it will have acquired traditions and precedents, and its General Assembly may have acquired more corporate feeling.

The weakness of the United Nations is that there is too little unity of feeling among its members. Nation-states find it hard to accept that the common good must outweigh their own selfish interests. Members of the United Nations will learn this difficult lesson gradually as they discuss the affairs of the world and practise the habit of acting together.

3 The Century of Imperialism

In the course of the nineteenth century, imperialism erupted in Western Europe like a volcano. The lava flowed out over Asia and Africa and the Pacific, obliterating the old landmarks. Now the fires have died down as suddenly as they burst forth, but the landscape has been permanently altered.

Sudden and violent as the eruption was, there had been preliminary rumblings for 300 years. Columbus discovered the New World in 1492, and six years later Vasco da Gama rounded the Cape and opened up the sea route to India. Within forty years of Columbus's first voyage, Spain had conquered Mexico and Peru and had planted colonies in Central and South America; while the Portuguese were controlling the whole of the Indian Ocean, with bases established at every exit: in the Persian Gulf, at the mouth of the Red Sea, and in the Straits of Malacca.

During the seventeenth and eighteenth centuries, Dutch and English and French settlers colonised parts of North America; the Dutch established themselves at the Cape and in the East Indies; and French and British intrigued and fought to control the trade of India. In the closing years of the eighteenth century the first British settlers landed in Australia.

While the seafaring peoples of Western Europe were fighting for the gold and gems and spices of the tropics, the peoples of Russia, with equal hardihood and endurance, were setting themselves to conquer the great plains of Asia. They crossed on horseback from one great river to the next; they launched their boats and explored and settled the new valley, until the day came when they once more felt the urge to push further towards the rising sun. In the first half of the seventeenth century, Russian horsemen reached the salt water of the Pacific.

There was an exciting fifty years or so of Spanish and Portuguese settlement and colonisation, but afterwards the process of European expansion settled down to a slow and painful routine. Trading expeditions set sail for tropical harbours, carrying cargoes which they hoped might prove saleable. Sometimes they did not return; sometimes they came back to port a year or more later, having lost half their men but bringing a cargo of gold or silk or

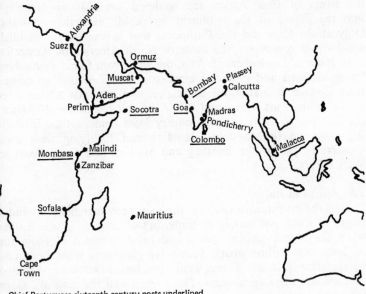

Chief Portuguese sixteenth-century posts underlined

Map 1. The Indian Ocean

spices or tobacco rich enough to tempt others to follow them. After long and difficult voyages, shiploads of settlers landed in North America or Australia or on sundry tropical islands, and faced the new hardships of pioneering.

Broadly speaking, there were two types of European settlement. In America and Australia, there was little effective resistance to the European conquerors, and conditions were reasonably attractive. In these circumstances, it was not too difficult to establish colonies. Latin America was settled by the Spaniards and Portuguese; and further north, the east coast was soon occupied by Dutch, French and English settlers.

In Africa and in tropical Asia, conditions were different. Along the African coast there was no African nation capable of making an effective resistance to a determined European conqueror. But except at the southern tip of the continent, Africa was defended against invasion by the malarial mosquito and by the geographical obstacles to penetration inland. The Guinea coast was so full of malaria that it became known as 'the white man's grave'. It was not until 1830 that the 'Oil Rivers' of Nigeria were found to be the delta of one of the great rivers of the world. The Congo and

the rivers of East Africa are rendered unusable as highways
into the centre of the continent by rapids near their mouths.
Only at the Cape did the Europeans find it possible to establish
a colony in conditions like those of North America or Australia.

In India and elsewhere in Asia, the white men found themselves
facing civilised and powerful kingdoms, which needed no advice
from Europe in matters of commerce, and but little advice even
in the military art. Here, and in the difficult conditions of Africa,
the Europeans, many months journey from home, settled in trading posts on the sea-coast, building and fortifying their own
quarters in places like Bombay and Madras, and Cape Coast in
West Africa.

The British in India

During the seventeenth century, the European merchants in India
began to think not merely of trade, but of empire. It was a time
when the Mogul empire, which had ruled so much of India for
so long, was falling apart. Provincial governors were becoming
independent princes. There were rivalries; there were disputed
successions; there were wars. The French and the English, eager
for commercial concessions, yielded to the temptation to intrigue
with the rival princes. From intriguing they passed to fighting. It
was the Frenchman Dupleix, the governor of the French station
of Pondicherry, who set the new fashion. In four years, from
1748 to 1752, by backing the right horse in one of these Indian
quarrels, Dupleix made himself master of the whole of south
India, and the British post of Madras was at his mercy. But the
whole glittering structure of French power in the south was over-
turned by the gallant leadership of the young Englishman Robert
Clive.

Soon afterwards, the Nabob of Bengal decided to confiscate
the wealth of the British merchants in Calcutta. He attacked and
took the British post and imprisoned the British inhabitants. Clive
was sent north with an army to punish the Nabob and restore
the situation. He retook Calcutta, and in 1757 defeated and
destroyed the Nabob's army at the battle of Plassey. With this
victory there began the gradual process by which the East India
Company ceased to be merely a commercial concern and became
an imperial body. Aided by seapower, Britain established her
position in India so firmly that the French could no longer hope
to overthrow it.

In 1857, just 100 years after the battle of Plassey, some sections
of the Indian army mutinied against their British officers and the
Company's government. Their mutiny was not put down without

hard fighting. It succeeded in drawing attention to various disadvantages and abuses which resulted from using a commercial company to administer an empire. The chief result of the mutiny was that the government of India was transferred from the Company to the Crown. It was the Crown that granted India her independence in 1947, just ten years short of the second century after Plassey.

The break-up of the Mogul empire left a power vacuum; and as things turned out, it was the British that filled it. The British empire over India created a new situation. Henceforth, the safety of the British communications with India became a vital British interest. Not only was the Indian trade valuable, but the Indian army was a military asset which might be of great importance, provided it could be brought wherever it was needed. In 1878 Disraeli brought a contingent of Indian troops to Malta as a warning to Russia. Much of British policy from Clive's day onwards, and throughout the nineteenth century, was determined by the need to keep open the route to India. In the Napoleonic wars, this led Britain to take over the Dutch settlement at Cape Town and the strategically important French island of Mauritius in the Indian Ocean, which had been often used as a French naval base, to the great harassment of the East India Company's trade.

The British in the Middle East

The Napoleonic wars produced another threat to the British position in India. Napoleon himself proposed to evade the British navy by marching to India overland, as Alexander the Great had done more than 2,000 years before. In 1798 he landed with his army in Egypt, proclaiming that with the help of the Indian princes he would overthrow the British rule in India and ruin Britain by destroying her trade. His scheme failed, and the danger to India passed away; but his expedition brought about a rare flurry of excitement all along his route. On the shores of the Persian Gulf, the Sultan of Oman was much alarmed. His country was under attack from two directions. His Arab neighbours were at war with him, and the neighbouring seas were infested with pirates, so that his seamen could not safely trade with India and East Africa. If a large French army came into the region, who could tell what might happen?

The Sultan weighed up the risks, and made his choice: he decided to seek help from the British against his immediate danger rather than await Napoleon's arrival and appeal to the French. He made an alliance with Britain, and a British naval squadron went to the Persian Gulf and cleared out the pirates for him. This

c

was the beginning of the British alliance with Oman, which lasted until our own day. At a later date, the British followed up this entry into Arab politics by occupying Aden as a convenient coaling station for ships on the Indian voyage.

These operations were all carried out long before there was any talk of oil. The world demand for oil began at the end of the nineteenth century with the development of the internal-combustion engine and the use of heavy oil as a substitute for coal in fuelling steamships. When that happened, the oil-fields of the Persian Gulf region became an area of intense rivalry among international oil companies. It was after 1919 that the demand for oil and for control of oil production became most acute: that is, at a time when Britain and Western Europe were weakened by the 1914–18 war. Iran and the other oil-producing countries were thus able to demand and obtain better prices for their oil. It was an unhealthy and dangerous state of affairs, and oil imperialism (American, Russian and British) tended to keep the politics of the region unstable.

These precautions of the eighteenth and early nineteenth centuries – the occupation of Cape Town and Mauritius, and the alliance with Oman – were taken by Britain while the only sea route to India was round the Cape of Good Hope. But from Napoleon's time onwards there was talk of shortening this sea route by cutting a ship canal through the isthmus of Suez, which would save some six thousand miles, and make Bombay rather than Madras the chief gateway to India. The scheme was suggested by French engineers; and in view of the Napoleonic dream, this in itself would probably have been enough to damn it in British eyes. But as the details were worked out, the matter became more and more complicated by international politics and intrigue, and British opposition became more and more bitter. Before long, Britain developed a vested interest in preventing the construction of a canal. British shipping companies ran regular lines of ships from England to Alexandria and from Suez to Bombay; British travel firms organised connecting coach and hotel services across the isthmus; and later on, British engineers built railways across it. But Britain was unable to prevent the canal from being built. It was built and run by an international company, though very few of the company's shares were held by British investors.

The opening of the Suez Canal in 1869 was thus a British defeat. Once the canal was open however, the whole position was changed. British interests in India were so important that it became one of the main objects of British policy to prevent the canal from falling into hostile hands, which in those days meant French or Russian hands. In this matter, Britain was luckier than she deserved to be. The Khedive of Egypt was at his wits' end for ready money; in 1874 Disraeli bought his Suez Canal shares for cash, and Britain thus became a major shareholder in the Suez Canal.

In 1882, thirteen years after the canal was opened, British troops occupied Egypt. They did not go there to take control of the Suez Canal. They went, on the orders of such a convinced anti-imperialist as Gladstone himself, to put down a nationalist Egyptian revolt against the Turkish ruling class, the Khedive and his circle. The Khedive had run his country heavily into debt, and the claims of the foreign bond-holders were a heavy burden on the Egyptian revenue. The Khedive had already defaulted on the interest payments, and it was generally feared in Europe that if the revolt succeeded, the new government would repudiate the debts altogether. The British expedition was sent with the approval of the other European powers, and in fact a French naval squadron at first co-operated with the British fleet off Alexandria, though at the last minute the French government changed its mind and withdrew it. Nevertheless, Britain might not have accepted the commission of Europe's debt-collector had not the government felt uneasy about the safety of the British 'life-line', the short route to India.

If Gladstone had known that the British troops were to stay in Egypt for seventy years, he would never have sent them there. He hoped that the work of pacifying the country and reorganising its finances would be finished in a few months, and that he could then bring the troops home again. But the British occupation of Egypt was one of the landmarks in nineteenth-century imperialism. It helped to start the rush.

There had been earlier beginnings in Africa. The French began their conquest of Algeria in 1830, and in the fifties they began advancing inland from their ancient trading posts at the mouth of the Senegal river. When the explorers had determined the course of the river Niger, it was tempting for the French to push inland up the Senegal and then make the short overland crossing to the Niger, which they did in 1880.

From 1876 onwards, King Leopold of Belgium was systematically building up a new kingdom in the Congo, which became known as the Congo Free State and later became a Belgian colony. About the same time the French explorer De Brazza was at work on the lower Congo, and his discoveries and treaties led to the beginnings of the French colony of Equatorial Africa.

There were preliminary expansionist moves in Asia also. From 1840 to 1842, Britain fought the so-called Opium War with China. In an attempt to stop the national habit of opium-smoking, the

Chinese government made it illegal to grow the opium poppy; those who could evade the law did so, and those who could not evade it sighed for an alternative supply of the drug. Opium was grown also in India, and it suited commercial men in India to export Indian opium to supply the demand in China. Chinese protests against the illegal landing of opium were met with British moralising on freedom of trade. There were incidents, and then there was war. It ended with the establishment of a British colony at Hong Kong and the beginning of a system of 'Treaty Ports', in which the Chinese, who wished to have nothing to do with foreigners, were compelled to allow European merchants to reside and trade.

In the fifties, a French expedition conquered three countries adjoining China, the states of Laos, Cambodia and Vietnam. In 1824, 1852 and 1885 Britain fought wars against Burma, the final result of which was to destroy Burmese independence and make the country a province of the British empire in India.

The American continent was protected from European encroachments by the Monroe doctrine. In 1822 President Monroe gave notice that the United States would resist any attempts by Europe to interfere in the affairs of any American country, or to establish fresh European colonies in the New World. In 1864, the United States was temporarily helpless because of its civil war, and France took the risk of occupying Mexico with French troops and setting up a so-called empire in Mexico under French protection. But as soon as the United States had finished its civil war and had leisure to deal with Mexico, it gave the French notice to quit, and the unfortunate puppet emperor was captured by his Mexican opponents and shot.

Imperialism in Africa

Africa was the great empty space on the map, the great question-mark. Its coastline was well known, but hardly anything of the interior. For more than 300 years European sea-captains had been loading their ships off the West African coast with gold, ivory, pepper, and above all, slaves. In 1807 the British navy began its long task of suppressing the African slave trade, and about the same time, the Liverpool merchants discovered a new article of commerce, palm oil. The new factories, with their humming machinery and their smoking chimneys, were beginning to multiply in Britain, and palm oil could oil the bearings and could be made into soap for washing away the industrial grime. Britain made no attempt to colonise the 'Oil Rivers'; the merchants, the 'palm oil ruffians', lived on hulks moored in the creeks, and bought their oil from the African waterside chiefs. Further west, on the Gold Coast, there was a string of fortified European trading posts. By 1872 Britain had bought out her Danish and Dutch competitors; and in 1874, after a long history of misunderstandings and wars with the Ashanti nation of the interior, Britain annexed a strip of country from the seashore inland as far as the Ashanti frontier. In 1861 the small island of Lagos became a British colony; it was the one place on the west coast where the navy had been unable to stop the illicit slave trade. The British government was determined at that time not to get involved on the West African mainland, and it was another twenty years before Britain began to think of setting up protectorates there.

Elsewhere along the coast there were small European posts. The French were settled on the Senegal. The British paid hard cash for a plot of land at Freetown, where they could settle the shiploads of miscellaneous slaves taken by the navy on the high seas. An American society made a similar settlement in Liberia for slaves liberated by American warships, and the settlement was given its independence in 1847. Spain and Portugal held a few islands and fever-ridden coastal towns. The Portuguese had at one time occupied a good part of the East African coast; but they had long ago abandoned nearly all of it to the Arabs, among whom the Sultan of Zanzibar held a vague pre-eminence.

Only in South Africa did European control, in the middle of the nineteenth century, stretch any considerable distance inland. It was a thousand miles from the British settlement at Cape Town to the northern frontier of the Transvaal republic.

That was all. The interior of Africa was almost entirely unknown to Europe till after the middle of the nineteenth century; except that the course of the Niger had been explored by 1830, and in the 1840s two German missionaries reported to a largely incredulous Europe that they had seen perpetual snow on the tops of two high mountains in East Africa.

Until the 1870s, Europe was afraid of Africa. The west coast had already gained the nickname of 'the white man's grave', and it was generally assumed that East and Central Africa would be as bad. Africa was supposed to be dangerous because of its wealth of tropical diseases, and because of lions and snakes and cannibals. It was Livingstone's long years of marching up and down Africa that convinced Europe that these dangers were less than had been supposed, and that it was possible for white men to live and work there.

Livingstone was more than an explorer; he was a missionary. He found the whole of East and Central Africa being riddled by the slave trade. Incalculable suffering was being caused by the Arab slaving caravans which made their forays into the interior from

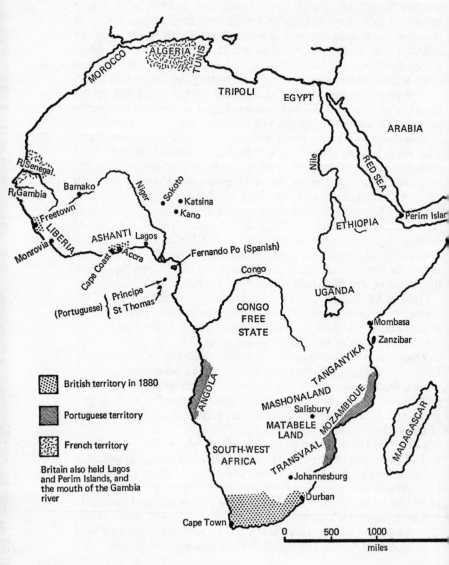

British territory in 1880

Portuguese territory

French territory

Britain also held Lagos
and Perim Islands, and
the mouth of the Gambia
river

Map 2.   Africa before the Scramble

Zanzibar and other bases on the east coast. There were treaties which prohibited the export of slaves to the Asian markets, but the enforcement of the treaties depended on the efforts of a small British naval squadron based on Simonstown at the southern tip of Africa. Livingstone urged that this naval patrol was inadequate to stop the slave trade; the only real way of stopping it was to penetrate into Africa and replace a bad trade with a good one. Before leaving England on his last journey, he told his audience, 'I go back to try to open up a path to commerce and Christianity. Do you carry on the work that I have begun.' It was as a direct response to Livingstone's plea that British missionaries entered Malawi, Tanganyika and Uganda between 1875 and 1877. They were quickly followed by Catholic missionaries from France.

Unfortunately, both Christianity and commerce were highly competitive. Before many years, the Protestant and Catholic converts in Uganda were fighting a full-scale civil war; and once European businessmen had overcome their fear of Africa, they came to regard it not as a menace but as a challenge. King Leopold of Belgium hired Stanley, the most famous explorer next to Livingstone himself, to go back into 'Darkest Africa' (the phrase is Stanley's own) and set up a trading empire in the Congo. France, angry with Britain over Egypt and smarting from her defeat by Germany in 1871, flung herself into the task of empire-building in West Africa, Equatorial Africa, and Madagascar. Germany, entering the competition rather late, made up for her late start by her energy; she secured two large territories, Tanganyika and South-West Africa, and two smaller ones, the Cameroons and Togoland.

Gladstone's government looked on in mild surprise and disdain at this undignified scramble for Africa. Gladstone was not interested in Africa; it did not touch his imagination as Ireland, Italy or Greece did. Britain was still the workshop of the world, and with reasonably free trade could undercut her competitors. Gladstone's policy was that of 'the open door'; as long as British traders had freedom to compete in Africa, they needed nothing more. Gladstone wanted no additional territorial responsibilities in Africa; it was bad enough being in Egypt, though he still hoped that we might soon be able to leave that troublesome country.

But by the 1880s, Gladstone's point of view was becoming out of date. British business interests in the Niger delta and elsewhere were too important to be abandoned to other powers like France, Belgium and Germany, which did not believe in the policy of 'the open door'. Empire-builders like Cecil Rhodes in South and Central Africa, Goldie in Nigeria, and Mackinnon in East Africa put pressure on the British government, and received first permission and then encouragement to open up the country and bring fresh territory under British rule.

Gladstone's hope of being able to leave Egypt was disappointed. In 1887 his successor, Lord Salisbury, decided that Britain must stay in control of Egypt for many years to come. This decision raised the question of Uganda, for Uganda contained the headwaters of the White Nile and was in danger of being included in the German protectorate in East Africa. In 1890, Salisbury made an agreement with Germany by which Uganda was recognised as a British sphere of influence. The main consideration was the little island of Heligoland, which lay off the western end of the Kiel canal and could be a nuisance to the young German navy in time of war. Salisbury offered to cede the island to Germany, and Germany jumped at the bait, whereby Heligoland became instead a nuisance to the British navy twenty-four years later.

In that same year 1890, Cecil Rhodes organised a pioneer column to advance from South Africa northward. The column occupied the African territories of Mashonaland and Matabeleland and organised them into a British protectorate which they named Rhodesia; their capital they named Salisbury in honour of the prime minister.

The missionaries, traders, police and adventurers of several nations were now competing for the honour of putting down the Arab slave trade and bringing Christianity and commerce to Africa. In the opening years of the twentieth century an exciting scramble occurred between British and French officers for control of the lower part of the Niger valley. The British held the delta of the river, the French held its upper and middle courses; in between there lay a group of independent Hausa-Fulani states – Sokoto, Kano, Katsina and others – who were, unluckily for themselves, slave-traders. The Englishman Lugard secured the greater part of this country for Britain, and in 1903 it became the protectorate of Northern Nigeria.

Imperialism Elsewhere

Imperialism was not confined to the sinful countries of the Old World; it spread to the young and relatively innocent United States. In 1898 the Spanish colony of Cuba was in revolt against Spain, and the American public could not stand the news of Spanish misrule and the horrors caused by the fighting. The United States declared war on Spain; the American victory was quick and complete; and at the peace conference the United States insisted on annexing not only Cuba but also Porto Rico and the Philippines. The Americans had already occupied Midway Island in the Pacific;

in 1887 they acquired the use of Pearl Harbor in Hawaii; and at the close of the century they strengthened their position in the Pacific by annexing Hawaii, Guam, Wake, and part of Samoa.

In 1869, the year of the opening of the Suez Canal, there was a ceremony at Promontory, Utah, to celebrate the driving of the final spike in the first continental railway to link California with the eastern seaboard. America now stretched from sea to sea, and the rail journey could be made within a week. But the sea journey from San Francisco to New York round Cape Horn took several weeks; during the Spanish war, the American battleship *Oregon*, in a hurry to reach the fighting zone near Cuba, took sixty-eight days over the trip. The Americans came more and more to feel the need for a canal through the isthmus of Panama. A French company had already obtained a concession to construct a canal. In 1902 Congress decided to buy out the French company and to negotiate with the republic of Colombia for the right to construct the canal and to control the canal zone. The Colombian government asked too high a price, and the United States was in a hurry. The Colombian province of Panama revolted from the mother country; Colombian troops moving to put down the revolt were prevented from doing so by United States marines; and the republic of Panama was quickly recognised as a sovereign state, its first act after independence in 1903 being to make the necessary concessions concerning the canal.

By 1914 the whole of Africa was under colonial rule, save for the republic of Liberia on the west coast and the ancient empire of Ethiopia or Abyssinia at the head of the Blue Nile. In Asia, only a few countries remained independent: notably Japan, Thailand, and China, with Tibet and a few states in the high mountains. All the Arab countries were under Turkish rule; Siberia was Russian; India, Burma and Malaysia were British; Indonesia was Dutch; Indo-China was French.

China was the great question. The states of Western Europe had forced the decrepit Chinese empire to grant them treaty ports and trading rights. Britain already held Hong Kong. Germany seized another Chinese harbour for a naval base. Russia, for ever searching for an ice-free port, laid hands on Port Arthur and built a branch of the Trans-Siberian railway through Chinese territory to link Port Arthur to her railway system. Britain protested, and seized another Chinese port for herself by way of compensation; France did likewise. There was a general feeling in the West that China was ripe for dividing into European spheres of interest, and Britain hoped to be allotted the Yangtze Kiang valley as her share. But this crowning triumph of Western European imperialism was prevented by the outbreak of war in 1914. After the war, Europe was in no condition to embark on fresh imperial adventures. China then lay helpless as a field for Japanese imperialism.

Causes of Imperialism

There were many causes that led to this rapid process of carving Asia and Africa into colonies and protectorates. One cause was commercial rivalry. Britain preferred to hold to a free trade policy and keep out of colonial responsibilities, since in a world of free trade her manufacturers could undersell their foreign competitors and she could draw supplies of cheap food from the virgin soils being exploited in North America. The price she paid was the ruin of British agriculture, but it was a price that she was prepared to pay.

But if it paid Britain better to follow the policy of 'the open door', it would pay her rivals better to protect their industries with tariffs; and thus Belgium, France and Germany had strong motives for annexing African territory. When they began to play at that game, Britain was compelled to join in.

British businessmen needed no compulsion; it was the British government – timid, cautious, and above all parsimonious – that needed compulsion. When diamonds were discovered at Kimberley in 1870, young Cecil Rhodes left his cotton plantation in Natal and set himself to acquire control of the diamond-field. When gold was found on the Rand in 1886, Rhodes was well forward in the rush; and at once he began to wonder what more Kimberleys and more Rands might be awaiting discovery further north. He was determined that his northward advance should not be halted by Afrikaners, Germans, or Portuguese; and it was in the hope of finding gold that he sent his pioneer column across the Limpopo in 1890.

Similarly, Goldie in Nigeria was determined to push inland and forestall the French, who were advancing down the Niger. For many years, Mackinnon in Zanzibar pressed the government in vain to allow him to open up trade routes in East Africa and develop the country as a sort of condominium, with Britain and the Sultan of Zanzibar sharing the profits.

Commercial rivalry was mixed with rivalry for national prestige. The German empire-builder Karl Peters surreptitiously visited East Africa and secured from a handful of unsuspecting African chiefs treaties by which they placed themselves and their people under German protection. Bismarck, the ruling German statesman of the day, had hardly any more interest in colonies than Gladstone; but even he dared not reject Karl Peters' achievement, and he accepted the treaties on behalf of the German government.

In China, prestige was as important as commercial profit in driving the European powers into competition. Britain already held one good commercial harbour and naval base at Hong Kong. But when Russia seized Port Arthur and Germany Kiaochow, Britain felt bound to take Weihaiwei, which she did not need, in order to demonstrate that she was still active and alert.

At the other end of Asia, the story goes that a French warship was sent with orders to hoist the French flag on the unoccupied island of Perim at the mouth of the Red Sea. The French captain was unwise enough to call at the British port of Aden and accept an invitation to dinner at Government House, at which he incautiously revealed the purpose of his voyage. The captain of a British cruiser slipped away early from the party; without Admiralty orders he put to sea and forestalled the Frenchman by hoisting the British flag on Perim.

Strategy was less important in imperialist thinking than we might suppose. Lord Salisbury, who presided over much of the British activity in the colonisation of Africa, dismissed the strategic possibilities of East Africa as worth very little. But one element in naval strategy, namely the establishment of coaling stations for the fleet, was very important in British thinking. If Britain had been left undisturbed, she would have left most of Africa alone and contented herself with snapping up a few harbours as coaling stations. There are some amusing papers in the Record Office in London describing the perplexity of a Portuguese slave-dealer in West Africa during the 1850s. He was making large profits out of his slaving, but the activity of the British navy was making the future of this business highly uncertain. He now had the opportunity of switching from slaves to coal, with much smaller profits but with respectability and complete safety. Had the moment come to make the change, or should he live dangerously for a while longer?

Britain was self-sufficient in coal, and the coal-burning steamships refuelled at Aden or Bermuda or Hong Kong with Welsh anthracite shipped out from Cardiff and Swansea. But in the latter years of the nineteenth century the internal-combustion engine was invented. The new 'horseless carriages' began to replace bicycling as the fashionable craze, and the demand for petrol began to grow. Oil also began to replace coal as a fuel for steamships; and the oil-fields near the Persian Gulf at once became of the highest strategic importance. There was no oil, as far as was known, in Britain, or indeed in Western Europe. The replacement of British coal by foreign oil weakened the British economic posi-

tion, and the decision to convert the Royal Navy from coal to oi
fuel was not taken without serious misgivings.

Strategy, prestige and commercial rivalry are of dubious mora
value, but in the scramble for colonies there were some highe
motives as well. In East and Central Africa especially, much effor
was spent in putting down the Arab slave trade. Lugard agreed with
Livingstone and other missionaries that the slave raiders had done
so much damage that Africa's first need was peace and security
which could be obtained only by bringing the country under British
rule. It chanced that the great explorations in that region took place
during the long European peace which intervened between the
Franco-German war of 1870 and the World War of 1914. Explorers
from Western Europe were horrified at the damage they saw being
done in Africa. One Englishman wrote, 'The Pax Britannica which
shall stop this lawless raiding and this constant inter-tribal war wil
be the greatest blessing that Africa has known through the age
since the Flood'. It was ironical that within a few years, the riva
colonial powers involved the African peoples in a far greater
war in a quarrel which was no concern of theirs.

The Colonial Period

There will always be room for controversy over the balance-shee
of imperialism – or colonialism, as it is often called today. Nearly
everyone will agree that the economic development it brough
was a good thing. Roads, railways and air services began to link
Asian and African villages with the outer world. Minerals and crop
were exported, and began to provide Asia and Africa with som
of the comforts and conveniences which were enjoyed in Europe
Under colonial rule, Asia and Africa received at least the beginning
of health and education services. It has been suggested that these
benefits could have been obtained, without the necessity of foreig
rule, by a sort of combined international technical assistance
scheme. Theoretically this may be so; but before the establishmen
of the League of Nations after the First World War, Europe woul
have been unable to conceive of any such scheme. The world being
as it was from 1890 to 1920, European governments would spen
money and effort on no one but their own subjects.

Asian and African critics accept that colonialism brought then
many economic and some social benefits, but they say that the
price they paid was too high. Far too large a proportion of the
proceeds of their crops and minerals went to pay dividends to
foreign shareholders; far too little was spent by the companies in
wages or taken in taxation to be spent by the government for the
public benefit. They say that if the colonial powers had been less

selfish, there could have been more education and a more purposeful preparation for independence. Worst of all, it was too generally assumed that because European troops had artillery and machine-guns, whereas the Africans had spears, the European was a superior being and the African an inferior. This insult hurt all the more because it was often made unconsciously by kindly and well-meaning Europeans.

Over most of Africa and much of Asia, the family, the clan or even the tribe was the unit rather than the individual. It was nobody's fault that by importing their own highly individualistic and competitive ways into such a society, the Europeans did a great deal to break down the social structure. There are some peoples in Africa whose social code lays great stress on causing no offence and avoiding all ostentation. When brought into contact with Europeans, such a people will go silently to the wall. It was nobody's fault that modern health services brought about a great increase in the human and in the animal population, so that traditional systems of agriculture broke down and the land suffered from over-cropping, over-grazing and erosion.

Colonialism, in short, brought some good and some evil; and one could argue for ever whether the evil outweighed the good, and whether it might have been possible to secure the benefits without paying the price for them.

The colonial period was short, and it would have been a heavy task to carry through the colonial system to success. Crown government in India began in 1858, and the annexation of Burma was completed in 1886; these two populous territories together had fifteen times the area of Britain. The total area of the British Crown colonies in Africa was twenty times that of Britain. Both in Africa and in Asia, Britain governed on the principle that no grants were to be made from the British Treasury unless a territory was too poor to provide even the bare essentials of government. Administrative and technical staff could be obtained from Britain; roads, railways, schools and hospitals could be built; but all expenditure on salaries and on construction and equipment had to be met from local revenue. Once they were provided with a skeleton administration, the colonies received no more Treasury grant, and thereafter they cost the British taxpayer nothing. In 1929 and 1940 two Acts were passed which enabled small grants to be made from British funds for directly revenue-producing projects like railways, harbours, or geological surveys. It was not till 1945 that an Act was passed enabling grants to be made not only for economic development but for welfare.

In Africa, the period of colonial rule lasted roughly from

1880 to 1960. In many colonies law and order were not completely imposed until the eve of the 1914 war; there was small-
scale fighting in Nigeria till 1912, and even later in Kenya and
Nyasaland. After the 1914 war came the long economic depression. Africa depended on the export of her raw materials, and
African governments drew most of their revenue from duties on
export and imports. After a short-lived post-war boom, the world
prices of African produce slumped, and it was only the rearma-
ment programme from 1935 onwards that began to push prices
up again. After 1945, thanks to the Colonial Development and
Welfare Acts, colonial governments for the first time had a fair
amount of money to spend on social services as well as on
economic development. But their time was short. Their people
were demanding self-government. Within twenty years all the
African colonies were independent, and the colonial governor was
a species that was nearly extinct.

Colonial Independence

The colonial system contained the seeds of its own decay. Asians
and Africans came to study in Paris and London. They obtained
professional qualifications, and they absorbed European ideas on
parliamentary government and liberty and civil rights. Some of
them were embittered by unhappy experiences in Europe; others
who enjoyed their student days, felt the contrast when they returned home and found themselves excluded from any effective
share in the government of their country. The Belgian authorities
observing this, hoped to avoid trouble in the Belgian Congo by
providing the country with excellent welfare services but seeing
to it that no university-educated Congolese ever returned to his
country to be a subversive influence there. They were disappointed
The Congolese were determined that the Congo too should become independent; and the result of the Belgian policy was that
the Congo began its independent life with fewer educated men
than the French and British colonies.

If Europe had been able to live in peace, the nationalist movements in the colonies would have developed more slowly. The
great mass of the people would have known nothing of the outside world, and the slowly increasing handful of highly-educated
professional men would have found it harder to arouse their
countrymen's political ambitions. But when Britain and France
went to war against Germany and her allies in 1914 and 1939
they raised large armies of Asian and African troops and threw
them into the fight. In the 1939 war, Indian divisions fought in
Africa, and West and East African divisions joined the Indian

army in reconquering Burma from the Japanese. It is not surprising that the Indian and African ex-service men came home after the war unwilling to submit tamely to whatever the white sahib or bwana proposed for their country. After the war there were difficulties over demobilisation, housing, employment, shortages, and rising prices. The ex-service men listened and believed it when they were told that these difficulties were caused by the white men's selfishness or incompetence, and that the remedy lay in their own hands.

The two World Wars gave imperialism a shock from which it could not recover. Turkey entered the 1914 war in occupation of all the Arabic-speaking region of Asia. She had recently lost her north African colony of Tripoli, which had been taken by Italy in 1911; her Egyptian province had been in British occupation for thirty years. During the war, all Turkey's Arab subjects revolted, with encouragement and help from Britain and France, and with leadership supplied by Lawrence and others, as well as by Sherif Hussein and his sons. As a result of the war, all the Arab countries were liberated from Turkish rule. But they did not, as they hoped, immediately obtain independence; the League of Nations placed Iraq, Transjordan and Palestine under British mandate, and Syria and Lebanon under French. This was a shock to the Arabs, who considered that they had been betrayed; and Britain and France lost much of the goodwill they had gained from the war of liberation.

The 1914 war destroyed not only the Turkish but also the German colonial empire. The German colonies were all confiscated, and were distributed among the victorious allies; though, like the Arab countries, they were placed under mandates from the League of Nations, so that there was some measure of international supervision over the way in which they were administered. Much was said in allied countries about Germany's alleged unfitness to govern colonies. A good deal of this criticism was based on an inquiry held by the German government itself, some years before the war, into the administration of German East Africa, which (like both the Rhodesias at that time) was governed by a chartered company. The inquiry produced evidence of a good deal of maladministration and cruelty; it shocked the German public. The German government at once acted just as the British government acted after the Indian Mutiny: it took the country out of the hands of the chartered company and set in hand a thorough overhaul of the administration, which by 1914 had already had much good effect. No similar inquiry was ever held into French or British colonial administration. The British Labour

Party did indeed suggest that all British colonies should be placed, like the former German colonies, under League of Nations supervision. But this suggestion was quietly smothered.

Independence came first to the Indian sub-continent, which had been much longer under British rule than any of the African colonies.[1] For many years the British had foreseen that the day would arrive when the British raj must come to an end. In 1900, 1919 and 1935 India had been granted increasing instalments of self-government. In later years the British authorities had been exasperated by terrorism and embarrassed by the movement led by the saintly but elusive Hindu leader Mahatma Gandhi, whose tactics of non-violent non-co-operation were much more difficult to deal with than terrorism. In the closing years of the 1939 war, and immediately afterwards, the British were striving not to postpone Indian independence, but to hold the sub-continent together as one independent state. In this they failed. The antagonism of the Hindus, led by Gandhi and Nehru, and the Muslims, led by Jinnah, proved too strong. The predominantly Hindu area became the independent state of India; the two Muslim areas on the east and west of India, a thousand miles apart formed the independent state of Pakistan. Burma, which had been completely occupied by the Japanese during the war, chose to revert to her ancient condition of complete independence. India and Pakistan became independent in 1947, Burma and Ceylon the next year.

From the constitutional point of view, the British colonies in Africa were a generation behind India; as regards economic development, they were still more backward. There were no large steel works or textile mills in colonial Africa. The British were very conscious of what had happened in India since 1900. They assumed that some day the African colonies would be ready for independence, but they believed that independence was far ahead; there was much patient work to be done first in economic and social development, and in extending self-government by carefully graduated instalments.

These calculations were upset; partly because African leaders were not willing to go forward at the slow rate which the British thought advisable, and partly because the United Nations brought continuous pressure to bear on the colonial powers. The old League had supervised the administration of the mandated territories, the former German and Turkish colonies; but it regarded the British administration of Mauritius or Sierra Leone and the

[1] Though the English fort at Cape Coast in Ghana dates from the beginning of Charles II's reign, and Freetown in Sierra Leone from 1787

French administration of Madagascar or Senegal as domestic affairs which were outside its jurisdiction. The United Nations took a different view. It invited all colonial powers to send it annual reports on the educational, social and economic progress of all their colonies; it drew up a standard form of questionnaire; it set up a committee to examine and discuss the reports; and it invited the colonial powers to send representatives to meet the committee for the discussion. The UN committee made it quite clear that the purpose of every colonial administration should be to prepare its country for independence as rapidly as could be.

The British were ready in principle to accept this; they disagreed only over the timing. They hoped that funds provided under the Colonial Development and Welfare Acts would speed up not only economic but also social and educational development; and they had a scheme for increasing African share in government. In 1946 they gave the Gold Coast and Nigeria an unofficial majority in their legislative councils, and later did this in other African countries. They increased the African representation in the governor's executive council. They introduced a ministerial system. They planned that when Africans had become accustomed to ministerial responsibility, the governor's executive council should be replaced by a council of ministers, and that this should later develop into a cabinet, responsible no longer to the governor but to an elected legislature. They hoped that the elected legislatures would develop a system of parties, divided not over personal or tribal rivalries, but over principles; and they hoped that national leaders would arise among the tribal chiefs who had become accustomed to dealing with national affairs.

The British timetable broke down. A series of riots in the Gold Coast, the richest and supposedly the happiest colony in Africa, convinced the government in 1948 that progress towards self-government must be speeded up. A series of national leaders appeared – men like Nkrumah in the Gold Coast, Azikiwe and Awolowo in Nigeria, Kenyatta in Kenya and Nyerere in Tanganyika – who were not tribal chiefs and did not believe in the British policy of ruling through the tribal chiefs. The Gold Coast became completely independent (under its new name of Ghana) in 1957, and all the other British colonies[1] followed it within ten years.

French colonial methods were somewhat different from British.

[1] The white minority government in Southern Rhodesia declared the country independent in 1965; but Rhodesian independence was not recognised by Britain, or by the black African countries, or by the United Nations.

D

French Africa was more centralised. The French administration did not trouble to uphold the social standing of the tribal chiefs but treated them frankly as subordinate officials. The French drew a clear distinction between French citizens and France's colonial subjects. There was less lip-service paid by the French than by the British to African languages and culture, and there was less trouble taken to develop representative government. On the other hand, the French did take some Africans into the parliament at Paris, and one of them at least became a cabinet minister; it never occurred to the British to have a Nigerian sitting at Westminster to represent Lagos, much less to appoint him secretary of state for the Colonies.

In practice however there was a good deal of similarity between British and French administration. Both countries were short of administrative and technical staff, though after the 1939 war both provided considerable financial assistance to their colonies from metropolitan funds. Everything really depended on the relationship between the white administrator and his African people; and the more the administrator was overworked and overloaded with paper, the more remote he became.

In 1945, after the war, France summoned a constituent assembly, which included a block of African representatives. The Africans were dissatisfied with the assembly's proposals, and in 1946 they held a conference of their own at Bamako, and formed a party of their own, the *Rassemblement Démocratique Africain*, to express their views in the parliament at Paris. In 1956 the RDA members succeeded in getting the French government to pass a law which permitted colonial territories to take over a good deal of self-government. In 1957 the new law was applied in one territory after another, so that all the African colonies were equipped with responsible legislatures and ministries.

The decisive moments came in 1958 and 1960. In 1958 General de Gaulle became ruler of France, and began to draw up a new constitution for the French Community. The draft would give the colonies full internal self-government, but their foreign and defence policy and certain other affairs would be controlled by the Community's executive council. A referendum was held in 1958 on the question whether the constitution should be accepted. One colony, Guinea, voted against it, and immediately received its independence; all the others voted in favour. But in 1960 all the other French African colonies changed their minds and decided to quit the Community and become independent. They continued however to receive French financial and technical assistance, and the links between France and her former colonies seem much closer than those between Britain and the former British colonies.

Just as it can be argued whether colonialism did more good than harm, so it can be argued whether the colonies received their independence too soon. In one sense, they certainly became independent too soon: none of them had enough educated citizens or enough economic development. Economically, they were still too much dependent on exporting raw materials, and their communications and their economic resources were greatly underdeveloped. They were short not only of doctors, but of dispensers; not only of engineers, but of draughtsmen; not only of accountants and works managers, but of typists and filing clerks. Such shortages were bound to cause inefficiency; and the inefficiency would be all the more obvious because in their inexperience, the newly independent governments would undertake ambitious projects which the colonial governments would have known to be impracticable.

On the other hand, one cannot learn to swim without getting into the water; and one cannot learn the arts of administration and government without having responsibility. For a few short years, the British system of having African ministers in power, with the governor holding reserve emergency powers to prevent disaster, served as a sort of dual-control training machine. But very soon the African ministers insisted on taking over sole control. They enforced their demand by boycotts and walk-outs which could make all effective government impossible. Ultimately, all government depends on consent. African leaders were in a position to withhold their people's consent; and if they did so, the colonial power must either call up the guns, or must give way. In dealing with a sectional revolt, like the Mau Mau in Kenya, the colonial power might call up the guns; but faced with a truly national movement, it must give way, as Britain, France and Belgium all did.

4 Marxism

The severest and most vociferous critics of imperialism are the spokesmen of communist governments. It is mainly through the work of Marx and Lenin that communism is today such a mighty force, and that so many countries have communist governments.

Communistic ideas and practices of one sort or another are ancient and widespread. Over most of the world there has existed the primitive, unselfconscious communism of the agricultural village community, which holds its land in common and allows each member of the community his fair use of it, regulating his usage by strict custom. This primitive village community existed in England and elsewhere in Western Europe until it began to crumble in the troubled times of the fourteenth and fifteenth centuries; it still survived in Russia at the beginning of the present century; and it can be found in Asia and Africa today.

The medieval English village system began to crumble when the Black Death in the middle of the fourteenth century killed so many people that there were barely enough to work the land, and the feudal lords began to abandon corn-growing and switch to the profitable and labour-saving practice of sheep-rearing. The village decayed as the town and the textile trade developed and capitalism was born. England began by exporting raw wool, and passed on to exporting finished cloth. Capital was needed to produce the cloth, to build the ships, and to maintain the export organisations; but enough was left over to build the magnificent churches that stand today in the main wool-producing districts of East Anglia and the Cotswolds. Free capital available for investment piled higher and higher as a result of the sixteenth-century explorations, the opening up of India and the New World, the African slave trade, and the West Indies sugar industry. By the time that the industrial revolution began in the eighteenth century there was plenty of capital available for building canals, railways, machinery and factories.

Marx (died 1883) and his friend and colleague Engels (died 1895) lived in Victorian England and saw the evils of early nineteenth-century industry: the slums, the ugliness, the exploitation of labour. Novelists like Dickens, reformers like Lord Shaftesbury and William Plimsoll saw these evils just as clearly as Marx and Engels. The reformers thought it possible to improve the industrial system by legislation, keeping the benefits of capitalism but getting rid of the defects. Marx and Engels thought this a vain hope. They thought the evils inevitable because they were inherent in the nature of capitalism; the only remedy was to destroy capitalism and replace it by a better system. Marx did not think that this would necessarily mean a bloody revolution. He was prepared to see the working classes acquire political power by a gradual peaceful process. When the First Socialist International Conference was held in London in 1864, Marx's inaugural address congratulated the British workers on the recent Ten Hours Act and the young co-operative movement. To conquer political power, he said, was now the great duty of the workers, and he advised them to set up their own political party. The continental socialists who were listening to Marx accepted this, and proceeded to set up Social Democratic parties. In England, the workers preferred for the time being to ally themselves with the Liberals, and it is only in the present century that this alliance has broken down.

What is this capitalism, which Marx criticised so strongly? In Marx's view, it is an economic system in which the prime object is to accumulate capital. The most successful business is not necessarily the one which gives the public the best service or pays its shareholders the highest dividend. It is the business which accumulates the biggest reserves of capital, and uses them to establish new branches, to expand into new lines of activity, or to take over a rival firm. The capitalist erects and equips a factory, lays in a stock of material, hires his labour, and sets the machines running; he sells the manufactured product and enjoys the proceeds. In the comparatively small-scale business firms that Marx knew, the owner set aside what he thought necessary for ploughing back into the business, and spent the rest as he pleased. Today the picture is more complex. The huge limited company has to make elaborate provisions for taxation (perhaps in several countries in which it operates) and distribute its available profits in dividend to large numbers of shareholders. But the principle is the same. The capitalist is in business to make as much profit as he can; he pays his staff at the agreed rates, and keeps the surplus for himself, either to distribute in dividend or to plough back into the business.

Marx was a realist. He knew full well that a business cannot be started without capital, and that the capital invested has been accumulated through labour performed in the past. He would agree that the man who provides the capital to start a new business is performing a service, and is entitled to a fair reward. He always distinguished between the capitalist as a concept in theoretical economics, and the human being who lives under the capitalist system and invests his savings in company shares. We may guess that he would have approved when the British government nationalised the mines and the railways and compensated the shareholders with fixed-interest stock. Marx was not criticising capital; he was criticising capitalism.

Marx's criticism of capitalism was that when the buildings and plant and raw materials have been provided and the costs of production – including wages and a fair return on capital – paid, the whole of the remaining surplus has been provided by the workers, and should belong to the workers. But under the capitalist system it does not belong to the workers; it belongs to the shareholders, to the capitalist. Marx recognises that the owner of a family business may work hard in it as the manager. As manager, Marx would agree that he is entitled to an appropriate salary, and entitled, like other workers, to a share in the profits; but not to the whole. This argument is not invalidated by the enormous development of limited companies in modern times. The doctor or bank clerk who saves £100 and invests it in company shares is making no real contribution to the welfare of the company. He buys shares which someone else wishes to sell, and the company's total capital is unaltered. But the shareholder has money; and capitalism is a system in which the man who has money has power over the man who has nothing to sell but his labour. The manager, the technologist, the accountant, the man on the production line, the van-driver, these men make profits for the firm and have a personal interest in it. The firm is their livelihood. The investor has usually no such personal interest; he is interested only in his dividends. And yet the board of directors, however enlightened, regards itself as responsible mainly to its shareholders. Labour, like raw materials, is an item in the costs of production, which the management will try to keep as low as possible. The board's first concern is to remain in business and increase its profits; if it can produce a better balance-sheet by closing an unprofitable works and laying-off men, it will do so. Marx would reverse this order of priorities; instead of a system in which the capitalist can employ or dismiss labour, he would prefer one in which labour can employ and control capital.

However enlightened and well-intentioned management may be, the everyday working of capitalist industry always produces enough instances of inequality and hardship to make such criticisms as these attractive. But Marx was not content with criticising the economics of industry. He drew elements from the thought of his contemporaries to work out a philosophy of history: the theory of the class struggle.

The Class Struggle

As Marx looked at world history, he saw political power passing from one class to another. Primitive village communities become organised into kingdoms and empires as groups of warrior nobles establish their leadership. In western Europe, feudalism develops; and gradually the feudal kings and barons become weaker and their power passes into the hands of merchants and capitalists. In Marx's view, political power is based on economic power; in fact, we might almost say that economic power is the only true power. In a modern Western industrial state, Marx regards the economic classes as reduced to two. The class of feudal lords has lost all effective power, and there now remain only the workers (often referred to as the proletariat) and the capitalists or employers, whom Marx often calls the bourgeoisie, because capitalism develops in towns, not in country villages.

As Marx watched this development, he saw in it a process whereby the worker loses control over his means of production. In a primitive village, the worker owns – or at any rate controls – his own means of production. He has his own potato-patch and spade: his own loom and stock of yarn: his own hammer and anvil and stock of iron: his own knives and needles and stock of leather. But as a result of the modern factory system, the worker has lost this control; he is helpless without the conveyor-belt and the expensive machinery which stands beside it. For Marx, the question was how to restore to the workers control over the means of production – and for that matter, the means of distribution and exchange as well – which they have long since lost.

It seemed to Marx that men's actions, even if they do not always realise the fact, are mainly determined by their economic interests. Sooner or later there is bound to be a struggle between the workers and the bourgeoisie, the workers demanding more economic and political power and the bourgeoisie striving to hold on to its privileged position. Competition, said Marx, will tend to reduce the rate of profit on capital. The pioneer in any field of business will make very satisfying profits. His success will attract a host of imitators and rivals; the cream of the market will be skimmed off, and what remains will become less and less attractive. To counteract this tendency for the rate of profit to fall, capitalism strives to develop itself, to extend its search for new products and techniques, for bigger and richer markets. It will seek overseas for new markets, new sources of raw materials, new supplies of cheap labour. And thus imperialism develops, imperialism being regarded by Marx as capitalism's last desperate resource.

By this hard work and ingenuity, the bourgeoisie will postpone as long as it can the decisive struggle with the advancing proletariat; but sooner or later, said Marx, the struggle was bound to come. It would be a hard struggle, for the bourgeoisie in a highly developed country possesses political and military power, which it would not, Marx thought, hesitate to use against the workers, invoking (quite sincerely) ideas of national patriotism in support of its own class interests.

Ultimately, however, the victory of the proletariat was sure; and what would happen then? Since the workers (the proletariat) in every country form the great majority of the population, power would pass finally from the hands of the bourgeoisie into the hands of the workers. The immediate result would be what Marx and Engels called a dictatorship of the proletariat, a government which would put down all enemies of the revolution, very likely (though in Marx's view, not necessarily) shooting some handfuls of bankers, conservative politicians, financiers, company directors and right-wing journalists in the process. But when the process was complete, the power of the state would be, for the first time in history, in the hands of the great majority of its citizens. Capitalism would be no more; the state would own the means of production, distribution and exchange; there would no longer be any conflict of interest between the state and the mass of the people, as under capitalism there must be. What then would be the need of the state machinery? None, said Marx; when the dictatorship of the proletariat had done its work, the state would no longer be needed, and (as Engels put it) the state would 'wither away'.

Brief though this summary of Marxism has been, it shows how varied is its appeal. There is of course an underlying assumption: namely, that as the state withers away, such human frailties as laziness, selfishness and greed will likewise vanish. Provided we can accept this, Marxism has something for almost everybody. To the manager or technologist in industry it says, 'Why work for the benefit of the shareholders, for a board which screws you down on money for equipment and research? Work for the public, for the people.' To the lower-grade worker it offers better pay and conditions, for no longer will the company be preoccupied with the need to satisfy its shareholders. To the man growing

cotton or sugar or coffee under the tropical sun it offers freedom
from exploitation by foreign capitalists and an equal footing with
his fellow-workers in Europe. To the plain man who is weary of
the wrangles of party politics, Marxism offers an honest policy
based on the true economic interests of the whole people. To all,
it offers an analysis which seems to make sense of history, and
the comforting assurance that time is on its side and so its fore-
casts must inevitably come true.

Marx was a revolutionary, but he died in 1883 without seeing
any permanently successful revolution carried out by his disciples.
He was more successful in analysing the capitalism of his own day
than in foretelling its future development. He did not live to see
the managerial revolution of our own day, or to study and
analyse the practical working of such experiments in socialism
as the British nationalised industries. Marx recognised that
capitalism had advantages as well as disadvantages. He had no
opportunity of observing any weaknesses in the practical applica-
tion of his own ideas.

Eagerly scanning Europe for signs of the coming revolution,
Marx had great hopes of the revolutions of 1848, which overthrew Metternich in Austria and Louis-Philippe in France, and
produced a wave of nationalist feeling in Italy. This year of
revolutions, 1848, produced an important document in the history
of socialism, the Communist Manifesto, with its rousing finish:

'The communists consider it superfluous to conceal their
opinions and their intentions. They openly declare that their
aims can only be achieved by the violent overthrow of the whole
contemporary social order. Let the governing classes tremble
before the communist revolution. The proletarians have nothing
to lose in it but their chains. They have the whole world to
gain. Proletarians of all countries, unite!'

The detailed proposals of the manifesto do not all appear nowadays as terrible as they did to the 'governing classes' in 1848. Its
main proposals are:

1. The nationalisation of land.
2. A high and progressively graded income tax.
3. The abolition of inheritance.
4. The confiscation of the property of emigrants and rebels.
5. The nationalisation of credit through a monopoly state bank.
6. The nationalisation of transport.
7. The nationalisation of a great part (not necessarily all) of
   industry, and the planning of land use.

8. The universal obligation to work, and where necessary the establishment of labour armies, especially for agriculture.
9. Agricultural labour to be treated in the same way as industrial labour; living and working conditions in town and country to be gradually equalised.
10. State education for all children; child labour in industry to be abolished; education to be linked with economic production.

Marx was disappointed in his hopes of 1848. The German and Austrian liberals failed to secure the adoption of a parliamentary constitution on British lines. Though disappointed in this, Marx thought that the bourgeois revolution which was carried out in Europe in 1848 must surely one day be followed by a socialist revolution on the lines of the Communist Manifesto. In France, there occurred the short-lived proletarian dictatorship of the Paris Commune in 1871. In England, Marx found much to encourage him. The working class still had no votes. But in 1844 the Rochdale pioneers opened the first co-operative shop; in 1833 the government passed the first effective Factory Act, and in 1847 the more sweeping Ten Hours Act. By these developments, and by the second Reform Act of 1867, Marx was encouraged to hope that in England the socialist revolution might come about gradually with little or no bloodshed; but he saw that the process would be slow.

Russia

At the other end of Europe there was Russia: a vast country, hardly at all industrialised and almost entirely agricultural; the mass of its people illiterate and ignorant of the outer world, practising subsistence agriculture in their village communities. From the point of view of a practising revolutionary, it seemed an unpromising field.

Nevertheless, from this point of view Russia had one advantage. The Russian government was despotic; it ruled with the aid of a secret state police and used the vast spaces of Siberia as a penal settlement for political offenders. But there existed in Russia a class of educated people who were able to compare the rigid Russian system with the more liberal ideas of the West; and the very comparison made them revolutionaries. During the second half of the nineteenth century, the Russian government saw the need for change. In 1861 it set the servile villagers free and made it possible for them to acquire land of their own. Later, it introduced other reforms: trial by jury, more education, freedom to move about Russia and to emigrate, even some amount of local self-government. But such reforms as these did not satisfy the revolutionaries, especially after they had read Karl Marx. They were all agreed that Russia needed a revolution, but how could a revolution be brought about in Russian conditions? There was hardly any capitalism in Russia, but Marx said that the proletarian revolution would be brought about by those who had suffered under capitalism. Could the Russian villagers – ignorant, deeply religious and fervently loyal to the Emperor and to the Church – be transformed into a revolutionary proletariat? Marx himself thought it unlikely, and the Russian revolutionaries were deeply divided over the question of strategy.

Most of the Russian Marxists thought that Russia might be an exception to Marx's general theory. Generalising from what had happened in western Europe, Marx said that society developed from feudalism to capitalism and from capitalism to socialism. But, they asked, need this always be so? In Russia the village commune was still very much alive, almost as much alive as the village communes in the West had been before capitalism developed and sucked the life out of them. It should surely be possible for Russia to pass straight from the village system to socialism, without passing through the intermediate stage of capitalism. The revolutionaries who thought in this way called themselves Narodniki or Populists, because they believed in the revolutionary possibilities of the Russian people.

This view was strongly opposed by a small group of Russian Marxists under the leadership of Lenin (1870–1924). In Lenin's view, there was no hope of transforming the Russian villagers into a revolutionary force. The Russian villager, or peasant as he was often called, was not interested in socialism or revolution. He was incurably 'petty-bourgeois', that is, narrow-minded and selfish: all he wanted was more land and freedom to use it as he pleased. The Populists were deceiving themselves if they thought that Russia could by-pass capitalism. Certainly there was very little capitalism in Russia as yet, but it was developing fast; and it was beginning to suck the life out of the village commune in Russia just as it had done in England and France long before.

In Lenin's view a Russian revolution could be carried out only by an industrial proletariat, and even then only if it was led by professional revolutionaries like himself. Lenin was above all a practical politician. He took over any of Marx's teachings which suited his purpose and ignored the rest. He cared nothing for consistency, and bewildered his colleagues by the way in which he changed his policy to suit changing circumstances. Since he

regarded the villagers as 'petty-bourgeois', he regarded them a
potential enemies of the revolution. When he came to power, i
was easy for him to use force against these 'enemies of the
revolution': to requisition their grain, to stop their private market
ing, to confiscate their land, and to conscript them as workers or
collective farms in the country or in factories in the town. Kar
Marx, and Lenin himself in his younger days, intended the socialis
revolution to produce a free society, with all the civil right
which were taken for granted in England. But when Lenin se
himself in opposition to the Russian villagers, who formed the
overwhelming mass of the Russian people, he destroyed this hope
of a free society. In the thought of Marx and Engels, the dictator
ship of the proletariat was to be a temporary phase. No one aske
who would actually exercise power during this phase, or how
long the phase would last, or what could be done if those who
exercised power refused to give it up. When the question arose
not as a matter of revolutionary theory but as a practical problem
Lenin's answer was that the mass of the workers was incapable
of exercising power. Only professional revolutionaries were fit to
lead the revolution; they would exercise power, and only they
would decide when the time had come to resign.

From 1897 to 1900, Lenin was exiled to Siberia, and fo
some years after that he lived in exile in western Europe: in
London, Geneva and elsewhere. All the time he kept up his
correspondence with his fellow-revolutionaries in Russia, and he
held conference after conference to discuss plans and strategy
At a conference held in London in 1903 there was great debate
over the constitution of the party. Lenin was in favour of limiting
membership of the revolutionary party to a selected few; other
preferred a wider membership. Lenin was in a minority, but he
refused to accept the majority decision. Instead, he set himsel
to split the hostile majority. He took immense pains to inter
view opponents singly and win them over to his point of view. He
called a private meeting of his own supporters, with sentries
posted outside who had orders to admit none of the majority
party. In the end, Lenin's tactics caused several delegates to with
draw from the conference in protest; and instead of being in a
minority of six, Lenin found himself in a majority of two. It wa
a tiny majority, and a very temporary one; but Lenin immediately
adopted for his group the name Bolsheviki ('majority party') and
his opponents were called the minority party or Mensheviki. Fo
the rest of his life, whatever the voting figures might be, Lenin
insisted that his faction, however small, was the true majority o
the Russian Marxist party.

5 The Russian Revolution

The split between Bolsheviks and Mensheviks became of great importance when the Russian revolution came about in 1917. The Mensheviks were at a disadvantage in being called, and in allowing themselves to be called, 'the minority'; especially as in fact they were at first a great majority. Not that Lenin or his intimate colleagues among the Bolsheviks attached any real importance to democratic procedure as it is understood in the West. The success of the revolution was more important than democratic procedure. Lenin's respected teacher Plekhanov, speaking on the party's draft programme at the 1903 conference, was asked how any form of dictatorship could be reconciled with a free democratic republic. He replied that if the people were to elect a parliament favourable to the Marxist programme, the party would keep it in being as long as possible: but if the elected parliament were unfavourable, the sooner it was dissolved, the better – in two weeks, let us say!

The hopes of Lenin and his fellow-exiles were raised in 1905, when the Tsar granted a constitution and Russia for the first time had a parliament. But it was not until 1917, when Russia was exhausted by her losses in the First World War, that Lenin's opportunity came. The war was still going on, and the nation seemed to be cracking under the strain of its terrible losses. As the last hope of holding it together, the Tsar's advisers talked of a constituent assembly to devise a new constitution. But the military situation was desperate. The army was almost in a state of dissolution; more than a million deserters were roaming about behind the lines; the transport system was breaking down. Early in March there were serious riots in Petrograd (now Leningrad), the capital and the meeting-place of the parliament. 'Bread, peace, freedom' was the cry; troops who were ordered to disperse the mob failed to do so, and many of them joined it. The Tsar's autocratic government lost control of the capital, and never regained it.

What was to replace the autocracy? The great majority of the parliament hoped for a ministry composed of members of parliament and responsible to it: a cabinet system like that of Britain. But the Tsar and his advisers would not face this possibility.

On 11 March the Tsar prorogued the parliament; four days later he abdicated in favour of his brother. Thus there was a power vacuum; it was a question of organising something to fill it. A group of members of parliament formed itself into a provisional committee under the chairmanship of the president, and it began urging the Tsar to authorise it to act as a provisional government.

But the provisional committee had a rival. During the rioting, the industrial workers in Petrograd began electing a soviet. The word soviet means simply a committee. At the time of the unsuccessful revolution of 1905, such committees of workers had been formed in many towns, and they were not abolished when the Tsar's government resumed control. In fact, the formation of soviets was encouraged by the law governing elections to the parliament. Workers, peasants, landowners and owners of town property voted in separate classes. In each factory the workers elected a soviet to represent them on a higher body; this higher body elected representatives to serve on the general electoral college of the city; and this city electoral college elected the city's representatives in parliament. Elections to parliament were indirect, and voting was carried out in three or four stages.

Thus, there was nothing novel about the idea of a soviet in Petrograd; and on 9 March the workers began electing their soviet, which they speedily enlarged to include representatives of the troops. At this stage the provisional committee of parliament and the Soviet of Workers' and Soldiers' Deputies were not rivals for power, and neither was consciously revolutionary. Many men were members of both bodies. The two did not amalgamate, but they speedily agreed on a short-term programme of reform. The mob's cry had been for 'Bread, peace, freedom'; it was easy to issue a series of proclamations on civil liberty, but the questions of bread and peace were much more difficult.

On 16 April, Lenin returned to Petrograd from exile; the German government arranged his rail journey from Switzerland in the hope that he would bring about Russia's withdrawal from the war and thus enable Germany to turn all her forces against the allied armies on the western front. With Lenin's arrival, the hesitating and reluctant Russian revolution acquired its leader.

Lenin immediately announced a programme which startled and alarmed his fellow-revolutionaries. He proposed that as a temporary measure the soviets should assume complete power; they should refuse to collaborate any longer with the provisional government; they should nationalise the land, setting up a system of agricultural soviets for making the arrangements locally; they should work towards state capitalism as an intermediate stage in the development of true socialism; and the soviets should arrange to summon a constituent assembly. Lenin was uncompromising on the subject of the war: the Russian troops, he said, must fraternise with the soldiers of the enemy so as to encourage socialist revolution in Germany and Austria.

It was his talk of nationalising the land and fraternising with enemy troops that particularly startled his colleagues. Since the abortive revolution of 1905 the Tsarist government had had a deliberate policy of helping peasants to acquire land of their own, knowing that land-owning peasants would be conservative – pettybourgeois, as Lenin would call them – and opposed to any talk of revolution. By 1917, three-quarters of the agricultural land of Russia was already in peasant hands. It seemed to Lenin's fellow-revolutionaries that in his Swiss exile he had lost touch with realities; he was proposing to alienate four-fifths of the Russian people on a point of principle.

Similarly with his proposal to fraternise with the enemy. The International Socialist Congress, meeting shortly before the war, had agreed that it would be the duty of all socialists to oppose any war measures on the part of their governments. Yet when the war came in August 1914, these resolutions went for nothing: the socialist parties in Germany and France voted almost solidly for the war credits. Lenin, still in exile, had refused to believe the news when he heard it. A big European war seemed to him – and to many other socialists – a heaven-sent opportunity for the socialist revolutionaries in each country to launch their revolution: so much so, that he thought it most unlikely that national governments would be so foolish as to provide such an opportunity. But in April 1917, all that was nearly three years ago. German troops were entrenched deep into the heartland of Russia, and even the Bolsheviks held that Russia must hang on and defend herself against further invasion. They did not believe that German socialists, who had been unable to resist their government in 1914 when it took the risk of declaring war, would be able to resist it now, when the German armies, both on the eastern and the western front, stood deep in enemy territory. Fraternisation with the enemy, thought Lenin's colleagues, would not bring about revolution in Germany; it would merely demoralise the Russian troops, and throw Russia wide open to the enemy.

So Lenin was outvoted, but to him that was no new experience. He replied that his opponents were living in a world of theories; he had to take account of facts. He set himself, as so often before, to split his opponents, conciliating those who could be conciliated, proclaiming the stubborn as heretics. And constantly he preached his doctrine and slogan of 'All power to the soviets'. So great was his personal reputation and influence, that many members of soviets up and down the country came to believe that if Lenin said so, it must be so.

In June, there assembled in Petrograd the first All-Russian Congress of Soviets of Workers' and Soldiers' Deputies. Of more than 1,000 members, only 108 were Bolsheviks; the two biggest parties were the Social Revolutionaries (the successors to the Populists) and the Menshevik group of Marxists, which together made up more than half the total membership. Lenin and his faithful few had a long way yet to go. Much of the history of communism since 1917 comes from the fact that Lenin and his Bolsheviks were a small minority in Russia, and were determined to gain power and hold it until they could mould the Russian people according to their own ideas.

Then, in mid-July, a Bolshevik rising went off at half-cock. A regiment of troops in the Petrograd garrison, which had become deeply infected with Bolshevism, attempted to capture the city and compel the soviet to take power. There were two days of rioting and disorder, and then dependable troops entered the city and put down the rising. Lenin was furious: he knew that the time had not come for the soviets or the Bolsheviks to try and seize power, and this stupid undisciplined rising had put the clock back. Naturally the provisional government arrested a number of the Bolshevik leaders and imprisoned them; Lenin escaped by bolting to Finland, and he stayed there for several weeks.

This July crisis brought about the resignation of the aristocratic leader of the provisional government. He was replaced by Kerensky, a socialist who, like many others, had been elected to the parliament in 1906 by peasant votes because all the Marxists both Mensheviks and Bolsheviks, had boycotted the elections Kerensky was as far to the Left in 1906 as any member of parliament could be; but in 1917 he was at best a middle-of-the-road man: a sound liberal, full of sympathy for the peasants whom he represented, but anxious that Russia should avoid the mistakes of the French revolution. He wanted no Robespierre, no reign of terror, and no Bonaparte. Kerensky was clear about what he wanted to avoid; he was not clear about how he could avoid it. If there had been a strong middle class to support him, Kerensky might have succeeded. But in Russia there was no middle class. There were the aristocrats and the generals, there were the land-hungry peasants, and there were the revolutionary worker and soldiers. Kerensky had no chance against Lenin.

In September, it was the turn of the generals to attempt a rising. The war was still going on; the Germans were still advancing, and had just captured the important city of Riga; the Russian offensive of July had failed; the Kerensky government seemed to be doing nothing but talk. Generals Kornilov and Krymov, apparently thinking that they were called upon to save the Kerensky government from Bolshevik control, marched on the capital. But there was no such danger from the Bolsheviks, and Kerensky had no intention of putting himself into the hands of the generals. He released the Bolshevik leaders from prison and called on the people in general to rally round him and save the revolution. Krymov shot himself, Kornilov submitted to arrest; their rising was a failure. Its main result was a great wave of support for the Bolsheviks all over the country. Lenin's lieutenant Trotsky became chairman of the Petrograd soviet, replacing a Menshevik; the Moscow soviet and many others too came under Bolshevik control. Lenin began to think the moment was approaching when the soviets might safely seize power.

Kerensky had summoned a second All-Russian Congress of Soviets to meet in Petrograd. It was possible, Lenin thought, that this second Congress might be more favourable to the Bolsheviks than the first had been. On 22 October Lenin came back from Finland, urging that the moment had come for the seizure of power. He overcame the hesitation and opposition of his colleagues; he even overcame the opposition of Trotsky, who feared that a premature Bolshevik revolution might be crushed by the capitalist states of Western Europe. The Congress was to meet on 7 November. On the 6th, Lenin wrote words that sum up his whole outlook as a practical revolutionary: 'If we seize power today, we seize it not against the soviets but for them. Seizure of power is the point of the uprising; its political goal will become clear after the seizure.' That night, Trotsky took command. With the troops loyal to the soviets he captured all the strategic points in the city against weak opposition. Kerensky escaped and went into exile; his colleagues were arrested. The Congress of Soviets met next day in a city which was in Bolshevik hands. To the Social Revolutionaries and Mensheviks, this was an uncomfortable situation. The Bolsheviks were far stronger in this second Congress than they had been in the first; and the SRs and Mensheviks, knowing Lenin of old, feared that he was aiming at a Bolshevik dictatorship. Their fears increased when they found that the chairman of the Congress, and fourteen out of the twenty-two members of the presidium, were Bolsheviks. One of the Menshevik leaders, Martov, demanded that the Congress should choose a government representing all the socialist parties. When this demand was refused, the Mensheviks and most of the SRs walked out of the Congress, leaving the Bolsheviks and their allies in control.

Seeing that the Congress had been duly constituted, had elected its chairman and presidium, and had the full support of the revolutionary troops under Bolshevik control, the SRs and Mensheviks had made a fatal mistake in walking out. In their absence, the Congress proceeded to establish a new provisional government, to hold office until the promised constituent assembly should meet and draw up a permanent constitution. This provisional government was called the Council of People's Commissars, and all the commissars were Bolsheviks. The Council was to be responsible to a central legislative body of 110 members; 62 of its members were Bolsheviks.

Lenin and the Bolsheviks now had the power; and with it they had the responsibility for giving the Russian people what they were demanding: 'Land, peace, bread.'

Lenin himself laid before the Congress his proposals on the land question. Not for the first time, he provoked a storm. The orthodox Bolshevik attitude to the land was that it belonged to 'the people', and should therefore be nationalised. But Lenin was faced with the fact that three-quarters of the arable land of Russia had already been seized by the peasants. In this, as in every other matter, the essential thing for him was the success of the revolution. If the Congress were to propose to the peasants that they should give up the land, it would lose the support of the peasants on the farms and of the peasants' sons in the army. There was no surer way of bringing down the revolution. Lenin therefore proposed that the final settlement of the land question should be left to the constituent assembly; but that meanwhile, all landlord rights should be abolished without compensation, and that those who had seized land should be allowed to keep as much as they could work with the members of their own family, hired labour being forbidden. In other words, the protection of 'temporary law' should be given to all family farms.

Lenin's audience of Bolsheviks protested that his proposals were un-Marxist and un-socialist; they were the ideas of the old Populists and their successors the Social Revolutionaries, those who had walked out of the Congress the day before. So they were, said Lenin, but what did that matter? The essential thing was to gain peasant support for the revolution, not to preach pure Marxism, antagonise the peasants, and so bring the revolution down. As usually happened, Lenin won the day.

The final settlement of the land question was thus left to the constituent assembly. No doubt Lenin and the Bolsheviks would gladly have dropped the idea of the constituent assembly if they had dared. There was no doubt that the assembly, like the two congresses of soviets, would be a mosaic of different political parties and dominated by peasant representatives. Lenin meant his revolution to be directed by one party, his own. But all Russia was awaiting the constituent assembly. Not only was it to draft a constitution and deal with the land question, but it was also to decide what terms of peace Russia would accept from Germany. The Council of People's Commissars was a temporary body, to hold power only until the constituent assembly should have done its work. In November 1917 the Bolsheviks did not venture to drop the idea of a constituent assembly.

Having placed Lenin and his friends in power and referred the questions of land and peace terms to the constituent assembly, the Congress had done all that Lenin needed it to do. Having met for the first time late at night on 7 November, it was dissolved, after an all-night session, at five in the morning of the 9th.

Elections to the constituent assembly were held late in that same month. The Bolsheviks obtained 9 million votes, the Social Revolutionaries 21 million; other parties further to the right obtained over 4 million. Of the 707 deputies, 175 were Bolsheviks, and over 400 Social Revolutionaries. The assembly met in January 1918; it elected a SR chairman, and rejected a Bolshevik motion for debate, whereupon Lenin and the Bolshevik members walked out in protest. There is an important difference between this Bolshevik walk-out and the Menshevik and SR walk-out from the Congress a few weeks before. The Mensheviks and SRs did not believe in force; Lenin did, and he had the backing of the troops.

After the Bolsheviks had left, the remaining members of the assembly speedily agreed to the Leninist land programme, which was entirely in line with their own Social Revolutionary ideas. They went on to proclaim Russia a federal socialist republic, and to resolve to seek a 'universal democratic peace'. That was all they were given time to do. Lenin and the Bolsheviks decreed the assembly dissolved; they sent in the troops to clear the hall by force and to disperse the crowds demonstrating outside the building in support of the assembly. The constituent assembly, so long awaited, was dissolved on the very day it first met. Like its predecessor, the second Congress of Soviets, it had done all that Lenin needed it to do, and he had no further use for it.

Between the meetings of the second Congress and of the constituent assembly, the provisional government took two steps which made the position of the Bolsheviks impregnable, as long as they retained the support of the troops and did not quarrel among themselves. One was the establishment of a political police. Under the Tsarist government, the political police had been successful in infiltrating into revolutionary organisations and sending revolutionists to Siberia or (as in the case of Lenin's own brother) to trial and execution. To be free from the fear of the knock on the door at night was one of the chief hopes of many an idealistic Russian revolutionary. But the Bolsheviks, knowing themselves to be in a minority, could not dispense with a political police. Under Bolshevik control, the political police became much stronger and much more brutal than under the Tsarist government. It was used on a large scale to crush all opposition to the regime, whether real or imaginary. The death penalty was abolished (greatly to Lenin's indignation) by the Congress of Soviets; but the political police ignored the abolition, and used 'merciless annihilation' against all 'counter-revolutionaries, spies, speculators, ruffians, hooligans, saboteurs and other parasites'.

The other step was the establishment of press censorship. All hostile papers were suppressed; all private printing-presses and stocks of paper were confiscated. Nothing could be printed without government approval; and even after every word had been checked and passed by the censor, the luckless author might find, years later, that approval had been withdrawn and he was required to write a retraction and apology, if indeed he was not handed over to the political police. Trotsky dealt roughly with those who protested that he himself had complained about the Tsarist press censorship: the revolutionary government could not allow itself to be weakened by press criticism.

For Karl Marx, socialism meant a classless society, a society in which there would be capital, but no capitalists; in which the workers controlled the means of production, distribution and exchange, so that there was no longer any need for the state. This socialist ideal had become immensely popular, and socialist parties of one kind or another, all influenced more or less by Marxism, existed all over Europe and in many countries elsewhere. The Social Democratic Party of Germany had over a million members in 1914, and had 110 seats in the German parliament. There were international socialist conferences: the First International in the sixties and the Second International of 1913; the latter spent much time in trying to heal the cleavages in Russian and in English socialism. Most socialists believed in evolution, not revolution; they hoped that the evils of capitalism could be gradually removed by parliamentary and democratic means. For socialism of this type Lenin had nothing but contempt. Not only were these socialists utterly mistaken in imagining that the bourgeoisie would ever give up the essentials of power without a fight, but any success that they won in gaining better pay and working conditions would weaken the workers' revolutionary fervour and make them into petty-bourgeois like the Russian peasantry. And so in March 1918, after he and his Bolshevik friends had consolidated their power, Lenin abandoned the name of socialist and called his party the Communist Party. He cut himself away from the Second International and founded a Third International of communist parties, with the avowed aim of winning the world for communism after the Russian model.

Communism today is thus deeply stamped with the mark 'Made in Russia', and it carries also Lenin's personal tag. All the witnesses agree that Lenin was a charming man. He captivated men and women by the affectionate respect with which he listened to them – as long as he hoped that he could win their support. He dazzled them by the clarity of his intellect and the brilliance of his oratory; as a debater he was unrivalled. He awed them by his power of hard work and concentration; no one ever caught Lenin uninformed or unprepared. This formidable character was sweetened by an intense love of nature and the open air, and an impish sense of humour. His friends and political followers adored him.

But Lenin had his other side. He was first and foremost a practical politician. His whole life was spent in planning and preparing for a revolution, and he allowed nothing to stand in its way; he was fond of music, but gave up going to concerts so as to have more time for studying Blue Books and writing letters and articles in the cause of the revolution.

Lenin divided revolutionaries into 'soft' and 'hard'. Lenin himself was hard, and he had no patience with soft revolutionaries. Soft revolutionaries wanted a large party, open to all who accepted the broad lines of policy and were prepared to work under party direction. Soft revolutionaries were anxious that the party should be run on democratic lines; that the majority view should prevail; that the minority should accept their defeat and should remain honoured members of the party; that every member should have his say in framing party policy. To Lenin, this meant that there would be interminable talk while the revolution waited; there would be protests, amendments, points of order and compromises instead of clear-cut decision and swift action. To Lenin, the successful revolution was the one thing that mattered, and it was impossible to look too far ahead and plan for every contingency; one should seize power, and then decide how to use it. He had no objection in principle to democratic procedure, but there was no time for it until the revolutionary government had gained power and was so firmly established as to be in no danger from the capitalist world. To make the revolution possible, iron discipline was needed, and it was for Lenin himself to apply the discipline. He changed his policy, contradicted himself, intrigued, bullied, excluded his opponents from the meeting, expelled them from the party: always guided by the principle that the speedy and successful revolution was the only thing that mattered. What Lenin was from 1900 till his death in 1924, international communism is today.

6   Russia under Lenin

Karl Marx thought Russia an unpromising country for revolution, because it was economically so backward. Industrial countries like Britain, France and Germany, with their highly developed capitalism, seemed to him more likely to provide the ground for the successful proletarian revolution. In spite of Russia's economic backwardness, Lenin had carried his revolution to success; but no one knew better than Lenin himself the danger in which the young revolutionary government stood. Russia was still at war with Germany, and a victorious German army was entrenched far into Russian territory. The Russian army was powerless to attack it. In spite of their name, the Bolsheviks were not the majority party in Russia; their strength lay not in their numbers or voting power, but in their discipline. Lenin had given the people the land they demanded, but he had yet to give them peace and bread.

Among all his brilliant scheming, Lenin had made one serious miscalculation. It seemed to him, as indeed it did to most socialists, that modern capitalism could not survive a big war between great powers. In one international socialist conference after another, socialists from different countries promised each other that the workers would not tolerate a war; they would vote against the granting of the necessary funds, and if necessary they would revolt. In 1912 a conference at Basel reminded governments that the Franco-German war of 1870 brought about the Paris Commune, and the Russo-Japanese war brought about a revolutionary movement in Russia. The socialists of Austria-Hungary must work to prevent an attack on Serbia, while those of Russia must work to restrain the Russian government. It was an accepted article of faith among European socialists that the outbreak of a really big war would bring about world revolution. Lenin fully shared this faith. In 1913 he said that a war between Austria-Hungary and Russia would be a great help to the revolution all over eastern Europe; 'but it is not likely that Franz Joseph and Nicholas [the two emperors] will give us that pleasure'. They would have too much sense for that, he thought.

But when war broke out in 1914, all these hopes failed. There were no revolutions, no general strikes, no refusals to vote the war credits – except by a few small groups: Ramsay MacDonald and Snowden in England, and the Russian Marxist members of parliament. Except in Russia, the capitalist governments came through the war intact. Even in the defeated countries, Germany and Austria-Hungary, there was no sweeping revolution. The German monarchy fell, and was replaced by a republic with a Social Democrat at its head; but the Weimar republic made no attempt to break the power of the army and the old ruling classes. There was a short-lived revolutionary government in Bavaria, but it was crushed. Austria-Hungary broke up into a group of Danubian succession-states. In Hungary, as in Bavaria, there was a Marxist revolution; but the revolutionary government was soon crushed.

To Lenin and the Bolsheviks, all this was a bitter disappointment. They had brought off what seemed almost a miracle; they had achieved the socialist or proletarian revolution in the most backward country of Europe. But their fellow-socialists in the West, with so much greater opportunity, had utterly failed to stop the war, to bring about a democratic peace, to overthrow their capitalist governments. And their failure placed the successful Russian revolutionaries in great danger. How could the Russian revolution achieve permanent success unless it was accompanied by revolutions in other capitalist countries? It could be assumed that all capitalist governments would be hostile to the revolutionary Russian government, just as their predecessors had been to the French government after the French revolution, more than a century before. Lenin and Trotsky, like Danton and Robespierre, felt that all peoples were their friends, and all existing governments their enemies.

In fact, the Soviet government soon had good evidence of the fear and hatred with which other governments regarded it. Even among the revolutionaries in Russia, the Bolsheviks were in a minority; and there were large sections of the Russian people who disliked the Bolshevik behaviour. Among them of course were the nobles and the generals, who still supported the Tsar and were prepared to fight for his restoration. They did fight, and they found Russian troops who were prepared to follow them. They were supported by the British and French governments, who were terrified at the thought of having to face the large German armies released from the eastern front.

For Lenin insisted on giving the Russian people peace, at whatever price. The Russian army was in no condition to continue the war against Germany, and what the Soviet government needed above all was time in which to consolidate the revolution. For two months, from December 1917 to February 1918, Russian and German delegates haggled over peace terms at the small town of Brest Litovsk. Trotsky himself headed the Russian delegation, and his aim was to spin out the negotiations and hope for a revolutionary movement among the German troops. But in the end, though Lenin had to fight hard to get his colleagues to support him, the severe German terms had to be accepted. Poland, Finland, Esthonia, Latvia and Lithuania, all of which had been part of Tsarist Russia, had to be given up; so had the Ukraine and other provinces. Russia lost about a quarter of her European territory, including most of the industrialised area and some of the most fertile agricultural land. It was a severe peace, and it was dictated by Germany. On this precedent, Germany had no right to complain of the *Diktat* of Versailles.

The treaty of Brest Litovsk was signed early in March 1918, in time to release large German forces for their final desperate offensive on the western front. But if Lenin had obtained peace with Germany, he was still far from having internal peace in Russia. From several directions the Soviet government was being threatened by armed forces. There was a strong army of Czecho-slovak troops in Russia; they were prisoners of war from the Austro-Hungarian army, who had surrendered in large numbers rather than fight against their fellow-Slavs. It had been arranged that these men were to be sent along the Trans-Siberian railway to Vladivostok and thence to fight against the Germans on the western front. But things went wrong. The arrangements were altered; there were misunderstandings; the Czechs were suspicious and angry. Trotsky ordered them to give up their arms, and they refused; he ordered that their battalions should be broken up and disbanded, and they decided to hold together as an army and make war against this government that was ill-treating them. They found a leader, the Russian admiral Kolchak, and for a time they occupied the whole length of the railway from Irkutsk westward as far as the Volga. At Samara on the Volga an anti-Bolshevik government was set up, composed of members of the constituent assembly and protected by the Czechoslovak troops. A similar government was set up at Archangel in the north; and in the south-west a group of generals was forming a large volunteer army to fight against the Bolshevik government in Petrograd.

Russia's allies in the war against Germany, notably the French, British, and Americans, were at first inclined to welcome the Bolshevik revolution; they saw it as a victory for democracy over old-fashioned absolute government, and they hoped that it would put new life into the Russian armies. When the Russian resistance collapsed, the first idea of the Allies was to safeguard the arms they had supplied to Russia from being captured by the advancing German forces. For this purpose, a small British force was landed at Murmansk; it was welcomed by the local soviet (much to Trotsky's anger) and it detached a small garrison to protect the anti-Bolshevik government at Archangel. Japanese and American troops landed at Vladivostok to take control of the eastern end of the Trans-Siberian railway and protect the retreat of the Czechoslovak troops.

When it became clear that the Bolshevik government of Russia was a minority government determined to impose its authority by force, the attitude of the Allies changed; the more so as in February 1918 the Bolsheviks formally repudiated all debts which the Tsarist government had incurred, and never wearied of calling on the workers in all countries to rise and overthrow their capitalist governments. The Allies then swung round to the idea of supporting the anti-soviet movements on the Volga, in the north, and in the south-west. As long as the war continued, there was nothing that the Allies could do to help the anti-soviet forces in the Black Sea region, for Turkey was fighting on the German side, and the Allies had failed to force their way through the Dardanelles and the Bosphorus into the Black Sea.

But in November 1918 the war ended, and the way was then open to the south of Russia. Arms and supplies were sent to General Denikin, the commander of the volunteer army of the south-west. French troops landed at Odessa, British troops further east at Batoum. Supplies were sent to anti-Bolshevik forces in the Baltic provinces. For a time, the situation of the revolutionary government in Petrograd looked serious. It was ringed round with hostile armies; food and military supplies were scarce; the mass of the people were sick of war and revolution and wanted peace and bread.

Trotsky was in charge of the war, and he and Lenin never lost courage. They had a central position, for they moved their capital from Petrograd to Moscow, where it has since remained. Their enemies had immense distances to cover without the aid of mechanical transport: Kolchak in Samara was 800 miles from Denikin in Kiev, and Denikin was 600 miles from Yudenich in the Baltic provinces. The French and British troops had no interest in the business; they had been recruited for the war against Germany, and they were impatient to get home and be demobilised. By the end of 1919 they had all gone, except for a British detachment at Batoum, which held on for six months longer. In any case, these foreign troops were never dangerous;

they were stationary garrisons, not mobile armies. It was the counter-revolutionary Russian generals who were to be feared. But the further their troops advanced from home, the less heart they had for fighting; they were more anxious to defend their own region than to attack the government in Moscow. Similarly, the nearer they came to their objective, the less support they received from the local people. To the peasant farming his newly-won land, all armies were a nuisance, all of them demanding to be lodged and fed, all of them damaging crops and killing live-stock. These strangers, with their Tsarist officers, were no better than the Red Army. And so the Soviet government won its war; by the end of 1920 the last of the Russian counter-revolutionary armies had been disbanded or been evacuated by sea.

The British and French efforts had been ineffective; but they enabled Lenin to proclaim with some justification that Britain and France had done just what all capitalist governments must be expected to do. The bourgeoisie in all countries would naturally follow their class interest and combine to crush the workers' revolution. If they could not crush it by force, they would at least try to confine it to Russia by erecting a *cordon sanitaire*, a barrier of small states with a petty-bourgeois mentality, who would see to it that the revolutionaries in Russia could not combine with the revolutionaries in Germany to overrun the whole of Western Europe. This in fact is what happened. Finland, Esthonia, Latvia, Lithuania, Poland, Czechoslovakia and Rumania were set up to form such a barrier. Only Rumania of these had been independent before 1914, and she received an additional province which had formerly been part of Russia.

This was an unhappy start for the relations between Soviet Russia and the West. At first, the Western powers refused to recognise the Soviet government. In 1922 an international con-ference was held at Genoa to discuss the question of war repara-tions and the whole political and economic situation in post-war Europe. Germany and Russia were invited, and it was under-stood that the conference might also consider the matter of the international debts owed by the Tsarist government. The Bol-sheviks had repudiated these debts, but they were prepared to consider coming to some arrangement over them if they could thereby secure recognition and trade agreements.

As far as the Western governments were concerned, the con-ference was a failure, for Britain and France disagreed both over Germany and over Russia. For Russia the conference produced one happy result. The Russian and German delegates, unable to make any headway against the French attitude, slipped away

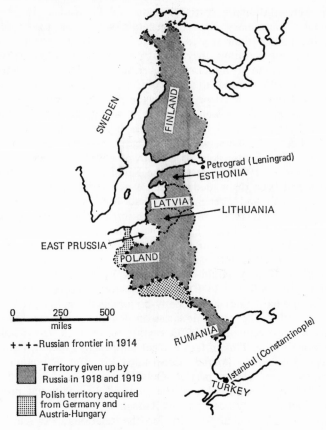

Map 3.   Russia's Western Frontier 1914–1919

together a few miles down the coast to Rapallo, and there they came to an agreement. Germany gave formal recognition to the Soviet government and extended a large credit for the purchase of German goods, notably the machinery which Russia so sorely needed to equip her industry and agriculture. Britain and France were indignant, but they could not upset the treaty, and they dared not allow Germany to acquire a monopoly position in the valuable Russian market. Britain and Italy recognised the Soviet government in 1924, France following a few months later. The United States did not recognise the Soviet till 1932.

The post-war world was a very different place for Russia from the world of 1914, when Russia was the ally of France and Britain, and entered the war with high hopes of gaining the city of Constantinople and the control of the Straits as the prize of victory over Turkey. Constantinople was still in Turkish hands and the Straits firmly barred; Russia was shut off from the West by the *cordon sanitaire*; the Western governments took little pains to disguise their hostility. Russia felt herself ringed with enemies, the workers (to use Marxist language) ringed with hostile bourgeoisie. Clearly, Russian policy must be two-fold: to preserve and strengthen the revolution at home, and at the same time to stimulate revolution abroad.

The difficulty was that if the revolution was to be preserved, Russia must trade with the West to secure machinery and equipment of all kinds; and if you wish to trade with the bourgeoisie, you must not be too active in urging workers to rise and overthrow them. This posed a difficult choice of priorities for men of principle. Trotsky held that world revolution was the most urgent need. He distrusted the Party's strong tendency towards autocracy, and longed for a genuinely democratic workers' republic, which would be much more attainable when the workers in the capitalist countries of the West had seized power from the capitalists, so that Russia was freed from the fear of foreign hostility. Stalin and others held that nothing must be allowed to endanger the security of Russia's industrial development. The first task was to make Russia strong so as to preserve the revolution; stimulating revolution in foreign countries, however desirable, must take second place. Trotsky was defeated and exiled, and was later murdered while living in Mexico.

It was convenient for Stalin to be able to brand his rival Trotsky as a traitor to the revolution because of his erroneous ideas on strategy. Stalin succeeded so well in this that Trotskyism became synonymous with the movement for world revolution, and inside Russia it came almost to mean treason against the Soviet state. For all that, Stalin and his friends had no intention of neglecting the possibility of revolution in the West. They too regarded it as important; but they preferred to work for it like a lioness hunting her prey: cautiously, slowly, freezing into immobility when they felt themselves being watched.

The Comintern

Owing to its failure to prevent the outbreak of war in 1914, the Second Socialist International had disintegrated. In 1919 Lenin founded a Third International, which – to mark his break with the old 'soft' socialists of the Second – he called the Communist International, or Comintern for short. The first conference of the new Third International was held at Moscow in March 1919, and naturally it was dominated by the triumphant Russians. This Third International was to remain in being as the body responsible for organising world revolution as circumstances might permit. Lenin himself laid down some of its guiding principles. Expediency must be the watchword; there must be no sacrifices made for the sake of communist dogma. Parliaments and trade unions in the West were bourgeois in their outlook, but a good communist must not boycott them on that account. On the contrary; he must contrive to get into them and work on them from the inside. Trade unions were especially important. No doubt the union leaders would try to exclude communists from membership or from office, but if necessary the communists must use 'all sorts of strategems, double-dealing, illegal methods, reticences, concealment of the truth, if only they penetrate the trade unions, stay in them, carry on communist work in them'.[1]

The second conference of the Comintern, held in 1920, adopted a sort of constitution. Twenty-one principles were laid down, and it was decided that no communist party could be accepted for affiliation with the Comintern unless organised on these principles. It must be run on Leninist lines, with iron discipline. The members must give unquestioning obedience to the central committee, and the central committee in turn must give unquestioning obedience to the executive committee of the Comintern. Any communists serving in the armed forces, elected to parliament or admitted as members of a trade union must take their orders from the central party committee, and in accordance with the party strategy, they must work to capture control of their organisation. Communist parties must be kept purged of all heretics, especially of socialists who believe in the possibility of gradual progress without violent revolution. A number of prominent socialist statesmen in several countries, including Ramsay MacDonald of Britain, were mentioned by name as men with whom no co-operation was possible.

There was nothing in all this to prescribe that the executive committee of the Comintern was to be controlled by Russians As a British or French cardinal is in theory eligible to be elected pope, so a British or French party secretary is in theory eligible to the supreme post of general-secretary of the Comintern. But since Russia was the only country that had successfully carried out a proletarian revolution, it was natural that the Comintern should hold its conferences in Moscow, and that Western communists attending them should look with reverence upon the

[1] Quoted in J. D. Clarkson, *A History of Russia from the Ninth Century* p. 627.

men who had carried the Marxist-Leninist tactics through to such success. Russia has in fact, though not necessarily in theory, always been the leader of world communism; though since the success of Chairman Mao in China, the Russians, to their indignation, find their leadership challenged.

Since all communists, whether they openly call themselves party members or not, are committed to the idea that violent revolution is the only permissible way of achieving their objects, there must always be a barrier between them and Western socialists. Socialists and communists alike look forward to the establishment of a classless society, and it was no doubt this agreement over aims that led a British Labour Party statesman to say that a Labour government in Britain could get on well with the Soviet Union, 'because the Left understands the Left'. But the disagreement over the means of achieving their aims prevents any true understanding between the man from the Second International and the man from the Third. The man from the Third International will make use of the man from the Second; he will work with him only until he thinks the moment has come to overthrow him and take over his power.

To Marx, and to Lenin too in his younger days, the classless society was to be free and liberal. But the Bolsheviks in Russia, knowing themselves to be a minority in the country, dared not abolish the censorship and the political police which they had inherited from the Tsarist government. Far from abolishing the political police, they enlarged and improved it. Lenin and his successors used it to crush 'counter-revolutionaries' and opponents of all kinds; and the secret political police became so powerful as almost to constitute a state within a state. In the early days of the Soviet government there were protests about the secret police, as there were about the censorship; but the Soviet government has never felt able to do without either.

To the end of his short career in power, Lenin retained his daring realism. The land policy which he had forced through was failing. The peasants were being compelled to hand over to the state all they produced over and above the rations which the state allowed them. But they refused to part with their grain and other produce in exchange for the rapidly depreciating Soviet paper money. Their reply to compulsory requisitioning was simply that they ceased to produce the goods. Lenin admitted that human nature was too strong for him; that people would work harder and produce more for themselves than for the state. He met the situation by abandoning his land policy and launching what he called the New Economic Policy. This new policy was to require the peasants to produce only a fixed amount for the state, and to allow them to keep for themselves all they could produce over and above it. Russia must be fed if the revolution was to survive; and to provide consumer goods, the rigidity of state capitalism must be relaxed and some private enterprise must be permitted.

Lenin's New Economic Policy was greeted with horror by some of his colleagues as an abandonment of the sacred Marxist doctrine: and with jubilation by many observers in the West, who saw it as evidence that Bolshevism had failed and might soon be replaced by some more liberal system. Lenin's critics spoke too soon. The NEP succeeded; production increased and the Bolshevik government survived. The NEP gave the Bolshevik government two things which were essential: time for pushing ahead with its policy of industrialising the country and educating the people for socialism; and a surplus of agricultural produce which could be exported to a hungry post-war world in exchange for machinery and equipment.

Lenin died in 1924 at the early age of 53, with his work far from finished. His power passed to Joseph Stalin, a Marxist and Bolshevik from Georgia in the Caucasus, nine years younger than Lenin himself. Stalin did not succeed without a struggle. His chief opponent was Trotsky, who was in a strong position, having been Lenin's right-hand man in the seizure of power. But Trotsky was no match for Stalin in political intrigue; he was defeated and exiled.

Russia Since Lenin

Lenin's successors have felt bound to continue the struggle which he waged against 'soft' revolutionaries and against those who were not interested in revolutionary ideals but in the more mundane matters of more land, better pay, more freedom. The most convenient means of maintaining the iron discipline they require is to impress on their people that Russia is ringed round with hostile capitalists or bourgeoisie, who are working night and day to overthrow the workers' government and wreck the socialist experiment. The Soviet government retains the Leninist idea (which Marx himself abandoned) of an élite of professional revolutionaries controlling the young state; and it seems ready to acquiesce permanently in Lenin's system of state socialism, which is very different from the socialist paradise that Marx hoped for.

The Communist Manifesto of 1848 contained the slogan, 'From each according to his abilities; to each according to his needs'. In 1936 the Soviet government modified this slogan for Russian purposes to read, 'From each according to his abilities; to each according to his work'. In Soviet Russia, as in Nazi Germany, the state is exalted at the expense of the individual citizen, to an extent which Karl Marx, writing in a more liberal-minded age, could never have imagined.

In 1928, four years after Lenin's death, Stalin began the first of Russia's five-year development plans, aimed at transforming the country into a modern industrial state. As part of the plan, Stalin abandoned Lenin's New Economic Policy; he carried communism into the villages, forbade private trading, and waged ruthless war on the more prosperous villagers, the kulaks. He paid a heavy price. The villagers refused to work on the collective farms, and destroyed their crops and their livestock rather than surrender them. There was much famine. Between 1929 and 1933 Russia's population of farm animals declined catastrophically: horses from 34 to 17 million, cattle from 68 to 39 million, sheep and goats from 147 to 51 million, and pigs from 21 to 12 million. Stalin himself showed his greatness by publicly admitting that he had made a mistake, and relaxing somewhat the rigour of his measures. It is seldom that any government admits to having been wrong.

Since 1928, as plan has followed plan, Soviet Russia has made enormous advances in industry, science and technology. There have been mistakes, some of them serious; in the years between the wars, the Russians had no more experience than any other people in planning a national economy, and they had to learn by their mistakes. Trotsky himself pointed out that the government established large collective farms before it had enough tractors to cultivate them, and supplied the farms with tractors before supplying mechanics to service them. But in spite of mistakes, Russia, which in 1914 was mainly an agricultural country living by subsistence farming, is now one of the greatest industrial powers in the world.

No doubt one reason for Russia's success is that the Communist Party is in undisputed control, and has rationed and disciplined the people in a way which would be impossible to a Western government which is elected on a party basis and is dependent on the popular vote for its re-election. But the Russian people have always been accustomed to autocratic government, and they have accepted the discipline. In 1914 there were Russian soldiers who marched into battle without rifles, waiting to pick up the rifle of a fallen comrade. Since 1928 the Russian people as a whole have shown the same patient valour. A Russian communist would say that in the inevitable struggle (whether military or commercial) between the communist and the capitalist worlds, this very discipline will ensure the victory of communism. It is for this reason that the communists claim that 'time is on their side'.

F

7 Russia as a Great Power

In the eighteenth and nineteenth centuries, Russia was one of the Great Powers of Europe. At the beginning of the eighteenth century, Peter the Great founded the city of Petersburg (later Petrograd, now Leningrad) and gave Russia access to the Baltic. Eighty years later, when Britain was making peace with George Washington and recognising the independence of her American colonies, Russia conquered the northern shore of the Black Sea from the Turks. Russian pioneers and fur-traders, like the Hudson's Bay men in North America, explored and occupied Siberia, pushing across from river to river and launching their boats to float downstream and explore the valley. In 1639 they reached the Pacific coast.

But Russia was still largely shut off from the Western world. The Baltic is frozen in winter; so is the Pacific coast of Siberia. The Black Sea coast is never frozen, but its exit into the Mediterranean was (and still is) held by the Turks. Russia has always felt suffocated. While the Portuguese and Spaniards, the Dutch, French and British were opening up the Americas and trading with Africa and the Far East, the Russians were shut out from the wider world by ice-bound harbours and the world's highest range of mountains. Russia has become obsessed with the ambition to secure warm-water harbours and free access to the high seas.

For a long time Russia was also shut out by land from effective contact with western Europe. Russia was Greek Orthodox in religion, her western neighbour Poland was Roman Catholic; the two Churches were bitterly hostile. While the English kings were fighting at Bannockburn, Crecy and Poitiers, the Poles and Lithuanians were building up, largely at Russia's expense, a great kingdom which stretched from Riga on the Baltic to Kiev on the Dnieper. Poland and Russia came to regard each other, like the English and French, as natural enemies. At one moment, while the English under King James I were planting colonists in Ulster, the Poles succeeded in occupying the Kremlin; they were thrown out by an explosion of Russian patriotism, and gradually the Russian Tsars began to liberate the Russian-speaking people who had been brought under Polish rule.

Russia, Poland and Turkey

It was through their constant wars with Poland that the Russians became drawn into European politics. In the eighteenth century, Poland slid downhill. There was a European war over a disputed succession to the Polish crown, Russia and Austria backing one candidate while France backed another. In the long wars which Frederick the Great of Prussia fought against Austria, the Russians fought on the Austrian side. They defeated Frederick more than once, for a time they even occupied Berlin. In 1762 Frederick was reprieved, for his great enemy the empress Elizabeth of Russia died, and her successor was Frederick's admirer. Russia and Prussia made peace, and a few years later they celebrated it by partitioning Poland. Russia took a slice on the east, Prussia a slice on the west, Austria a slice on the south. In 1793, Russia and Prussia, without Austria, helped themselves to two more slices, reducing Poland to a strip of country about 300 miles wide. Two years later they completed the process; Poland ceased to exist as a sovereign state, until she was reconstituted by the Treaty of Versailles in 1919.

In the Napoleonic wars Russia played her full part, and gained a great reputation when Napoleon invaded Russia and lost his army in the campaign. Russian troops were prominent in the decisive victory of Leipzig, and after Napoleon's exile they took their share in the army of occupation in France. Europe learned to respect and fear the Russian army, formidable in its patient valour and in its inexhaustible numbers.

After 1815, Russia possessed the world's strongest army, Britain the world's strongest navy. Russia was autocratic, and the Russian Tsar found it natural to combine with the autocratic rulers of Prussia and Austria in what they called a Holy Alliance, designed mainly for the purpose of guarding against any recurrence of liberalism or nationalism. They wanted Britain to join them, but Britain would have nothing to do with any such scheme. On the contrary, in 1821 when the Spanish colonies in South America revolted against Spain, the British foreign secretary Canning horrified the autocrats by promptly recognising the new republics.

Having digested her share of Poland, Europe's greatest military power began to think once more of her advance against Turkey, which had been almost at a standstill since her occupation of the Black Sea coast. In 1821 the Greeks revolted against Turkey, and a long and bitter war of independence began. Canning invited Russia, Prussia, Austria and France to join Britain in helping the Greeks to gain their freedom. Austria and Prussia refused,

France agreed; Russia, in spite of her membership of the Holy Alliance and her dislike of nationalist movements, eagerly accepted the chance of gaining something from the Turks in such a respectable way. The Turkish fleet was destroyed by the combined British, French and Russian fleets at the battle of Navarino, and a Russian army marched to Adrianople. The end of it was that a small Greek independent state was set up. Russia, which no doubt hoped for a commission on the transaction, received nothing; Britain and France feared the Tsar too much to add to his power.

Russia and Britain

From then onwards, Britain came to regard Russia as her chief rival. The Russian fleet was not to be despised; but one half of it was shut up in the Baltic, the other half in the Black Sea, to which Turkey held the key. It seemed to Britain that her policy must be to strengthen Turkey so as to bolt and bar the door more firmly. While Britain was consolidating her empire in India, Russia was developing hers north of the mountains. While the Greeks were fighting for their freedom, Russian troops were systematically conquering the tribes of the Caucasus. During the first half of the nineteenth century they conquered Turkestan; and by 1885 they had conquered the independent states of Bokhara, Samarkand, Khiva and others, and brought their frontier right up to Afghanistan and Persia.

In 1854, Britain and France actually went to war with Russia, the so-called Crimean War; they did so because the Tsar was openly reconnoitring his chances in a war with Turkey. He sent troops to occupy two Turkish provinces in the Balkans, and his fleet in the Black Sea destroyed the Turkish squadron there. Nobody gained much credit from the war, except the soldiers who did the fighting and endured the horrors of the hospitals before Florence Nightingale made her presence felt there.

Twenty years later, Russia tried again. The Serbs, Bulgars and Montenegrins were in revolt against their Turkish rulers; the Turks were fighting back, and Gladstone made fiery speeches to the British electors against the 'Bulgarian atrocities' that were being committed by the Turkish troops. Russian volunteers went to join the rebels, and Russia eventually declared war on Turkey. In March 1878 the Russian army was outside Constantinople, and Turkey was compelled to accept the Russian peace terms. The main proviso of the treaty was the creation of a self-governing state of Bulgaria, reaching from the Black Sea to the Mediterranean; for two years it was to be garrisoned by Russian troops.

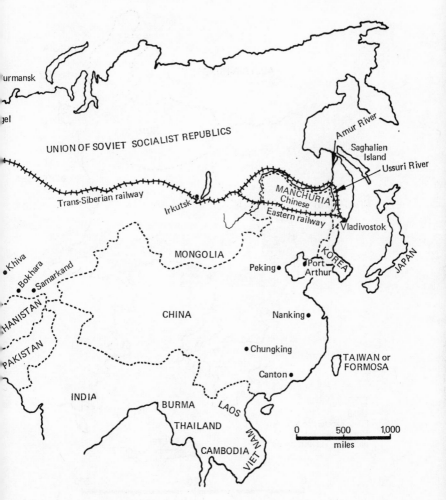

Map 4. Russia in Asia

RUSSIA

AUSTRIA-HUNGARY

RUMANIA

SERBIA

BLACK SEA

MONTENEGRO

BULGARIA

Constantinople

Adrianople

Salonika

GREECE

Navarino

European territory which
Russia proposed should
be left in Turkish hands

CRETE

0   250   500
         miles

Map 5.   Russia's Plan of a Greater Bulgaria, 1878

Britain, France and Austria had agreed that Turkey must reform her administration, and they had even contemplated joint intervention. But such a complete Russian victory as this alarmed them, and they told Russia firmly that this large Bulgaria under Russian protection could not be allowed. The London music-halls resounded with the hit of the day: 'We don't want to fight; but by Jingo! if we do, We've got the ships, we've got the men, we've got the money too.' The British fleet went through the Dardanelles and lay at anchor off Constintinople. As the German statesman Bismarck said, it seemed as if the whale and the elephant were about to come to blows. In the end, the business was settled by an international conference at Berlin. Bulgaria was established as a self-governing state; but she was to have no Mediterranean coast, so there was to be no chance of a Russian military and naval base in the Mediterranean. The British delegation at Berlin was led by Disraeli; he returned to London in triumph declaring that he brought back 'peace with honour'. Not only with honour, but with profit; for Turkey allowed Britain to occupy Cyprus, so that the British could more easily defend Turkish territory in the Levant.

Sucessive British ministers – Palmerston, Disraeli, Gladstone, Salisbury and Balfour – all kept a careful eye on Russia. In 1885, even Gladstone accused Russia of unprovoked aggression against Afghanistan, and parliament granted him a war credit of £11 million. But the crisis passed away without war. The Tsar turned his eyes away from Afghanistan and the Khyber Pass, and looked further east. In 1892 the Russians began to build the Trans-Siberian railway, and soon afterwards China agreed to allow Russia to cut off an immense corner by building a direct line to Vladivostok through the Chinese province of Manchuria. Not content with this, Russia hoped to develop Korea and Manchuria into Russian spheres of influence; and in 1898 she acquired from China the warm-water port of Port Arthur. This aroused the hostility of Japan, and a few years later the two countries went to war. In 1905 Russia was totally defeated by Japan; she had to surrender Port Arthur, evacuate Manchuria, and recognise Korea as a Japanese sphere of influence.

Russia, Germany and Austria-Hungary

The Russians are Slavs; so are the Serbs, Croats and Slovenes of Yugoslavia; so are the Czechs and Slovaks. During the nineteenth century, when so many of her fellow-Slavs were under Turkish or Austrian rule, Russia had a double motive for taking an interest in the Balkans, and so she had great opportunities of

RUSSIA

AUSTRIA-HUNGARY

RUMANIA

SERBIA

BLACK SEA

BULGARIA

MONTENEGRO

TURKEY

Adrianople

Constantinople

Salonika

TURKEY

GREECE

Athens

Navarino

AEGEAN SEA

Crete and half the Aegean
islands were Turkish in 1878

CRETE (Turkish)

0   250   500
              miles

Map 6. The Balkans in 1878

coming into friction with Austria-Hungary. For Austria-Hungary too had hopes of expanding south-eastwards into the Balkans at the expense of Turkey. Russia and Austria-Hungary gradually came to consider each other as natural enemies; and although in Bismarck's day Germany tried hard to maintain her alliances both with Austria-Hungary and with Russia, she found it more and more difficult, and eventually impossible. Germany found herself compelled to choose between them, and she chose Austria-Hungary.

Russia accordingly looked elsewhere for an ally, and in 1893 she formed a dual alliance with France. With much more difficulty, she came to terms with Britain; in 1907 the two countries settled their outstanding disagreements, and the Dual Alliance of France and Russia became the Triple Entente of France, Russia and Britain. As far as Britain was concerned, it was only an entente, not an alliance, for Britain was not yet prepared to make any formal alliance with any continental power.

Palmerston once commented on Russian behaviour. He said,

> The policy and practice of the Russian government has always been to push forward its encroachments as fast and as far as the apathy or want of firmness of other governments would allow it to go, but always to stop and retire when it was met with decided resistance, and then to wait for the next favourable opportunity to make another spring on its intended victim.

He might have pointed out also that when resisted at one point, the Russian government has always had a choice of other points along its lengthy frontier at which to probe the strength of the opposition. Russia was blocked in her attacks on Turkey in 1854 and 1878, blocked on the Afghan frontier in 1885, defeated by Japan in 1905 after a too incautious thrust, and allowed only a small part of what she hoped to gain in Persia in 1907. The Russian government then turned its eyes once more on the oldest of all Russian ambitions, the city of Constantinople or Istanbul. If Russia had avoided the Bolshevik revolution and had stayed in the war until the victory was won, it is probable that Istanbul would have been awarded to Russia by the peace treaty of Versailles. Russia's revolution and retirement from the war gave the victorious Western allies an excuse for insisting (or yielding to Turkey's insistence) that the Bosphorus and the Dardanelles should be demilitarised, but left under Turkish rule.

The events of 1945 enabled Russia to recover more territory than she had lost in 1918, though the great prize of Istanbul and the control of the straits still eluded her. She regained the Baltic countries (Lithuania, Latvia and Esthonia) and the easternmost province of Rumania.[1] To these she added new territory: part of East Prussia, part of Poland, and the eastern tip of Czechoslovakia. She improved her northern frontier at the expense of Finland, though she did not bring all Finland once again under Russian rule, as it had been before 1914.

But Russia extended her real power beyond her own frontiers. In compensation for the territory she gave to Russia, Poland was allowed to acquire as much new territory on the west at Germany's expense; she expelled the German population, and colonised her new western province with Poles drawn from the province now annexed by Russia. This new Poland thus incurred the hatred of all Germans, and became quite dependent on Russia; she was compelled to set up a communist government. In Germany, the whole area occupied by Russian troops at the end of the war was organised into a communist state. The two Germanies, East and West, remained hostile to each other until 1972, when they agreed to exchange ambassadors.

At various dates from 1945 to 1956, communist governments were installed in Rumania, Czechoslovakia, Bulgaria and Hungary, and these countries became Russian satellites. A revolt against the communist government of Hungary was crushed with the aid of Russian troops, and later on, Russian troops were brought into Czechoslovakia to overthrow the communist government there when its leader Dubcek tried to relax the rigour of the system and encourage closer contact with the West.

Yugoslavia too became communist at the end of the war, under its war-time communist leader Tito. But President Tito defied the 1921 resolution of the Comintern which declared that 'Unreserved support of Soviet Russia was and is the very first duty of communists in all countries'. Under his leadership, Yugoslavia has always gone its own way, maintaining contact with the West as well as with the Soviet group. Though communist, Yugoslavia cannot be called a Russian satellite.

The Cold War
In this way, Russia has succeeded in pushing her own frontier further westward, so as to lengthen the distance which a future invader, another Napoleon or Hitler, must advance over Russian soil before reaching the heart of the country. She has done more: she has protected herself with a barrier of satellite states more

---

[1] Rumania, spelt Roumania in England before 1914, now wishes its name to be spelt Romania, to emphasise the fact that it is a Latin country.

effective than the *cordon sanitaire* which the West erected against her in 1919. Moreover, since she has taken pains to shift as much as possible of her strategic industry into the heart of Asia, Russia is now as nearly impregnable as can be against any conventional military attack. We might expect that this would give her a feeling of strength and security, so that she would feel able to relax and allow the world to disarm and live in peace. But this has not yet happened.

Russia is the first and greatest communist state, America is the most powerful of capitalist countries. The West is prepared to accept communism in Russia as a fact, and would like to live on friendly terms with the communist states: to enjoy a 'peaceful coexistence', as the current phrase goes. But Marxist theory makes it hard for communists to believe this. Marx gives a vivid description of the development of capitalism, as it goes through its cycle of recurrent booms and slumps, becomes greedier as the rate of profit falls, stretches out rapacious hands to exploit the far corners of the earth. Marx died in 1883, and in 1910 the German economist Hilferding developed this thesis in the light of what had happened since Marx's day. He pointed out that large firms formed cartels or combines; they persuaded governments to protect their operations by tariffs; they squeezed out small firms and came more and more to dominate the scene; they competed in colonialist expansion; and (he predicted) would one day involve the world in war. Another Marxist, Parvus, went further. Hilferding described national capitalism, Parvus foretold the development of international capitalism. He said that modern capitalism had outgrown the existing system of independent nation-states. Nation-states were obsolete; in the coming age of world wars they would disappear, and only a few super-powers would be left standing among the wreckage. These Marxist authors did not claim that all this evil would be brought upon the world because capitalists intended it so; in their view it would come because capitalists blindly obeyed economic forces and sought to protect their own economic interests.

Even if we do not accept that the two world wars were caused by clashes between rival groups of capitalists, we must admit that in many respects Marx, Hilferding and Parvus have given us remarkably accurate predictions. To a Marxist, the accuracy of the prediction implies the validity of the underlying theory. Lenin accepted these views. In 1921 he told the Comintern that the international bourgeoisie, though temporarily unable to wage open war against Russia, was 'on the watch for the moment when circumstances permit it to renew the war'. Lenin never lost his belief that world revolution was inevitable, and that it was Russia's duty to support the revolutionary forces. The Communist Party in Russia has inherited this Leninist doctrine. If Russia is the friend of revolutionaries, it will be too much to expect a powerful and successful capitalist state to be able to tolerate the competition of an equally or more powerful communist state. Lenin was fond of asking the question, 'Who whom?' Who is to destroy whom? Inevitably, though perhaps with reluctance, capitalism would feel that it must destroy its communist rival, for fear lest the communist rival should destroy it. Thus, in Lenin's view the communists dared not relax their vigilance.

So it is natural for Russian leaders, remembering the way in which the Allies treated Russia in 1919 and later, to proclaim to their people that they are ringed around with capitalist foes (of whom America is the chief) and are living in a state of siege. The Russian people can believe this the more easily because for centuries they felt themselves shut away behind the ice of frozen harbours while more fortunate countries exploited the wealth of the tropics. On the other hand, it is understandable that this Russian suspicion of America should awaken American suspicion of Russia. Both countries have large military forces, both have the atom bomb. The fear of mutual destruction by nuclear warfare keeps Russia and America from open hostilities, but with unresting vigilance they carry on the so-called 'cold war'. This phrase is not so much used today as it was a few years ago, but it is a convenient term for the hostile rivalry between Russia and America, which so far shows no sign of being relaxed.

The idea of a 'cold war' ('cold' as long as the guns do not go off) comes from the German writer Clausewitz, whose book was published in 1832. Clausewitz held that there is no essential difference between peace and war. In his view, a state always has certain aims or ambitions, and negotiates to obtain them. If peaceful negotiations fail, and the state thinks its aims sufficiently important, it will go to war. If its neighbours know that the state will have no hesitation in going to war, they will be more disposed to give way to it. A state should always be prepared for war, and should cultivate the qualities which war requires. If war does come, it must be as short and decisive as possible; the enemy civilian population must suffer so much that it will compel its government and army to give up the struggle and make peace. These ideas of Clausewitz were drawn from a study of Napoleon's methods. They had immense influence in his native Germany, and have more recently been adopted in other countries. They have put an end to the old idea, which prevailed up to 1914, that war is the affair of the soldiers, and that civilians are not directly involved.

Had Martov and the Mensheviks defeated Lenin, Soviet Russia might today have been a liberal democracy: no less communist and Marxist, but based on the idea of individual liberties. But being based on Leninism, Soviet Russia is a totalitarian state. Western governments are based on the idea that the individual citizen has rights[1] and that the government exists to protect them; in a totalitarian state, like Nazi Germany, individual rights are of no importance compared with the interests of the party or the security of the state. Lenin and Trotsky imposed this conception of the state on Russia against the protests of the majority of their colleagues. In any sort of cold war, a totalitarian state will be at an advantage over a parliamentary democracy with a free Press like the United States. The Russian government can hold its cards close to its chest, whereas the American government has been compared to a card-player whose friend stands behind him calling out the cards in his hand and discussing aloud which is the best card to play.

Both countries have enormous armed forces, army, navy, and air. Russian policy has led many of the Western countries to form an alliance against her, called the North Atlantic Treaty Organisation; this NATO alliance is faced by the communist countries united in another alliance, the Warsaw Pact. Both alliances claim to be purely defensive. Canada and the United States are members of NATO, and allied troops garrison an advanced line in West Germany. The Warsaw Pact forces are much stronger in numbers and in their strategic position; Russia's military strength has always rested on her great numbers and the huge size of her territory. The NATO forces in Germany are supplemented by NATO missile submarines and by American air bases and missile sites in Britain and other parts of NATO territory. It is naturally a prime object of Soviet foreign policy to get the British and American troops sent home from Germany, all missile stations dismantled, and all military bases on foreign soil abandoned. NATO rejoins that this concession would leave Western Europe almost defenceless against a swift Russian attack, and no such concession can be made unless the West can be sure that no such Russian attack is to be feared. There is room for much negotiation on such points.

[1] Such as 'life, liberty, and the pursuit of happiness' as the American Constitution says: or the Four Freedoms of the Atlantic Charter. In Britain, a storm quickly blows up when any action is described as 'an infringement of individual liberty'.

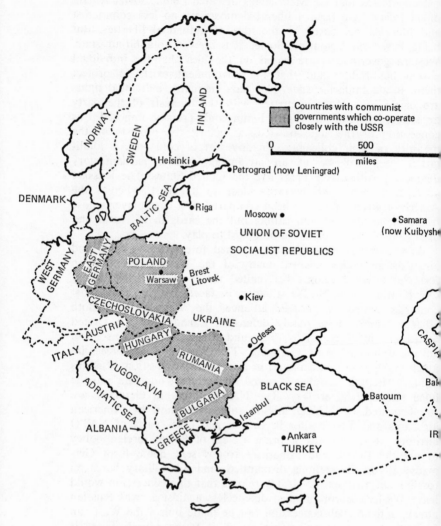

Map 7. Eastern Europe

In this uneasily balanced condition of cold war, both sides have their weaknesses. One Russian weakness is that although the governments of her satellite countries may be loyal and obedient, their peoples are not. The ancient enmities between Germans and Slavs and between Russians and Poles are not healed because there are communist governments in Warsaw and Berlin. The Soviet government has put forward a doctrine of 'limited sovereignty': Russia's interests are those of the whole communist world, and so Russia must always have the right to veto any action of a satellite government which she regards as being against her own interests. Russia cannot expect this doctrine to be popular in the streets of Prague or Bucharest.

Another Russian weakness in the cold war is that for the time being, citizens of the Western countries have more personal comfort, more consumer goods, and more civil liberty. The Russian people have always been accustomed to privation and discipline, and in the view of the Soviet authorities, this discipline must be maintained for the present in order to build up the strength of the Soviet state. The communist governments have a powerful secret police. They maintain a strict censorship over news and communications. They do not allow unrestricted travel to the West, and go to the length of erecting physical barriers along the frontiers to control it. The desire for more comfort is perhaps a human weakness which should not be indulged; but the desire for knowledge and for civil liberty is a noble thing, and this desire is still strong in Russia. Russian intellectuals know that whatever the limitations of Western democracy, the West has no secret police or censorship, and that a novelist or historian is free to write as he chooses without fear of being prosecuted as an enemy of the people or a slanderer of the state.

The West too has its weaknesses, notably those which can be summed up in the emotive words 'capitalist and colonialist exploitation'. It is easy for the poor in Britain or America to feel that their low pay or their unemployment is brought about by the capitalist system, and that they might be better off under communism. It is tempting to imagine that the manifest defects of life in the West could most easily be remedied by destroying 'the system'. People in Asia or Africa, who were formerly under colonial rule and are now independent, may sometimes reflect that their independence has not brought them much greater prosperity, and that this is somehow caused by the cunning of the imperialists or neo-colonialists. It is only natural that Russia should encourage such feelings. It is Marxist doctrine that imperialist exploitation is a necessary feature of capitalism, and that

political power is less important than economic. Thus, a Marxist
is bound to hold that it is not important whether a country is
governed by a British governor and British officials, or by an
African president or prime minister and an African staff. To a
Marxist, the important questions are: Who holds the economic
power? Who buys the country's produce, and who controls its
price? What chance has the country of finding alternative mar
kets? Who supplies the capital for developing the country's
industry, and on what terms? In drawing up the country's
economic development plan, are its planners free to consider the
country's own interest alone, or must they consider also the con
venience of foreign capitalists? A Marxist would ask these ques
tions not only about recently independent countries like the former
British and French colonies, but also about some older countries
like those of Latin America. He might also, for that matter
ask them about Poland, Hungary, or Czechoslovakia; but a
Russian Marxist would hardly be encouraged to do so.

The West, in short, is weak as long as its workers feel that
their interests are in conflict with those of the employers: as long
as anyone feels that he is being exploited.

There are communists in the West; in France and Italy one
voter in four votes for communist candidates at parliamentary
elections. In other Western countries the official Communist
Party is weaker; but there are presumably some communists who
follow Lenin's advice and conceal their party membership. The
West is weakened by industrial unrest; by excessive party political
squabbles; by anything which causes voters to become disgusted
with their political system, with their parliament or their civil service; by any events which cause the governments (and especially
the police) to become regarded as the enemies of the workers, or
which weaken the respect for law and civil authority. If such
events occur, Western communists would be neglecting their plain
duty if they did not seize on them, keep them going, and get the
maximum publicity out of them; for everything that weakens a
capitalist government or brings it into disrespect is helpful to
the Soviet Union.

This uneasy balance and struggle between capitalism and communism recalls the sixteenth-century struggle in Europe between
Catholicism and Protestantism. For a hundred years there were
wars of religion, and for a very long time it seemed as if no
compromise was possible, and no peaceful coexistence could
ever be achieved. But eventually the heat died out of the struggle,
and today's ecumenical movement is raising both Catholic and
Protestant Churches to new heights.

Marx used to say that progress is achieved by thesis, antithesis, and synthesis. A system or an idea exists; that is the thesis. It is attacked by a new system; that is the antithesis. In the end, both systems are replaced by a third, the synthesis; the synthesis embodies the best features of both the others. The struggle between Catholicism (the thesis) and Protestantism (the antithesis) may result in a synthesis, the union of both in something higher; this is not yet achieved, but is no longer regarded as unthinkable. Is it permissible to regard, similarly, capitalism as the thesis and communism as the antithesis, and to look forward to a future synthesis between them?

8 The Independent States of Africa

In the year 1914, nearly the whole of Africa was under foreign rule. Two countries were completely independent; they were Ethiopia (then usually called Abyssinia) and Liberia. South Africa was nearly independent; it was a self-governing member of the British empire, though it was not till 1931 that the constitutional theory was worked out and it was laid down that all self-governing members of the empire were equal in status.

All the rest of the continent was under foreign rule: British, French, German, Belgian, Italian, Portuguese, Spanish. The colonial frontiers of 1914 exist today with but few changes. There have however been many changes in the names of African countries, and the table on pages 114–7 may be helpful.

The 1914 war brought about one set of changes. The four German territories (Togo, Cameroons, South-West Africa and Tanganyika) were taken from Germany by the peace treaty. The League of Nations assumed responsibility for them, and entrusted the mandates for their administration to Britain, France and Belgium. Britain took Tanganyika, less two provinces which were entrusted to Belgium; South Africa took German South-West Africa; Togo and Kamerun were both divided between France and Britain, France in each case taking much the larger share. Italy received nothing; and since she had a secret agreement with Britain and France that if they added to their colonial empires through the war they would give her 'equitable compensation', Italy had some right to feel aggrieved. Some years after the war, Britain did indeed hand over to Italy a strip of Kenya to be added to Italian Somaliland, and a strip of the Sudan to be added to the Italian colony of Tripoli, the modern Libya. But these cessions were too small to be regarded as 'equitable compensation' for what Britain and France had received. In 1935 Italy attacked and conquered Ethiopia; it was liberated by British forces during the 1939 war.

Some great missionaries like Livingstone and some great administrators like Lugard were anxious to bring Africa under European rule because this seemed the only way to bring Africa peace and freedom, stopping the slave trade and the tribal warfare. But on the whole, the European powers partitioned Africa for their own convenience. They wanted sources of raw materials and markets for their manufactures; and more and more, as the partition proceeded, they wanted prestige. It was easy to pass from the idea of governing a territory to the idea of owning it; and if a small country like Belgium 'owned' a huge territory like the Congo, surely a great power like Germany or Italy was entitled to 'own' a slice of Africa in proportion to its own dignity?

African Frontiers

The colonial frontiers were drawn up by diplomatists in Europe by a process of bargaining. The European powers never went to war with each other over disputed African frontiers, but feeling was sometimes raised dangerously high by the marches and counter-marches made by soldiers and explorers of rival countries. In the last years of the nineteenth century it seemed for a time likely that Britain and France might go to war over Africa. British and French officers in the Niger valley were planting their national flags sometimes within a few feet of each other; and as soon as Kitchener had reconquered the Sudan by his victory at Omdurman, he had to hurry south to deal with the French Captain Marchand, who had made a gallant march right across Africa and planted the French flag on the banks of the Nile. Again, in Central Africa there were three important chiefs whose territories lay side by side. The two outer chiefs accepted British protection, but the chief in the middle declined it, so the British officer went away to allow him to think things over. Within a few weeks this chief was visited by a Belgian expedition; the Belgians gave him no time for reflection, but hoisted the Belgian flag, and shot the chief dead when he protested. This affair brought the province of Katanga under Belgian rule, and to this day it sticks like a horn into the middle of Zambia.

In drawing African boundaries, the diplomatists in Europe had no precise surveys to guide them. As a rule they took little or no regard to physical features. There were exceptions to this: for example, the kink in the frontier between Kenya and Tanzania was made because the German Kaiser asked his grandmother Queen Victoria as a favour to allow Germany the glory of ruling over the highest mountain in Africa, Kilimanjaro. Another exception is that Britain allowed German South-West Africa to have a long narrow strip reaching to the banks of the Zambesi; but as the German river frontage was above the Victoria Falls, it was useless for navigation.

The frontiers took no notice at all of existing tribal or linguistic boundaries. All over Africa there are examples of tribes cut in two, one part under British rule, the other under French or German; of sub-chiefs cut off from their paramount chief; of villages cut off from their markets or from part of their farmland. African unity today is made more difficult because part of independent Africa is English-speaking, the other part French-speaking.

The colonies and protectorates thus defined had no natural unity, either of physical or of ethnic geography. Their boundaries were like fishing nets containing a mass of fish of different species. Each territory contained a number of different peoples, with different languages, different religions, different customs, different foods and ways of farming. The peace imposed by the European conquerors put an end to inter-tribal warfare, but it did not put an end to the rivalries and ambitions which caused it. There were enmities in Africa as ancient and as bitter as the enmities between France and Germany, or Poland and Russia. Half a century of European rule could not hope to heal such enmities; in some cases, by allowing opportunities for the underdog to assert himself, European rule actually increased them. When the restraint of European rule was removed, it was to be expected that old rivalries would reappear, as they have done in the Sudan, the Congo, Uganda, Nigeria and elsewhere.

So one of the main tasks of every African head of state today must be to develop national spirit: to make his country into a nation-state. Even among highly educated Africans of today, there are few who feel any deep loyalty to the state, to Nigeria or Kenya or Zambia. There are many who feel such loyalty to a powerful ethnic unit such as the Yoruba or the Kikuyu or the Bemba. And there are many who belong to no such powerful group, and are loyal to a smaller unit such as a local clan. Nearly all political parties in independent Africa are organised on a tribal basis. They exist primarily to make sure that one particular tribe or ethnic unit receives its fair share of government expenditure on development and welfare, and that its members obtain a fair share of ministerial or civil service posts. Africans do not always find it easy to distinguish between the national government and the political party which for the time being is in power. A party in power is often tempted to maintain its position by raiding public money for the benefit of its own party fund, which can be used to bribe and intimidate voters.

Such political parties are divisive. That is one reason – as we shall see, there are others – why so many African states have abandoned the European system of party politics, and have become one-party states. In modern African conditions, there is something to be said for the one-party state, provided it is led by a statesman who is truly a national, and not merely a party leader.

If African frontiers are so arbitrary and artificial, an inheritance from European colonial rivalries, it may be surprising that independent African governments have done so little to rectify them. The problem is that once you begin altering frontiers, it is difficult to know where to stop. If Kenya, for example, were to cede to Somalia the region where the population is predominantly Somali, she might just as reasonably cede to Tanzania the region where the population is Masai, and hand back to Uganda the provinces which the British transferred from Uganda to Kenya in 1902. In a short time, Kenya might find herself completely dismembered. African leaders are conscious of the risk of 'Balkanising' Africa: of splitting it into hundreds of small weak states. They feel that Africa dare not allow discontented provinces to break away and become new independent nations. Unsatisfactory as the present frontiers are, it is better, they think, to preserve them and to develop national sentiment within them. When true nations have come into being, they may begin to think of combining into larger groups.

Africa's Poor Communications

Independent Africa is handicapped by poor road and rail communications. Both during the colonial period and since independence, African governments have been too poor to develop good roads and railways as much as they would have liked. But not only this. In colonial times, each colonial power developed its own system of roads and railways to feed the main seaport in the colony. The system fanned out from the seaport into the interior, and along the frontier there was a zone without motor roads. No roads or railways were built across colonial frontiers.[1]

In West Africa, the French in the Ivory Coast were more active in building railways than their British neighbours in the Gold Coast, now Ghana. The Ivory Coast railway system pushed much further north than the Gold Coast railways, and swung

[1] There is one important exception. The mineral wealth of the copperbelt in Katanga and Zambia led investors to compete for the profits to be made in carrying the mineral by building railways from Bulawayo, Beira and Lobito Bay. Today, political circumstances have changed. Zambia does not welcome Portugal and Rhodesia as business partners, so a new railway is being built to carry Zambian copper to the Tanzanian port of Mtwara.

eastwards, so as to take traffic by a roundabout way down to the Ivory Coast port of Abidjan instead of by a direct route to the Gold Coast port of Takoradi. In East Africa, there was a serious quarrel when the British governor of Tanganyika proposed to build a railway to Mwanza on Lake Victoria. This line would bring traffic down to Dar-es-Salaam, and the British governors of Kenya and Uganda went so far as to appeal to the government in London to quash the Mwanza project, because it would injure the trade of Mombasa. Independent Africa has not yet overcome the results of this policy; Africa is still poorly provided with lateral roads and railways.

The Colonial Period

When the First World War broke out in 1914, the colonial powers had only just established their authority. The whole of southern Tanganyika revolted against German rule in 1905. There was small-scale fighting in British and French West Africa in 1910 and 1912, and even later in Kenya; in 1915 there was a serious rising against the British government in Nyasaland (now Malawi). It was not until the end of the war that the colonial powers were able to settle down and make a real start on the task of developing their African territories. The European powers themselves were exhausted and impoverished by the war. They were tempted to use the resources of Africa for their own benefit, excusing themselves by the plea that Africans must surely profit by being brought into contact with the 'superior civilisation' of Europe, even if it were only as unskilled labourers on European-owned farms or mines. There were of course some European officials, settlers, businessmen and missionaries who did not yield to the temptation, and these altruistic people were sometimes supported by statements of policy from London. But after independence there came such a great spurt in economic development, as well as in education and other social services, that it is plain that the colonial powers could have done more than they did for Africa if they had been single-minded in carrying out their responsibilities.

Even so, we must not overstate the case. The period of effective colonial rule was short, only about forty years, from 1919 till 1960 or so. These forty years were broken by the terrible economic depression of the 1930s, and by the Second World War. Furthermore, it is more difficult to build the first fifty miles of road or railway, to establish the first secondary school, hospital and clinic, to introduce the first improvements in agriculture, than to continue and develop the system. In the beginning, your labourers are unfamiliar with pick and shovel and the technique of platelaying; they are unwilling to work for more than a few weeks at a time, and then they want to take their pay and go home to their villages. People are reluctant at first to bring their sick to the new hospital until the African medicine-man has given up hope; they bring them at their last gasp, and then complain that the white man's medicine is useless. As recently as the 1930s, many African parents were unwilling to send their children to school – 'to give them to the government', as they put it – because European education was beyond their comprehension and they needed the children's help in the house or on the farm. It takes time to build up a reliable labour force, to win confidence in Western applied science and education and medical care, and to educate teachers, dispensers, draughtsmen, clerks and subordinate staff of all kinds. If African countries had been given their independence in 1920, they would not have made such great strides as they did forty years later, when much preliminary work had been done. But, given the kind of technical assistance they are now receiving, they would have advanced further than they did in the forty years of colonial rule.

Egypt was granted formal independence by the Anglo-Egyptian treaty of 1936, though many Egyptians would say that their country was not fully independent until after the Suez affair of 1956, which abolished international control of the Suez Canal and expelled the British garrison from the canal zone. The Sudan became independent in 1956, Ghana in 1957, and most other African countries during the next ten years. In 1973 there were only five countries in Africa which were not under African rule. These were the three Portuguese territories (Guinea, Angola, Mozambique, with some small islands), which Portugal did not consider as colonies but as provinces of metropolitan Portugal; and the two states of Rhodesia and South Africa, in which political power was held by a white minority. We should perhaps add to these a sixth country, South-West Africa. This country, formerly a German protectorate, was taken over by South Africa at the end of the First World War, and administered as a mandated territory under the League of Nations. After the Second World War, the South African government refused to transform the League mandate into a United Nations trusteeship; it annexed the territory, and regarded it as part of South Africa. The United Nations did not recognise the annexation as valid, and regarded the country (which it called Namibia) as a colony wrongfully denied its freedom.

Difficulties Facing African Leaders

The whole of Africa is sub-tropical or tropical, and the continent is subject to natural disasters on a large scale: to droughts and floods and locust invasions, to pestilences and (in some areas) to over-grazing and soil erosion. Apart from such calamities, African leaders have other great difficulties to face. We have already mentioned three of these: artificial frontiers, lack of national unity, and poor road and rail communications.

Compared with Europe and North America, all independent African states except South Africa and Rhodesia are desperately poor. Most of them export raw materials and import manufactured goods. They are striving to develop their own manufacturing industries. But a factory needs power, raw materials, and a market for its produce; and few African factories can command all these on a big scale. Power is becoming available from big hydro-electric schemes like the Volta dam in Ghana and the Kariba dam on the Zambesi, and some countries are producing respectable quantities of consumer goods, such as shoes and textiles, beer and soft drinks, cigarettes, tinned fruits, and cement and steel rods for the building industry. They have assembly plants for producing machinery from parts made in Europe, but heavy industry is only in its infancy. However, in industrial development, as in railways and schools and hospitals, the beginnings must be slow but the speed of development will increase.

Africa's poverty is perhaps felt most in the scarcity of educated men and women. Secondary and higher education developed slowly in colonial times. The first African secondary school in Kenya did not open until 1926, and secondary education for Africans began in British Central Africa twenty years later. Uganda and the Gold Coast did rather better; Uganda opened its first secondary school in 1904, the Gold Coast as far back as 1876. But the Gold Coast, the wealthiest British colony in Africa, had only 3,000 children attending secondary school on the eve of the Second World War in 1939. University education followed later, though Fourah Bay College in Sierra Leone was exceptional; it became affiliated to the university of Durham as early as 1876, and all English-speaking West Africa owes much to the small but steady stream of Fourah Bay graduates. In 1920 a group of African leaders asked the British government to pro-vide a federal university for British West Africa, but nothing was done until after 1945. Then, with the advice of a Royal Commission and with money provided under the Colonial Development and Welfare Acts, university colleges (later developing into full universities) were opened in the Sudan, Ghana, Nigeria,

Uganda, Kenya and Rhodesia. Other institutions of higher education have been developed with technical assistance from Europe and America. In the Belgian Congo, and in French Africa south of the Sahara, the position in secondary and higher education was even worse than in British Africa; though throughout colonial times there were four communes in the Senegal whose people were regarded as French citizens, and were provided with *lycées* like those in France.

In spite of the efforts which African governments are making to train their citizens, and to send them to Europe and America for specialised courses which cannot yet be provided at home, Africa is still pitifully short of doctors, engineers, administrators, professional men and women of all kinds; and short too of the trained subordinate staff they need if they are to do their work efficiently.

One of the first results of independence was that some of the best African teachers were withdrawn from their classrooms to become ministers, civil servants, and ambassadors. At the same time, African governments aspired to universal primary education. Primary and secondary schools and colleges of education were multiplied, but the standard of education fell. In the last years of the colonial period the increase in school population was fast outrunning the supply of competent teachers: in the Gold Coast for example from 63,000 in 1935 to 456,000 on the eve of independence in 1957. African governments were prepared to accept a temporary lowering of educational standards; they thought this a lesser evil than limiting the number of school places and leaving many children without any schooling at all.

There is another difficulty which African leaders constantly denounce, and frequently punish, though often they can find no evidence to bring before a court. This is corruption. Corruption is not limited to Africa. From time to time there are scandals in Britain and other Western countries over bribes and secret commissions, and we may guess that for every such case which comes to light there are many which go unnoticed. It is to be feared that European firms competing for business in Africa do not always shrink from bribing an African official.

In one respect indeed, corruption in Africa can be understood, and to some extent excused. Before the coming of the Europeans, Africa had no system of salaries; it was run on a system of perquisites. A man had a duty to the other members of his family or clan, but none to strangers. Judges and officials of all kinds were paid in fees; the ordinary citizen might charge a fee or commission for a service which he rendered to a stranger.

To illustrate this we may take two cases from the writer's own experience. In one case, two Africans in a strange town had a quarrel, and wanted an arbitrator. They went to an African clerk in a business firm, and paid him a fee to induce him to ask his European employer to do them this kindness. In the other case, an African cook won a competition in cake-making, and offered a share of the prize money to his European employer, who had given him the recipe. This age-old African attitude easily adapts itself to modern circumstances. From this point of view, it is understandable that Africans whose position enables them to render great services, such as making appointments or granting contracts, should expect a percentage for themselves.

For themselves, or rather, for their family; for the African extended family is an extremely powerful social unit. A man's family will help him if he is in need or in trouble, and he must help his family if he becomes prosperous or powerful. African families will make great sacrifices to send a bright boy to Europe for study. They look on the enterprise as a long-term investment, for when he returns with a professional qualification, the young man will earn a good salary and as time goes on will have more and more influence; and his salary and influence must be at his family's disposal. We in Europe can have little idea of the pressure that is brought on an African departmental head to find jobs for his young cousins and nephews and fellow-clansmen. It will be a long time before the idea becomes generally accepted that a salaried position carries with it responsibility to the employer, whether the state or a business firm: and that a man's first duty is *not* necessarily to his family.

Understandable though all this may be, it is still corruption, and African leaders are right to denounce it. They will have an uphill task in putting an end to it.

The Independence Movement
No one was more conscious of these difficulties – corruption, artificial frontiers, shortage of competent trained staff, lack of national unity, poor communications and general economic backwardness – than the national leaders themselves. They knew that the problem of getting rid of their foreign masters would be as nothing to the problems that would face them when they moved into Government House and hoisted the new national flag overhead. They knew that in one sense, European critics were right in saying that Africa was being granted independence too soon. And yet they pressed on with their independence campaign. Why were they in such a hurry?

There were several reasons. One was that they did not trust the colonial governments to stand firmly for the cause of African progress against groups of people who seemed to have an interest in holding Africa back: the European farmers in Kenya, the big mining companies in Katanga and Zambia, the European export-import companies in West Africa. Another reason was the bitter disappointment they received when the League of Nations shrank from taking any effective steps to prevent Mussolini's conquest of Ethiopia. It seemed to them as though the white men would always stick together, and that Africa's only hope was to get her own spokesmen into international assemblies. A third reason was that African leaders were convinced that colonial governments could spend more on social services (especially education, which was always the Africans' first priority) if they chose; the reason why they did not choose was that education would put ideas into people's heads and threaten the colonial administrators' own peace and comfort.

Underlying these reasons was a general resentment at European assumption of superiority. Africans were weary of being told that they were like children: charming, amusing and lovable children, who must be handled 'kindly, but firmly'; who were incapable of holding down a responsible job; whose work must always be supervised and checked by a European; who could not be expected for a century or more to attain the political maturity and sophistication of Europe. In the Second World War, African divisions had played a large part in reconquering Ethiopia from the Italians, and had served with the Fourteenth Army in Burma. The Africans had been able to compare themselves with the British, the Americans, the Indians, the Italians and the Japanese; and they had no reason to be dissatisfied with the comparison. They were not prepared to return to the placid routine of colonial administration: to be told that finance, agricultural and mining policy, and the speed of advance in education and health, were matters which they must leave to the wisdom of the white bwana.

The African One-Party State

Within a few years of attaining independence, most African countries abandoned any serious attempt at party politics on European lines, and became one-party states. The outstanding exception was Nigeria, where three powerful parties, based on solid ethnic blocks, maintained an uneasy balance for some years. When two of the three parties formed an alliance, the balance was upset, and the country collapsed into civil war.

We have mentioned one reason for the African one-party state: the dislike which a national leader feels for parties which are based on local loyalties and rivalries. There are other reasons. All African governments are short of competent men, and face immense tasks of economic and social development. They have everything to do at once; the time has not yet come for differences of opinion over priorities. Any alternative government would face the same problems and would follow the same policy. It would be wasteful to leave good men idle in a shadow cabinet.

Another reason is that Africans like to take decisions by a unanimous or nearly unanimous consensus of opinion. They dislike the European custom of taking a vote and then of doing what fifty-one people wish and forty-nine people oppose. The African way is to discuss until a clear majority view emerges; and then it is the duty of the minority to abandon its opposition and to do its best to make the majority view work. Africans cannot understand an opposition which grumbles, shrugs its shoulders, and waits with glee to see the majority decision lead to trouble. Such opposition to them is almost indistinguishable from treason. In Ghana, many opposition members of parliament joined the government party, saying that they felt it their duty to support a government which had such important work to do. In Kenya, the opposition leader Mr Ngala, giving exactly the same reason, led the whole of his party to cross the floor of the House and join Mr Kenyatta's ruling party.

The British instinctively prefer a two-party system, but a one-party state need not necessarily be a dictatorship, nor need it adopt the totalitarian theory that the state is all and the individual is nothing. As long as the one-party government is seen to be ruling justly and efficiently, it may command general support, and may be able to maintain civil liberties. President Nyerere of Tanzania has said that his one-party government can profit from opposition and criticism, as long as the opposition is not organised.

There have indeed been African one-party states (notably the earliest of them, Ghana) which have developed into tyrannies, with government by decree, imprisonment without trial, strong-arm political police, and other defiances of the rule of law. Where this has happened, it has been through the leader's inability to keep his head and his sense of proportion, and his tendency to surround himself with yes-men and allow himself to become isolated from the general public. No African ruler can have the feeling of security that a British governor had. The governor, with a modest civilian police force and a bare handful of troops, was invisibly supported by the whole force of Britain. His African successor's main support is the loyalty of his fellow-tribesmen. He has always to reckon with the possibility of a blow from a discontented rival group.

The Policy of Non-Alignment

The first problem of every African leader (as of every party leader elsewhere) is to maintain himself in power: to crush or forestall or win over his political opponents and to convince his people that he and his party are the best conceivable government. His second problem is to develop his country: its education and health, its agriculture and mining, its communications and power supplies, its industry, and its prestige in the eyes of the outer world. For all this he needs money, skilled staff from overseas, and machinery and other equipment, supplied on credit terms. He is in the happy position of being able to apply for help to the United Nations and to three sets of outside donors: Britain, America and the West in general; Russia and her communist block; and China. He can play them off one against the other, and all of them are willing to help him in the hope of obtaining his sympathy and support in their rivalries. This is a vain hope; Africa will accept help from anyone, but will commit herself politically to no one. All African countries follow this policy of 'non-alignment'. They wish to have nothing to do with the rivalry between America, Russia, China and their allies. The colonial powers have already involved Africa in two world wars which were no concern of hers, and Africa is now anxious to be allowed to develop in peace.

Neo-Colonialism

Political colonialism is dead; the new national flag flies over Government House. But as Marx preached, political is less important than economic power. African leaders feel that their countries are not truly independent while they export little but raw materials and have to import most manufactured goods from abroad; while the prices of their raw materials are fixed for them on the London or New York markets; and while they have to employ so many foreigners in key positions. Their experience of Western capitalism has not been happy. European companies working in Africa have naturally done their duty by their shareholders, very few of whom were Africans. Royalties, wages and welfare expenditure in Africa on the other hand were part of their production costs, to be kept down. The companies were experienced and well organised, the Africans were not.

There were no African trade unions until after the Second World War.

This state of affairs, in which Africans hold political power but much economic power remains in the hands of European commercial interests, has been called neo-colonialism. African governments are determined to bring neo-colonialism to an end as soon as they can. They want to bring capitalism under control European firms must train Africans for senior technical and managerial posts, and must establish subsidiary companies based in Africa, with African directors. They must pay bigger royalties for their mining, timber or plantation concessions, and must plough back into Africa a bigger share of the profits they make there. In all this effort, African governments are conscious that they must tread with caution; they must allow a European firm to send back enough profit to Europe to induce it to stay in business and to attract investors' capital.

In defence against neo-colonialism, some African governments have introduced schemes of what they call African socialism they have placed their land, minerals, water supplies and essential services under public control. They welcome foreign capital under certain conditions and subject to certain regulations. The most heroic policy is that which President Nyerere of Tanzania announced in the so-called Arusha Declaration[1] of 1967. He declared that this sort of African socialism would be inadequate as a defence, and that Tanzania must do without the type of capitalist development that necessitates large inflows of foreign capital and foreign staff.

It is hard to see what President Nyerere or any other African leader can do about the basic trouble in neo-colonialism: the fixing of commodity prices in London or New York. It is there that the wealth and the financial experience and the markets are to be found. There are hardly any of Africa's commodities in which Africa is the major world supplier. Africa is in no position to bargain. President Nkrumah of Ghana, who was no economist had a scheme for holding a whole year's crop of Ghana cocoa off the world market to compel the world to pay a better price but the scheme failed. Africa has a genuine grievance here. If the world would pay better prices for African produce, it would bring about a great increase in African prosperity. But it may be a long time before voters in Europe and America will agree to pay still higher prices for their finished products in order to benefit the primary producers in Africa.

[1] Arusha is a town in northern Tanzania, at which the policy was drawn up and approved.

African Unity

Outside Ethiopia, Liberia, Egypt and South Africa, African independence is barely twenty years old. During this short period, no African states have gone to war with each other. There have been strained relations here and there; there have been large-scale civil wars in the Sudan, the Congo and Nigeria; and there have been many palace revolutions and *coups d'état*. In some countries the army has expelled the civilian government, usually claiming that civilian ministers were incorrigibly corrupt.

African leaders are aware of the dangers in this state of disunity. The history of Europe shows that a system of nation-states, each pursuing aims which are mainly selfish, produces quarrels and wars, and some kind of supra-national organisation is needed. In colonial Africa, such organisations were coming into existence. The French colonies in West and Equatorial Africa were grouped in two federations; the British territories in East Africa had the East Africa Common Services Organisation, with its own legislature and executive controlling a wide range of functions from railways and harbours to locust control. At independence, these relics of imperialism were dismantled, but there was a need for something to replace them.

President Nkrumah of Ghana was eager for political unification. He had something of Lenin's belief that the essential thing was to seize political power. In his struggle for the independence of his country, he disagreed with those who argued that he should obtain as many concessions as possible from Britain, but postpone political independence until the country had made more economic progress and had trained more of its citizens so as to make efficient government possible. Nkrumah adopted the slogan, 'Seek ye first the political kingdom, and all these things shall be added unto you' – 'these things' being prosperity, control over foreign capitalism, replacement of European officials by Africans, better social services, and greater international prestige. After Ghana's independence, Nkrumah preached the same gospel to his fellow heads of state. He urged them not to waste time in drafting treaties of commerce and friendship and mutual assistance, but to unite! To some extent, he practised what he preached. He united his country with the French-speaking republic of Guinea, and for a short time he managed to persuade Mali also to join the union.

But Nkrumah's preaching fell on deaf ears. Most African statesmen preferred to move more cautiously. It seemed indeed at one moment as though Kenya, Uganda and Tanzania might unite in some form of federation, and President Nyerere announced that he would be prepared to serve under anyone who might be elected as federal president. Commercial jealousies caused the scheme in its original form to fall through; but the three countries did succeed in 1967 in setting up a sort of economic federation the East African Community.

Four years earlier, in 1963, a conference held at Addis Ababa set up the Organisation of African Unity, a body somewhat on the lines of the Organisation of American States. The OAU is merely a consultative body: Nkrumah wanted it to have its own armed forces to enforce its decisions, but he found no support The OAU has had some successes. In 1964 for example, there were mutinies in all three East African armies, and at the request of the three governments, British troops were flown out to put down the trouble. This was politically embarrassing for newly independent states, and the OAU organised the replacement of the British troops by contingents from West Africa. The OAU has been useful in co-ordinating the views and the policy of its member states in such matters as Rhodesian independence and the civil wars in the Congo and Nigeria. The value of the OAU will grow as the years pass, through the opportunities which it gives for African statesmen to get to know each other and to discuss their common concerns. The habit of consultation and co-operation may in time lead to regional groupings and perhaps closer political unity.

To be profitable, any discussion of African affairs must bear in mind the immense size and variety of Africa. Travelling from Tunis to Cape Town and from Dakar to Socotra, you fly nearly one-fifth of the circumference of the world, a distance about the same as from Anchorage in Alaska to the Panama Canal, or from London to Irkutsk in the middle of Siberia. Africa has many hundreds of languages, some resembling each other as English resembles German, but others as different from each other as Gaelic, Czech, and Finnish. To expect an instinctive feeling of brotherhood between the Masai herdsman, the Bushman hunter and the Yoruba businessman is no more reasonable than to expect it between the Yorkshire mill-owner, the Greek fisherman and the Russian worker on the collective farm. All African problems are on a large scale; and first building, and then transcending national unity in Africa is a problem large enough to tax the greatest statesman in the world.

The Countries of Africa

The table on pages 114–15 and 116–17 lists the countries of Africa in alphabetical order, calling each by its modern name

The third column gives the name by which the country was formerly known in Britain. The fourth column gives the name of the colonial power which rules it, or used to rule it. The fifth gives the date of the country's attaining independence, if it has yet done so. The sixth column, headed 'Area', needs a word of explanation. It gives the ratio of the country's area to that of the United Kingdom. Algeria for example is roughly nine times the size of the United Kingdom, Sierra Leone is only about one-third the size of the United Kingdom. Readers in the United States can think of the state of Oregon instead of the United Kingdom; Oregon is only very slightly larger. Another way of looking at it would be to think of Algeria as being more than three times as big as Texas. Sierra Leone is roughly the size of South Carolina.

In the map on page 118, Africa is divided into five regions: North, West, Central, East, South. Each country is given a letter to show which region it is in, and a number to identify it within the region. The British Isles, on the same scale, are shown on the map in black. The African continent is over 120 times the size of the United Kingdom, and well over three times the size of the United States. Put Canada and the United States into Africa, and there would still be room for Europe as well.

H

Map Number		Modern Name	Former Name	Ruled or formerly ruled by	Date of independence
N	4	Algeria	Algeria	France	1962
C	9	Angola	Angola	Portugal	—
E	2	Afars and Issars, Territory of	French Somaliland	France	—
S	2	Botswana	Bechuanaland	Britain	1967
E	7	Burundi	Urundi	Belgium	1962
C	8	Cabinda	Cabinda	Portugal	—
W	17	Cameroun	Cameroons	France and Britain	1960
C	3	Central African Republic	Ubangi-Shari	France	1960
N	3	Ceuta and Melilla	Ceuta and Melilla	Spain	—
C	1	Chad	Chad	France	1960
C	6	Congo, People's Republic of	French Congo	France	1960
W	15	Dahomey	Dahomey	France	1960
N	7	Egypt	Egypt	Britain	1936
W	18	Equatorial Guinea	Rio Muni and Fernando Po	Spain	1968
E	1	Ethiopia	Ethiopia	—	—
C	5	Gabon	Gabon	France	1960
W	4	Gambia	Gambia	Britain	1965
W	13	Ghana	Gold Coast	Britain	1957
W	6	Guinea	French Guinea	France	1958
N	1	Ifni	Ifni	Spain	1969
W	11	Ivory Coast	Ivory Coast	France	1960
E	5	Kenya	Kenya	Britain	1963
S	5	Lesotho	Basutoland	Britain	1967
W	10	Liberia	Liberia	—	1847
N	6	Libya	Tripoli	Italy	1951
E	10	Malagasy Republic	Madagascar	France	1960
C	11	Malawi	Nyasaland	Britain	1964
W	7	Mali	French Sudan	France	1960
W	2	Mauritania	Mauritania	France	1960
N	2	Morocco	Morocco	France and Spain	1960
E	9	Mozambique	Mozambique	Portugal	—
W	8	Niger	Niger	France	1960
W	16	Nigeria	Nigeria	Britain	1960
W	5	Portuguese Guinea	Portuguese Guinea	Portugal	—
S	3	Rhodesia	Southern Rhodesia	Britain	—

Remarks	Map Number	
regarded as part of France, not a colony	N	4
yet independent, 1973	C	9
nal self-government 1973, 'to remain part of the French Republic'	E	2
—	S	2
of German East Africa till 1919	E	7
inistered as part of Angola	C	8
nan till 1919	W	17
—	C	3
regarded by Spain as colonies	N	3
—	C	1
—	C	6
—	W	15
pied by Britain 1882–1936, but nominally Turkish till 1914	N	7
ned by the union of Rio Muni and the island of Fernando Po	W	18
ays independent except for the Italian conquest 1936–41	E	1
—	C	5
—	W	4
—	W	13
sely joined with Ghana, 1958	W	6
ed by Spain to Morocco, 1969; will now disappear from the maps	N	1
—	W	11
—	E	5
—	S	5
nded by Americans as a settlement for freed slaves, 1821	W	10
ish till 1911; a trust territory, 1945–51	N	6
—	E	10
—	C	11
sely joined with Guinea and Ghana, 1960	W	7
—	W	2
nerly divided into French and Spanish zones	N	2
yet independent, 1973	E	9
—	W	8
war 1967–70	W	16
yet independent, 1973	W	5
ared itself independent, 1965; but independence still not generally cognised, 1973	S	3

Map Number		Modern Name	Former Name	Ruled or formerly ruled by	Date of independence
E	6	Rwanda	Ruanda	Belgium	1962
W	19	St Thomas	St Thomas	Portugal	—
W	3	Senegal	Senegal	France	1960
W	9	Sierra Leone	Sierra Leone	Britain	1961
E	3	Somalia	Somaliland	Britain and Italy	1960
S	6	South Africa	South Africa	Britain	1909
S	1	South-West Africa	South-West Africa	South Africa	—
W	1	Spanish Sahara	Spanish Sahara	Spain	—
C	2	Sudan	Sudan	Britain and Egypt	1956
S	5	Swaziland	Swaziland	Britain	1967
E	8	Tanzania	Tanganyika and Zanzibar	Britain	1961–4
W	14	Togo	Togo	France	1960
N	5	Tunisia	Tunisia	France	1956
E	4	Uganda	Uganda	Britain	1962
W	12	Upper Volta	Upper Volta	France	1960
C	7	Zaire	Belgian Congo	Belgium	1960
C	10	Zambia	Northern Rhodesia	Britain	1964

Remarks	Map Number	
man till 1919	E	6
yet independent, 1973	W	19
—	W	3
—	W	9
ned by the union of British and Italian Somaliland	E	3
pendent member of Commonwealth 1909, left Commonwealth 1961	S	6
nan till 1919; South Africa's annexation not recognised by UN	S	1
yet independent, 1973	W	1
lo-Egyptian condominium 1882–5 and 1898–1956	C	2
—	S	5
ganyika German till 1919, independent 1961; Zanzibar independent 64; the two countries join, 1965	E	8
man till 1919	W	14
—	N	5
—	E	4
—	W	12
some time after independence called Congo (Kinshasa) to distinguish from Congo (Brazzaville), the former French Congo	C	7
—	C	10

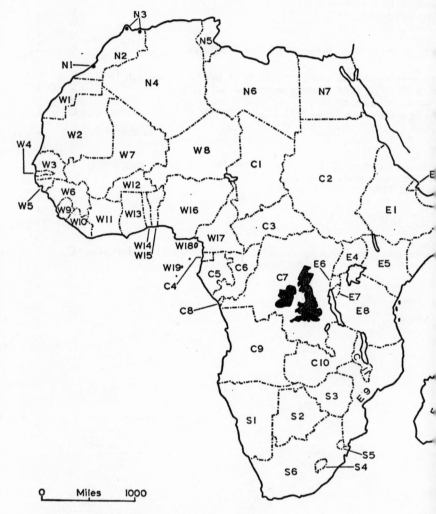

Map 8. The Countries of Modern Africa

9 China

China, as we all know, is a country with an ancient civilisation. In the valley of the Yangtze Kiang a civilisation which is recognisably Chinese had developed nearly 2,000 years before Christ; about the time when the first bronze-using people were invading Britain, and a thousand years or so before the Greeks sacked Troy, though quite late in the history of the Pharaohs of Egypt. China is a large country, about 1,200 miles by 800, with one great advantage and one disadvantage. The advantage is that the great river-basins are extremely fertile and can support a large population. The disadvantage is that the country has no natural frontier on the north and west. It is easy for the nomadic tribes of central Asia to invade the fertile Chinese plains, and China has many times seen foreign conquerors overthrow the native rulers and set up new dynasties.

There is a regular pattern which has recurred in Chinese history. During a period of peace, the population of the fertile valleys increases. Great irrigation works are then undertaken to bring more land into cultivation, and they can be carried out only by levying vast numbers of men under a system of forced labour. Then there is a threat of invasion, so heavy taxes have to be imposed and more men recruited to provide a defending army and to build defence works along the frontier. We admire Hadrian's Wall in Britain, which is some seventy miles long; the Great Wall of China, begun about 220 B.C., is over a thousand miles in a straight line from its eastern end to its western, and far more if we follow its curves. The burden of taxation and forced labour causes discontent, and young men who cannot get land either raise an open rebellion or else take to the mountains and forests and live as outlaws and brigands. Thus there ensues a time of troubles, which is eventually brought to an end by a strong emperor, and the cycle begins afresh.

In spite of foreign invasions and civil wars, Chinese civilisation has endured for 4,000 years: largely because of the admirable administrative system, which was established very early. Everything depended on the civil service, which was selected on the basis of competitive examinations, in theory open to all, though in practice weighted in favour of candidates whose families could afford to maintain them during the long years of study. The central government departments were directly responsible to the emperor, and in each local area the emperor was represented by an official very much like a district commissioner in the British colonial service. The local mandarin was appointed to his post for three years, and care was taken never to post him to his own locality. Within his district he was responsible for all aspects of government: for revenue, police, public works, and justice. Being a stranger to the district, and moving every three years, he had no local power of his own, and might be reasonably expected to be impartial. No system is perfect. The mandarin might be lazy or corrupt, and if his district was a month's journey from headquarters, his people might find it difficult to get him removed. But the Chinese emperors were governing their vast country through this hierarchy of scholar-administrators at a time when the medieval kings of England and France were marching up and down the country trying to keep their illiterate and rebellious barons in order.

Gradually the Chinese people spread into the neighbouring lands, especially into the pleasant warm country to the south. They came into contact with peoples of similar race to their own, and from time to time there were wars and peace treaties, and commerce and Chinese culture were gradually extended. About 100 B.C. the Chinese subdued the tropical coast lands from Swatow past Canton and Hanoi as far south as the 18th parallel. Some of this country they organised into the modern Chinese provinces of Kwangsi and Kwangtung; the rest of it, which corresponds closely to the modern state of North Vietnam, they held, and effectively civilised, for a thousand years, until they were thrown out by a Vietnamese revolt in A.D. 939.

The Chinese were an inventive people. For many centuries they had a monopoly of the art of rearing silkworms and making silk. They invented various machines for irrigation; they invented paper, ink and printing; they invented gunpowder and rockets. In shipbuilding they were far ahead of medieval Europe, and they would have laughed at the Spanish galleons of the Armada. During the fourteenth and fifteenth centuries, encouraged by the Chinese invention of the compass, Chinese seamen were no longer content to go coasting down the shores of the South China Sea, but sailed boldly out over the Indian Ocean. Their ocean-going ships reached East Africa, and a regular trade sprang up; African ivory came to China, and Chinese porcelain decorated the rooms in Arab houses in Mombasa and Kilwa.

In the middle of the fifteenth century, the emperor of the day made a fateful decision. He felt it impossible for China to indulge in this adventuring over the blue water, and at the same time to keep up her watch on the immensely long land frontier. The Chinese sea captains had found no strong civilised states beyond the seas. The overseas trade brought back no gold, no valuable produce unobtainable in China itself: nothing but ivory and similar trash. The emperor decreed that long ocean voyages must cease. All large ocean-going vessels were to be scrapped, and no more were to be built. Chinese shipyards must content themselves with small coasting craft, built not to exceed a specified maximum size. He marked a point on the chart, and forbade Chinese seamen to sail beyond it.

China thus turned her back on the ocean and adopted a continental policy. At the end of that same century, the Portuguese found the way round the Cape into the Indian Ocean, and it was not long before they made themselves masters of the Indian Ocean and its trade. What would have happened to Asia if the Portuguese on arriving had found the Chinese navy, with superior ships and at least equal seamanship, in command of the Indian Ocean? It is one of the great might-have-beens of history.

The Ming dynasty, which had ruled China since 1368, came to an end in 1644. It was overthrown by the Manchu invaders from Manchuria, northerners who came from outside China proper, and who (like the barbarians who overthrew the Roman empire) felt a proper respect for the civilisation which they had conquered. Conquering invaders themselves, they were determined that no other invader should conquer them; and they concentrated on the defence of the Great Wall and the northern frontier in general.

They could not realise the mistake they were making. One great disadvantage from which China suffered was her isolation. The Chinese never came into effective contact with any other civilised country. They exported their silk to Rome and Byzantium; but it was a year's journey, and the silk passed through many hands on the way. China was sometimes visited by Arab merchants, and by Muslim and Buddhist holy men. In the fourteenth century, the Spanish-Arab traveller Ibn Batuta set out to cross the Sahara desert and visit the kingdoms of the Niger valley; he spent a night or two as the guest of a man in Morocco, and discovered that his host was the brother of a man whom Ibn Batuta had met in China some years before. But the Arab civilisation in Cordova, or even in Baghdad, was several months' journey away by sea; China might hear travellers' tales of it, and receive occasional visitors, but there was never any close commercial contact. Western Europe was unvisited and unknown. South of China there were the states of south-east Asia, all of them drawing much of their culture from China. The rest of it they drew from India, but India also was far away; the sea journey was several weeks long – and anyway was now forbidden to Chinese seamen – and the land route over the mountains was one of the most difficult journeys in the world. The Chinese government had every excuse for believing that China was the centre of the world and of civilisation, and had nothing to learn from abroad.

Secure in their isolation, and defended by the armies on the Great Wall, the Manchus left out of account invaders who might come by sea; and they did not reckon on the other possibility that the land frontier might be attacked by an enemy more powerful than the nomadic tribes they were accustomed to deal with. In due time the Manchu emperors had to face attacks from the sea by the peoples of Western Europe; from the east by Japan; and along the northern frontier by Russia. Under these bewildering and re-peated attacks the Manchu empire tottered and fell.

China's first contact with Britain came in 1793, when the government of King George III sent Lord Macartney on a special embassy to Peking to try and conclude a treaty of trade and friendship. The mission was unsuccessful. Lord Macartney brought back to London a message from the Son of Heaven, accepting King George's humble and dutiful message and the gifts he had sent by way of tribute, but assuring him in lofty tones that since Britain produced nothing that could be of use to a civilised country, there could be no point in entering into a treaty or exchanging ambassadors.

As we have seen in Chapter 3, in the 1840s Britain fought the so-called Opium War with China. The Chinese government had the best of reasons for objecting to the opium traffic. Opium-smoking was a national addiction, and when the government banned the growing of opium in China itself, the drug was smuggled in whole-sale from abroad and paid for in Chinese silver, causing an un-acceptable drain on the Chinese currency. It suited the British merchants in India to sell the drug; and eventually the Chinese authorities behaved as the Americans had done in the Boston Tea Party of 1773: they destroyed large quantities of British-owned opium in Canton harbour. Britain declared war, and two years later imposed peace by the Treaty of Nanking. Not only did the treaty cede Hong Kong to Britain and grant Europeans the right to live and trade in Shanghai and four other so-called 'treaty ports', but – worst of all from the Chinese point of view – it com-pelled the Chinese government to accept European ambassadors in residence at Peking and to treat with European governments on terms of equality.

In 1856 Britain fought a second war against China, this time in alliance with France; the French, though as eager as the British to open up China to their trade, were brought into the war ostensibly because a French missionary had been killed in southern China. The peace treaty of 1858 required the Chinese government to tolerate Christianity, and to accept further advances by European businessmen. The European 'treaty ports men' became a privileged class: they lived in their own settlements in the ports, with extra-territorial rights; the Chinese customs duties were eased in their favour; before long the Chinese had to submit to having their whole customs administration overhauled and placed under foreign control, an Englishman, Sir Robert Hart, being placed in charge. These were the 'unequal treaties' of which China has long complained. There were more of them to come. China had to accept a line laid down by the British as her frontier with India, and in 1885 she had to acquiesce in the French annexation of Indo-China. In the 1890s Germany, Russia, France and Britain all annexed Chinese ports, and each expected to develop the adjacent country as its sphere of interest. Britain's sphere of interest was to be nothing less than the whole of the Yangtze valley.

Britain, France and Germany were content for the time being to carve out for themselves 'spheres of influence' in China; Russia demanded more. The frontier between Russia and China ran along the river Amur and its tributary the Ussuri. Almost at the southernmost tip of her territory, Russia built the port of Vladivostok; but Vladivostok harbour was frozen in winter, and Russia, always searching for a warm-water harbour, cast envious eyes on Port Arthur on the Yellow Sea, beyond the peninsula of Korea. But here Russia came up against the interests of Japan.

Like Britain, Japan consists of a group of islands lying close to the shores of a great continent. Like Britain, she has drawn from that continent her people and her civilisation; she looks to China much as Britain looks to mainland Europe. Like Britain again, Japan lies so close to the continental shore that she will never allow long stretches of it to be controlled by one potentially hostile power.

For some hundreds of years past, Japan had been in no danger. China under the Manchus was not as strong as formerly, and in any case, the Manchu government, as we have seen, was looking north and west, not eastwards to the sea. Korea, even when in-

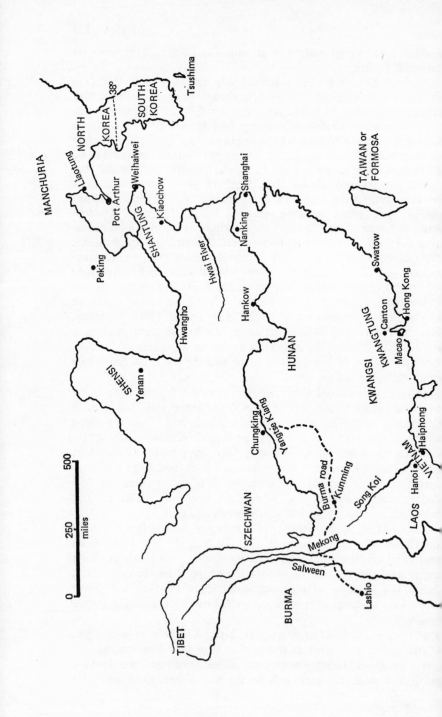

dependent, was not large enough to be a serious threat to Japan, and for some time Korea was part of the Chinese empire.

Until 1853, Japan herself had been as remote from the Western world as China. In that year, Commodore Perry with an American naval squadron did to Japan what the British had done to China eleven years before. Japan henceforth was to be open to foreign trade. But Japan's reaction to this violation was quite different from China's. China learned that she could make no effective resistance to European attacks, and she shrank back into her shell. Japan determined to modernise and westernise herself enough to beat the Europeans at their own game. With immense energy she set herself to build up her manufacturing industry. She copied the German army and the British navy. By the end of the century she felt strong enough to defend her interests against the intruders from the West.

Like the Western powers, Japan was now an industrial state, and like them she needed a market for her exports. China was the obvious market for Japan; but China was rapidly being carved into different European spheres of interest. If Japan was not to be squeezed out altogether, she must find a way of asserting herself on the Chinese mainland.

In 1894, there was a revolt in Korea against Chinese rule, and a Chinese army entered Korea to suppress it. This seemed to Japan a suitable opportunity for establishing herself on the mainland. She declared war on China, and quickly compelled her to sue for peace. By the treaty of Shimonoseki in 1895, Japan annexed the island of Formosa and the Liaotung peninsula, including Port Arthur; and she compelled China to recognise the independence of Korea. This Japanese victory was an unpleasant shock for the Western powers. Russia, France and Germany – but not Britain – joined in ordering Japan to give up Port Arthur and the Liaotung peninsula. Japan did not feel strong enough to defy all three, and she obeyed; but she determined to have her revenge in due time.

The immediate threat to Japanese interests came from Russia. Only three years after Japan had evacuated Port Arthur, Russia herself seized the port; and thus she had at last a warm-water harbour on the Pacific, the object of her ambition for so long. But Port Arthur was useless to Russia unless she could control the country behind it and could build a railway to link the new harbour with her own railway system. The country behind Port Arthur was the Chinese province of Manchuria, the native land of the Manchu dynasty which ruled China. It was plain that Russia's intentions were to link Port Arthur with the Manchurian railways and with her own Trans-Siberian line, and to develop Manchuria in her own interests. Moreover, if Russia occupied Manchuria, she would cut Korea off from contact with China, and Korea too would become in effect a Russian province. Japan was utterly opposed to all this, for she had set her heart on developing both Korea and Manchuria herself. If Russia continued her policy, a conflict would become inevitable.

For the moment however Japan had to postpone action against Russia. The Chinese government was unable to prevent the humiliations which Japan and the European powers forced upon it. There was a section of government opinion which wished China to follow Japan's example and modernise herself; but most of the Manchu governing class dared not risk it, for a modernised China might be strong enough not only to stand up to foreign aggression but even to overthrow the Manchu government. Moreover, the government was facing great internal difficulties. The cycle of Chinese history was working: the population had increased from about 100 million in the eighteenth century to four times that figure in 1850, and there was the usual poverty, land-hunger, discontent, and rebellion. General Gordon the Englishman had helped the government to put down the formidable Taiping rebellion in the 1860s; but thirty years later a new rebellion was started by a society calling itself the Society of Righteous Harmony Fists – a title which the irreverent British rendered as 'the Boxers'. The society's idea was that if its members could obtain no weapons to help them to restore righteousness and harmony, in accordance with the ancient ideas of Confucius, they would be ready to go into action with their bare fists. To the Boxers it seemed plain enough what were the unrighteous and inharmonious forces at work in their country. First of all, there was a foreign government, the Manchu dynasty and its Manchu officials: a government which had 'lost face' in so catastrophic a fashion during the last fifty years. Then there were the Christian missionaries, the foreign merchants in their 'concessions', the foreign railway staff and manufacturers: foreigners of all kinds who were upsetting the old Chinese customary way of life and depriving the gods and the ancestral spirits of the reverence which was their due.

The Boxers began as an anti-Manchu and anti-Christian movement; but the old dowager empress who was supreme at Peking cleverly diverted their attack away from the Manchu government by promising them the help of government troops if they concentrated their attack on the foreigners. This they did, and for nearly two months in 1900 the foreign embassies in Peking were besieged by a force of Boxers and of Chinese regular troops. An international force was raised in Europe and Japan, and the siege was relieved. After their victory some of the allied troops behaved like barbarians; the city of Peking was looted, and fresh humiliations were imposed on the Chinese government.

Japan took part in this affair. In 1902 she strengthened her position by an alliance with Britain, and two years later she decided that the moment had come to settle her account with Russia. She demanded assurances that Russia had no intention of annexing Manchuria or Korea; Russia refused to give them, and Japan declared war. The affair was soon over. The fighting took place in Manchuria, that is to say on Chinese soil. The Russian army was handicapped by being four thousand miles from home at the far end of a single-track railway line; Japan was a highly industrialised state fighting near its home bases. The Japanese navy quickly disposed of the few Russian warships based on Vladivostok, and thereafter had complete command of the sea. The Russian Baltic fleet left its home port and steamed half-way round the world towards Vladivostok. Off Tsushima island, with 600 miles to go, it found the Japanese admiral Togo waiting for it, and was destroyed. By the terms of the peace treaty, Russia surrendered to Japan all the rights that she claimed in Korea and Manchuria; Japan took back Port Arthur from China, and took from Russia the southern half of the island of Saghalien. This treaty gave Japan a commanding position in Manchuria, which she steadily developed for the next forty years. In 1910 she quietly annexed Korea.

It seemed as if China was destined to be carved up not merely into spheres of influence but into colonies, with Japan replacing Russia as a colonising power. China was saved from this by two events: the revolution of 1911, and the World War of 1914.

The old dowager empress was the strongest person in China; but she died in 1908, and her son the young emperor died in the same year. Another man to be reckoned with was the soldier and politician Yuan Shi-Kai. Yuan had betrayed to the dowager the men who proposed to modernise China, and he had seen to it that all his rivals were among the men executed for taking part in the movement. At the time of the Boxer rebellion Yuan commanded a division of troops, and had been ordered to bring his troops into action against the international force; he had disobeyed his orders, and had succeeded in convincing the dowager that he had acted for the best. The new emperor Pu Yi was a child, and those about him thought Yuan Shi-Kai too dangerous; so they dismissed him. Yuan retired into private life and bided his time.

As the Taiping and the Boxer rebellions had shown, there were revolutionary forces in China. There was a revolutionary leader, the westernised medical man Dr Sun Yat-Sen, who had been stirring up rebellions, without any great success, since 1906. Sun Yat-Sen was no Lenin. He was a revolutionary more like Kerensky, a Chinese patriot who wanted to get rid of the useless Manchu government and equip China with a modern representative parliament, so that his country could break out of her chains and take her rightful place in the world. His luck turned in 1911: in that year some government troops mutinied and joined him. By the end of the year nearly all the country had joined his rebellion, and Dr Sun Yat-Sen was elected president of the Chinese republic.

He still had to reckon with Yuan Shi-Kai. The six northern provinces had remained faithful to the Manchus, and the government called Yuan out of retirement and appointed him to command the loyalist troops. But Yuan preferred negotiating to fighting, and the two men came to terms. The young emperor Pu Yi was to abdicate, and China was to have a republican government and a democratically elected parliament. But Sun Yat-Sen did what Lenin would never have done: he stood down from his position as president, and supported Yuan Shi-Kai as his successor.

Yuan Shi-Kai was installed as president in March 1912. Much of the imperial civil service had broken down in the general disorder, and Yuan appointed a number of officers as military governors in the provinces. China's first parliament met in 1912, but it did not last long; in 1914 Yuan dissolved it and took dictatorial powers. Yuan died in 1916, and after his death the only effective powers in China were the military governors (the 'warlords') whom he had appointed. For ten years these men fought and intrigued against each other, bringing chaos and misery to the whole of China. Sun Yat-Sen established himself at Canton, in alliance with the local war-lord, and there he gathered as many as he could of the surviving members of parliament, organising them into a party calling itself the Kuomintang or National People's Party. Later, with the help of a young army officer named Chiang Kai-Shek, who had been trained in Japan, he was able to form his own army and dispense with the help of the local war-lord.

Sun and his National People's Party were now in control of one province, the southernmost of the eighteen provinces which make up China. Although he had the support of the young students and of the Chinese businessmen, he would have had little hope of recovering control over the rest of the country had it not been for the events of 1919.

Japan joined Britain and France in their war against Germany in 1914, and profited by the war to take over all German concerns in China. Many of these were concentrated in the peninsula of Shantung, and Japan simplified matters by annexing the whole peninsula; she also reoccupied Port Arthur. She put to Yuan Shi-Kai a list of Twenty-One Demands, amounting to complete economic control of Manchuria and a good deal of control over the rest of China; and Yuan had to grant them. Britain and France had to pay Japan her price for her help in the war: the price was that they should support her when (at her own convenient time) she should propose to keep Shantung for good. Britain and France made a secret agreement with Japan to this effect, and in return for a financial loan, the Chinese government made a similar agreement. These secret agreements became known in 1919, and there was an explosion of anger throughout China. All the best Chinese patriots rallied to the Kuomintang, and Kuomintang cells and groups sprang up all over the country.

It was natural that the Russian revolutionaries should seek to make common cause with the revolution in China. Both the Bolsheviks and the Kuomintang were fighting to free their countries from exploitation by foreign capitalists and from the results of feeble and corrupt government. Both had reasons to dislike Britain and France. Both hated Japan, which had occupied Shantung and Manchuria, and now held Vladivostok, awaiting an opportunity to push westwards along the railway and occupy as much of eastern Siberia as she could conveniently digest.

True, the Kuomintang revolutionaries were not Marxists, but this defect could perhaps be remedied in time. It would be unthinkable that a good Bolshevik should lose such a chance of weakening Japan and capitalism. The Soviet government announced to China that it would forego all the unequal treaties which Tsarist Russia had imposed upon the Chinese government. Soviet agents were a great help to the Kuomintang in carrying out underground propaganda and in keeping alive the opposition towards the foreign capitalists. A young man named Mao Tse-Tung was converted to Marxism, and in 1921 he, with Chou En-Lai and a few others, founded the Chinese Communist Party.

In 1925 Sun Yat-Sen died, and Chiang Kai-Shek took over his power. In June 1926 the Kuomintang felt strong enough to set out from their base at Canton to conquer the rest of China; in January 1927 they occupied Hankow, next month Shanghai; and in June 1928 Peking. Chiang Kai-Shek chose to establish his capital at Nanking in the south; and in October 1928 he formally announced the establishment of Nationalist China. For the

I

time being the Kuomintang was to be the only permitted political party, but the Chinese people were somehow to be trained for democracy. Although there were still outlying areas of China under the control of local war-lords, the Nanking government seemed so firmly established that the Western powers gave it formal recognition.

Chiang Kai-Shek was now more or less the ruler of China; but apart from the immense tasks of national reconstruction that faced him, he had three serious problems. One was the Japanese; the second was the European control of China's economy through the concessions at Shanghai and elsewhere; the third was the small but active Chinese Communist Party.

One thing was certain: he could do nothing against the Japanese, or the remaining war-lords, without weapons and money. Since only from the foreigners could he obtain either, Chiang decided to remain on good terms with them. This meant that he must damp down the anti-foreign agitation among his people; and if the Chinese communists insisted on following the Bolshevik line and fighting the Europeans and the Japanese at the same time, he must be prepared to break with the communists.

Chiang would have preferred to lead a national war, in alliance with the communists and supplied by the Western powers, against the Japanese. But the communists forced his hand. They encouraged the land-hungry villagers to rise up against the gentry and landlords, and the factory workers to strike against their capitalist employers. Mao Tse-Tung and a few others actually led a rising in Hunan province, and set up a number of soviets in the two provinces of Hunan and Kwangsi, an area which was important because it lay between Canton and Nanking and threatened the whole of the Yangtze valley. The Chinese and foreign businessmen became alarmed, and Chiang saw that he must choose. He chose the side which could supply him with money and arms; he banned the communist party, and slaughtered thousands of communists and left-wingers in and around Shanghai.

After such a drastic step as this, it was difficult to see any hope of an alliance between the Kuomintang and the communists. The two parties were rivals for the leadership of China; and if Chiang did not crush Mao, sooner or later Mao would crush him. From this time onward, Chiang seems to have become more and more obsessed with the communist danger.

But what was to be done about the Japanese? Chiang decided that there was no urgency about the Japanese problem. The Japanese were firmly in control of Manchuria, but it seemed likely that for the time being they would advance no further, and if so, the Kuomintang would have time to consolidate its position and push on with its enormous task of reconstruction. In 1922 a conference was held at Washington about Far Eastern and Pacific affairs. It brought about an agreement between Britain, the United States and Japan on the limitation of naval armaments; and it led also to a series of political agreements. The Anglo-Japanese treaty of alliance was replaced by a Four-Power Treaty, by which these two states, with France and the United States, undertook to respect each other's Pacific territories. As for China, the four powers undertook to respect China's independence and to help China to get on her feet again. In accordance with the agreements, Japan gave up Shantung, but she held fast to her economic control of Manchuria. As long as Japan adhered to her promise, there need be no fear of further Japanese aggression into China.

Japan adhered to her promise for nine years, from 1922 to 1931. Then she decided that the time had come to annex Manchuria completely. A Japanese officer was murdered – presumably by Chinese hands – in Manchuria; Japan immediately ordered all Chinese troops to leave the province, and proceeded to expel them by force. There were anti-Japanese demonstrations at Shanghai, so Japan landed an expeditionary force there. China appealed to the League of Nations, of which both she and Japan were members. The League sent out a commission of inquiry, which recommended that Manchuria should remain under Chinese sovereignty, but that it should be given a good deal of self-government, and economic help from outside – 'outside' no doubt meaning principally, but not exclusively, Japan. Japan ignored the report; she set up a puppet state in Manchuria called Manchukuo and made a defence agreement with it. She withdrew her troops from Shanghai, but she gave a blunt warning to the League that she would oppose any schemes of international technical assistance to China; she considered herself the power most interested in China, and would not allow any other country to share with her 'the responsibility for the maintenance of peace in East Asia'. To make a thorough job of the business, Japan gave notice of withdrawal from the League. None of the great powers which were members of the League was ready to send troops to oppose Japan or to undertake serious economic sanctions against her, so Japan's aggression was successful, and she occupied the neighbouring Chinese province of Jehol and added it to Manchukuo. The members of the League naturally refused to recognise the state of Manchukuo; but they did nothing more. This affair was the first really serious blow to the League in its peace-keeping capacity. One member state had forcibly occupied part of another member state, and retained it in defiance of the League. Four years later, Japan's example was followed by Mussolini.

If the Kuomintang was really the Chinese National party, this Japanese aggression, condemned by the rest of the world, seemed the opportunity for the party and its leader to stand forth as leaders of the national resistance to Japan. But Chiang was more immediately concerned with crushing the communists. He embarked on a series of manœuvres aimed at encircling the communist strongholds, but Mao Tse-Tung was an accomplished guerrilla leader, and Chiang's swoops failed. Then Chiang tried new tactics: he blockaded the communist areas with fortified posts to cut off their supplies. Chiang was implored to go into action against the Japanese. He refused; and it must be said in his favour that the Japanese navy commanded the sea, and no foreign shipments of arms would have got through to him. Nevertheless, Chiang's refusal to fight the Japanese allowed the communists to lead the Chinese resistance and to gain the credit for it. Chiang would not fight the foreign capitalists, he would not fight the Japanese enemy; could he be regarded as the national leader? Many of the best men in the Kuomintang lost faith in his leadership, and drifted away to follow Mao.

In October 1934, the communists of the south, dangerously short of food and supplies, broke out of the ring in which Chiang had enclosed them. Under bombing and shellfire they marched westwards, 100,000 strong, hoping to be able before long to turn north. But Chiang's troops barred their way across the Yangtze river, and they had to march further and further west into the mountains. Eventually they crossed the Yangtze much higher up, and after a march of 368 days and more than 5,000 miles they reached a new base in the Yenan district of Shensi province, just south of the Great Wall. This was the famous Long March, a tale of hardship, discipline and valour which stirs the heart of others besides Chinese.

From their new base in the Yenan district, Mao and his men organised national resistance to the Japanese; and they also organised great social changes in the district. Mao had progressed in his thinking beyond such crude measures as confiscating land from the landlords and throwing it into collective farms. He limited himself for the time being to regulating the rents which landlords were allowed to charge, and developing self-governing village communes, in which landlords of good will were allowed to take part as equal members. This kind of policy produced much support for the communists; the villagers could see that

Mao's brand of communism was bringing them improvements in their condition.

Meanwhile, Chiang kept to his policy of crushing the communists before dealing with the Japanese, so that his party became more and more identified with the interests of landowning, business, and banking. In 1936 Chiang left his base in the south and flew north to the headquarters of Chang Hsueh-Ling, the war-lord of Manchuria. When the Japanese attacked his native province in 1931, Chang had wished to defend it, but Chiang Kai-Shek ordered him to hold his fire and abandon his country so as to keep his army intact for future operations. Chang reluctantly obeyed. But that was now five years ago, and Chang and his men were still impatient to be allowed to launch an attack on the Japanese army of occupation. When his chief, Chiang Kai-Shek, arrived at his headquarters, not to tell him that the moment had come and to hurl himself at the Japanese, but to urge him to throw his troops into action against the communists in their base at Yenan, Chang's patience was at an end. He refused. He arrested Chiang Kai-Shek, got in touch with the communists, and compelled Chiang Kai-Shek to sit down and discuss matters with a communist representative, Chou En-Lai. Chiang Kai-Shek saw that unless he agreed to begin operations against the Japanese he was finished as a national leader, and he might even lose his life. He agreed to make a common front with the communists against Japan and to recognise the communist territory of Yenan as a self-governing region. In return, the communists recognised the authority of the Kuomintang goverment at Nanking and agreed to place their army under Chiang Kai-Shek's orders.

These things happened in the winter of 1936–7, and Japan replied in July by invading the whole of northern China and sending troops to Shanghai. Chiang Kai-Shek attacked Shanghai, and full-scale war quickly spread all over eastern China. By the end of 1937 the Japanese troops had occupied Nanking; next October they took Canton and the important commercial cities in the middle course of the Yangtze. Chiang Kai-Shek moved his capital to Chungking in the mountainous province of Szechwan, and kept what was left of his army intact and idle, leaving it to Mao and the communists to carry on the war against Japan by guerrilla tactics and sabotage. Chiang felt sure that before long Japan would be involved in a world war, and when that was over the stage would be clear for him to deal with Mao and the communists.

At Chungking, the Kuomintang and their army were quite cut

off from the outer world, except for the slender link of the Burma road, which was constructed for that special purpose, over a thousand miles of the most difficult country in the world, between Chungking and Lashio in Burma. Lashio was the terminus of a railway from Rangoon and Mandalay. Along this road came a stream of lorries bringing food and medical supplies, raw materials and military stores. After Japan entered the World War and occupied Burma, the road was closed, and supplies could then come to Chungking only by the dangerous air route 'over the hump' from India. Everything was scarce at Chungking, there was rationing and a black market, and there were great opportunities for profiteering and speculation. Chiang and the Kuomintang had shown great energy and efficiency in getting their army to Chungking, and in stripping the country as they went of plant and machinery. But while they stayed quietly at Chungking from 1938 till the end of the war in 1945, Mao and the communists were carrying on their guerrilla war against Japan. By 1945, Mao was the national leader; by remaining immobile, Chiang had lost his claim to the position.

When Japan surrendered in 1945, both Mao and Chiang had large armies in the field ready to take over control of China. This was the moment that Chiang had been waiting for: Japan was no longer an obstacle, the European concessions in the treaty ports had been destroyed in the fighting, the United States fleet commanded the sea. The way was clear for him to settle his account with Mao.

The United States, with its distrust of communism, preferred to deal with Chiang, whose government after all had been formally recognised in 1928 and could hardly now be disowned without very strong reasons. The Americans provided Chiang with large quantities of military equipment, and moved his army down from its mountain province into lowland China. The Americans nevertheless hoped that Chiang and Mao would be able to come to terms and co-operate in building China afresh. Chiang refused; nothing would persuade him to abandon his obsession with the idea of crushing the communists, and moreover by now he was quite identified with the interests of the businessmen and the country gentry. The Kuomintang had lost much of the idealism with which it began; for so many of the idealists had left it and thrown in their lot with Mao.

The first armed clash came in Manchuria in July 1946, and Mao's men, the People's Liberation Army as they now called themselves, had overwhelming popular support. The Kuomintang army began to dissolve; whole units surrendered, or went over to the communists taking their American equipment with them. By the end of 1948 the whole of Manchuria was in communist hands, and in January 1949 the communist army won a decisive victory in a full-scale battle at the Hwai river. Three months later the communists took Nanking. Chiang and the remnants of his army took refuge first at Canton and then at Chungking; finally, in December 1949, they abandoned mainland China and took refuge in the island of Formosa (Taiwan), where for the time being they were safe under the protection of the United States navy.

Mao Tse-Tung was now the undisputed ruler of mainland China, and he proclaimed that at his convenience he would invade and subdue the Chinese island of Taiwan. Chiang Kai-Shek retorted that his was the only lawful government of China, and that he fully intended to land again on the mainland and destroy the communists. As long as the United States navy commanded the sea, it was certain that neither party could carry out its threat without American permission. The United States recognised Chiang, and intended to go on doing so. China had a permanent seat on the UN Security Council, and this seat was occupied by a representative of Chiang Kai-Shek, who claimed to speak for the whole of China. It was not until November 1971 that the Assembly voted to withdraw recognition from Taiwan and to recognise the government of Mao Tse-Tung as the true government of China.

For more than twenty years, Mao Tse-Tung has been able to carry on with his work of rebuilding his country, with no interference, and very little help, from outside. In his early days he received advice and help from Russia, but before long he came to the view that Russian advice was unsuitable for Chinese needs, and all the Russian technical advisers left. Russia believed in building the communist state on heavy industry, Mao believed in building it on a strong village life. From the Chinese point of view, Russia has been too ready to work towards agreements with the West, especially with the United States, the country which has always stood by Chiang Kai-Shek. Russian advisers have been too dogmatic in insisting that methods which work in Russia are the only methods for a good communist. In 1950, Mao was in the middle of his schemes for land reform, and was massing troops in the south for the invasion of Taiwan; he felt it as inconsiderate of Russia that she should choose that moment for launching the invasion of South Korea and thus involving China in war against the United Nations forces when they crossed the 38th parallel. Russia still regarded herself as the leader of the communist world, and acted in matters of foreign policy without consulting China. Soviet Russia still held territory, both on China's northern and western frontiers, which had been occupied long ago by the Tsarist government and which the Chinese regarded as unjustly occupied under 'unequal treaties'. At various times since Russia withdrew her technical advisers in 1960, there have been frontier clashes between Russian and Chinese troops. There was a similar clash with India in 1962, when Chinese troops attacked India and occupied territory which they claimed had been wrongfully taken from China when the frontier line was fixed by British surveyors in the nineteenth century.

Another military adventure was undertaken in 1950, when Chinese troops invaded Tibet. Tibet had always recognised a vague sort of Chinese suzerainty, but when the Manchu dynasty fell, the link with China was broken, and Tibet became independent. Whether under Chiang Kai-Shek or under Mao Tse-Tung, no Chinese government could submit to this loss of face. The communists had special reasons for objecting to the Tibetan government, in which the villagers were completely dominated by the landowning nobles and monasteries. Nevertheless, in Tibet the Chinese were regarded as foreigners; and they may have behaved as tactlessly there as the Russians in Manchuria. In 1958 there was a Tibetan revolt against Chinese rule, and the Chinese had to undertake a second expedition in force, expelling the Dalai Lama and setting up a puppet government of their own – just as the Japanese had done in Manchuria a generation earlier.

China's foreign policy under Mao's leadership has been restrained. China has sent advice and help to African states, and in this and other ways she has been eager to show her independence of Russian influence. She sent 'volunteers' into North Korea when the UN troops, against the advice of India, crossed the 38th parallel. But after the Chinese had halted the UN advance, China made no attempt to annex North Korea, although the whole of Korea had until 1895 been part of the Chinese empire. China stopped her invasion of India when she had taken the country she claimed as hers, though she might easily have taken more had she chosen. She has not sent troops or volunteers into the Vietnam war, though Indo-China, like Korea, was always a Chinese sphere of influence, and North Vietnam was at one time a Chinese province. It remains to be seen whether Chinese foreign policy will continue to be so restrained.

The social and economic problems of such a vast country with a rapidly expanding population are difficult enough to give any government sufficient occupation for a long time to come. All revolutions are experimental, and today's orthodoxy becomes tomorrow's heresy. In China, as in Russia, the twists and turns of policy are accompanied by personal rivalries, and the appearance and disappearance of aspirants for power, in a way which we in the West find bewildering. After more than a hundred years of foreign exploitation, and forty years of almost continuous fighting on Chinese soil, the process of building up a strong and prosperous communist state will be a long one.

10   South-East Asia

South-East Asia forms a peninsula, separating the Indian Ocean from the Pacific, and forming the meeting place of the Indian and Chinese civilisations. The peninsula runs down into the tail of Malaya: and beyond Malaya there is the long chain of islands, 3,000 miles long from the tip of Sumatra to the western end of New Guinea, which we used to call the East Indies, and which now form the state of Indonesia.

INDO-CHINA

The peoples of Indo-China, whether of Malayan or Mongoloid race, seem to have arrived there fairly recently, coming down the great river valleys from the mountainous country of central Asia. The earliest waves of immigration may have arrived about 1500 B.C. or even earlier, but new waves were still arriving in the thirteenth century of our era. The first people came down about the time that Stonehenge was being built, the last of them about the time of Magna Carta.

As they spread out and colonised the new lands, they came under the influence of two ancient cultures, those of India and of China. Hinduism and Indian culture came by sea along the eastern shores of the Bay of Bengal, Chinese culture spread southward along the coast. In the country which today forms the states of Thailand, Vietnam, Laos, Cambodia and Indonesia, the two cultures met and to some extent blended. Today, Vietnam is more strongly influenced by China, Laos and Cambodia by India. The abandoned temple-city of Angkor in Cambodia is one of the show-pieces of Hindu architecture, and Hinduism is an important element in the culture of Bali and parts of Java.

The history of Indo-China has been greatly influenced by its physical geography. There is a chain of mountains running parallel to the east coast, leaving only a narrow plain between mountain and sea. This narrow coastal plain is Vietnam. In the north of the region the mountains expand westwards into a rugged plateau; this is Laos. Through narrow gorges the river Mekong flows down from the mountains of western China; and in the lower part of its course it forms a wide plain before entering the sea through its delta. The Mekong delta, with the port of Saigon, is in southern Vietnam; the southern half of the river valley is Cambodia, the northern half is Thailand. Six hundred miles away to the north is another river, the Song Koi or Red River; this has built up a smaller plain and delta in north Vietnam, and in the delta are the towns of Hanoi and Haiphong. Indo-China is a region of heavy rainfall and tropical forest.

The broad outlines of the modern situation in Indo-China began to emerge about the time that William the Conqueror was reducing the unruly English to order. The coastal plain was occupied by the Vietnamese people, closely akin to the Chinese. The northern half of the plain had in fact been ruled by China for a thousand years, but in A.D. 939 the Vietnamese revolted and threw off Chinese rule.[1] The southern half of the coastal plain had originally been occupied by a state called Champa, which had reached a high degree of civilisation under Indian, not Chinese influence. When the Vietnamese revolted from China, they began fighting their way southward at the expense of Champa, gradually conquering the country and setting up a series of Vietnamese lordships in it.

An area covering a great part of modern Thailand and the whole of modern Laos and Cambodia formed the Khmer empire, another Indianised state, with its capital at Angkor.

About the year 1250, another wave of immigrants came down from the northern mountains. These were the ancestors of the Thai, Lao and Shan peoples of today, all very closely related. The Lao peoples colonised the modern Laos, setting up a series of small Lao states in the hills. A century later, in 1353, these hill states united into one kingdom called Lan Chang.

The Thai people attacked the Khmers further south, and conquered more and more of the Khmer country until in 1431 they captured the Khmer capital, Angkor. They did not hold it; but the Khmers abandoned Angkor, and built a new town at Phnom Penh, leaving Angkor to be swallowed up by the forest. The Thais went on fighting and conquering, at the expense both of the Khmers and of the Laos. The Khmer state was reduced to the small kingdom of Cambodia, and about 1700 the Laotian kingdom of Lan Chang split into two. One part was called Luang Prabang

---

[1] After losing this province, the Chinese gave it a new name. They called it Annam, meaning 'the pacified south' – as if to avoid losing face by admitting that it was not pacified. This name Annam has tended to stick.

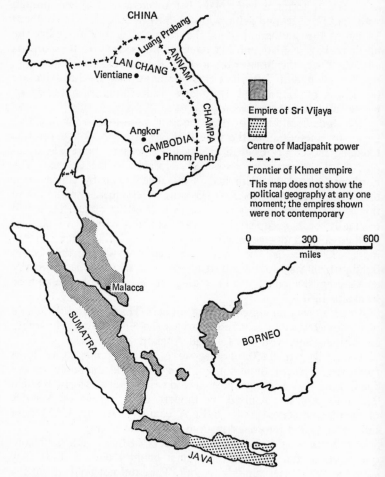

Map 10. South-East Asia before the Europeans

(the name of its capital town), the other was called Vien Chang;[1] in 1827 Vien Chang was conquered by the Thais.

When Portuguese, Dutch and English arrived in the region of South-East Asia, great rivalry ensued for the valuable spice trade of the archipelago; but the mainland states of Indo-China were somewhat off the main trade route, and produced nothing

[1] Through French influence (for France has been active in these parts) the name Vien Chang is nowadays usually spelt in the French way, Vientiane.

that was specially required in Europe; so for a long time they were left alone. The first significant contact that the states of Indo-China had with Europe came about through the arrival of Christian missionaries, at first Portuguese but later French. In the seventeenth century French missionaries were active both among the Thais and in the coastal strip of Vietnam. They found it hard going against the Hindus and the Buddhists, and in the eighteenth century they almost abandoned their work. Nevertheless, France did not forget this early missionary effort, which began as part of the great expansion of French influence under Louis XIV. In modern times she used it as the basis for renewed French expansion.

The Vietnamese state was organised as one kingdom; but the country was so long, and so much cut up by spurs of hill country, that the kings found it difficult to control their barons who were fighting and conquering in the south. The situation was much like that in Britain when the Norman barons were busily conquering estates for themselves in Wales, and resented interference from the king of England. During the seventeenth and eighteenth centuries, the Vietnamese barons conquered all the remainder of Champa, and occupied the whole of the Mekong delta at the expense of the Khmers. Thus the whole of modern Vietnam became nominally one state, and Cambodia was cut off from the coast of the South China Sea, though she still had a coast on the Gulf of Siam.

Eventually a baronial family named Nguyen brought the turbulent barons of the south under control, and formed the southern half of Vietnam into a separate state, the Nguyen ruler calling himself king. The boundary between south and north Vietnam was fixed (for reasons of physical geography) very close to the modern boundary. Though politically divided, the two Vietnams were now largely alike in population, the northern colonists with their Chinese culture having swamped the older Indianised Champa people. The two Vietnams began to be called by different names: the Europeans called the northern state Tongking, and the southern state Cochinchina.

So matters stood in the latter half of the eighteenth century: there were the two Vietnamese states of Tongking and Cochinchina, there were the two Laotian states of Luang Prabang and Vien Chang, and there was the kingdom of Cambodia. The expanding Thai state was exerting continuous pressure on Cambodia and the two Laotian states, and the unhappy Cambodia was under pressure also from the barons of Cochinchina.

In the last thirty years of the eighteenth century there were new developments. The ruling Nguyen family in Cochinchina was split by a family quarrel, and the whole of Vietnam, both south and north, collapsed into civil war. As it happened, this was a period when French and British rivalry in the Indian Ocean was at its height, and a French missionary in Cochinchina thought he saw an opportunity here for France. He backed the rightful Nguyen heir, Nguyen Anh, and managed to secure for him the help of a small contingent of French troops. With this assistance, Nguyen Anh fought a long and successful war. Not only did he reconquer the whole of Cochinchina, but he carried the war beyond the northern boundary and reunited the whole of Vietnam into one kingdom. France's price for this valuable assistance was the cession of a small island off the Mekong delta and a plot of land near Tourane (or Da Nang) on the east coast. The treaty setting out these arrangements was made in 1787, and two years later the French revolution began, so that France was in no condition to take advantage of the concessions. But she did not forget them.

Nguyen Anh fixed his new capital at Hué, and made Saigon and Hanoi into provincial capitals. To be on the safe side, he asked the Chinese emperor to recognise his authority, and the emperor did so, requiring him to send tribute every other year. This Chinese suzerainty was to prove important later on.

The nineteenth century was the great age of Western imperialist expansion. Britain had no special interest in Indo-China; she had no designs of conquest, and had not even any great design of controlling the trade of the region. But British expansion elsewhere led France to form designs of conquest in Indo-China. This is how it came about.

In the course of the French revolutionary wars, Holland was occupied by French troops and was compelled to become an active ally of France. This left the Dutch colonies open to attack by Britain; and the British navy had such complete command of the sea that Britain was able for the time being to do what she liked in the Indian Ocean and the neighbouring seas. She used her power mainly to secure her communications with India, taking the Cape and Ceylon from Holland and certain strategic islands from France. She also took the island of Java from Holland, but gave it back at the end of the war. Though Indo-China itself did not specially attract the British, their Chinese trade was immensely important: Britain imported Chinese tea and silk, and exported Lancashire textiles and other British manufactures, and also Indian opium. During the short British occupation of Java its governor was Stamford Raffles; when he was withdrawn from

Java he looked around for another convenient base in the region, and in 1819 he was authorised to annex the island of Singapore to command the vital trade route to China.

When you acquire a seaport on a foreign coast or a trading station in a foreign country, it at once becomes a matter of concern to you that its neighbourhood should remain quiet and peaceful, so that trade can flow naturally. Britain had no desire at that time to occupy Malaya, but she was anxious that the Malay states should not be upset by Siamese[1] intrigue and conquest. The Thais of Siam were still actively expanding; they were pushing westward into Burma and southward into the Malay peninsula. It thus became a British objective to limit the Siamese advance southwards. Luckily for Britain, this was made possible by events in Burma. The king of Burma had ambitions, and between 1813 and 1816 he pushed his frontier westward by conquering Manipur and Assam, two states on India's eastern border. Not content with this, he began assembling troops in 1824 for an attack on India itself, thus threatening the British position in Bengal. This time, the British forestalled the Burmese attack; they struck first. This was Britain's first Burmese war; it was ended by a treaty of 1826, by which Burma gave up its previous gains of Manipur and Assam, and ceded to Britain the Arakan coast and another coastal strip south of the Irrawaddy delta.

These events delighted the Siamese government. Burma and Siam were ancient enemies, and less than sixty years earlier, Siam suffered the humiliation of having its capital sacked by Burmese troops. Anything that weakened her enemy Burma was a service to Siam. In that same year 1826, Siam concluded a treaty with Britain, promising to go no further south into the Malay peninsula. Siam had plenty of scope for her ambitions elsewhere. Next year she destroyed the Laotian state of Vien Chang (Vientiane); she had recently taken two provinces from Cambodia, and she now resumed her pressure on that state. Though prepared to be friendly with Britain, Siam declined to admit British traders; she meant the 1826 treaty to keep Britain, and the West in general, at a distance.

Friction continued between Britain and Burma, and in 1852 Britain occupied the rest of the Burmese coastline, confining Burma to the interior. This British conquest put under British control the

[1] The name Siam is really the same as the name Shan; our English pronunciation Sye-am obscures the identity. We should pronounce it more like *sham*. Thailand is the largest of the many Shan states, and adopted the name Thailand only in 1939.

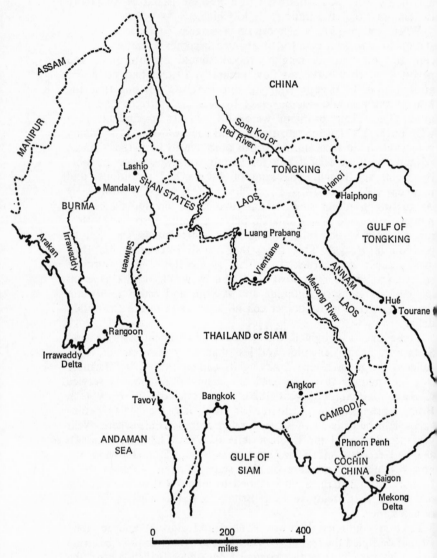

Map 11. Burma, Thailand and Indo-China

mouths of both of Burma's great rivers, the Irrawaddy and the Salween.

How did all this affect France? By the middle of the nineteenth century, France was an industrial and a colonial power, and was seeking for ways in which she could break the British control of the trade routes to China. It is a striking feature of Map 9 that three great rivers, the Salween, the Mekong, and the Yangtze Kiang run for a long way side by side in parallel valleys less than thirty miles apart. The British had occupied the lower Salween; could France perhaps find a way up the Mekong, cross over to the headwaters of the Yangtze, and so open up the interior of China to French commerce?

In 1856 France joined Britain in a war against China, and by the peace treaty, China undertook to tolerate Christian missionary work. French missionaries were working also in Vietnam; and after the treaty had been signed with China, the king or emperor of Vietnam (or Annam, as the Chinese called it) continued to show hostility to Christian missionaries. Relying on the fact that since 1803 Vietnam had acknowledged Chinese suzerainty and should therefore be bound by the new treaty, France attacked Vietnam. In 1862 Vietnam ceded to France the eastern half of Cochinchina, and a year or two later the French proclaimed a protectorate over the kingdom of Cambodia.

This gave France control of the Mekong delta, and French explorers at once set to work to map the upper course of the river and see if it offered a possible trade route into China. They were disappointed; the river came pouring down through dangerous gorges and rapids, and they saw no hope at all of establishing a line of steamers. Then what about the other river of Vietnam, the Song Koi or Red River: was that any more hopeful? This river entered the sea in the northern province of Tongking, and having traversed its valley a French explorer reported that it might be usable. The king of Vietnam made a fresh treaty in 1874, granting French merchants the right to trade in the Song Koi valley. But the treaty was found to be worthless, for Chinese bandits and others refused to allow anyone to use the river. After eight years of this frustration, France sent a strong force of troops to Tongking, and the king was compelled to accept a French protectorate. France organised her new possessions into the colony of Cochinchina and the two protectorates of Annam (based on Hué) and Tongking (based on Hanoi). China was compelled to acquiesce in these arrangements.

Britain was not anxious when the French occupied the Mekong delta, but matters were different when the French began to exploit

K

their new position in Tongking. The Song Koi might not offer a very convenient route into China, but it did offer one into Laos, and through Laos into northern Siam and Burma. The king of Burma was happy to have a different European power to deal with, and hoped to play France off against Britain. He concluded a trade agreement with France, which would provide him with a French-owned bank, a French line of steamers on the Irrawaddy, and a large consignment of arms for use against the British. The result of his playing at power politics was the third Anglo-Burmese war of 1885, which extinguished Burmese independence and put an end to French hopes in that direction.

Or perhaps not altogether; for although Britain had annexed Burma, the continuous mosaic of small independent states which stretched all the way from Burma to Vietnam was still open to penetration. The British knew some of them as the Shan States of Burma, but they were all very similar. Britain would have preferred to limit her territory to Burma proper, leaving the Shan States outside: but not if this meant seeing them fall one after another to the French and become part of French Indo-China. In the 1890s France did indeed annex a number of the eastern states, and made Siam give up all its territory east of the Mekong River. Britain thereupon annexed all the Shan States which had owed allegiance to the kingdom of Burma, so that British Burma met French Indo-China along a short stretch of the Mekong river. It was convenient however both for Britain and France to leave the remainder of Siam as an independent buffer state between British and French territory, and a treaty of 1896 put an end to Anglo-French rivalry in this way.

Vietnam, Laos and Cambodia were thus merged under French rule, and in 1887 the colony of Cochinchina and the four protectorates of Annam, Tongking, Laos and Cambodia were joined into an Indo-Chinese Union.

France had a difficult task. Much of the country was hilly, unproductive, and thinly peopled. Except for rice, Indo-China had no important export crop, though there were possibilities in rubber. Except for coal and a little tin, it was not rich in minerals. The physical geography made communications very difficult. The trunk railway line running parallel with the coast from end to end of Vietnam was not completed until 1936. The French built a railway line from Hanoi in the north up the Song Koi river to Kunming in western China. A small railway network was developed around Saigon, and a line was built in Cambodia to link the capital Phnom Penh with Bangkok in Siam. But there was no railway link between Phnom Penh and Saigon, and Laos had no railways at all. Economic development was concentrated near the tidewater, and much of the interior of the country remained under forest. Cambodia and Laos lagged behind Vietnam. The Vietnamese were proud of their own culture, and had no wish to be 'assimilated' and Frenchified. From 1905 onwards there was a nationalist movement in Vietnam. But the Vietnamese were quick to profit by the economic opportunities which French rule offered them. Laos and Cambodia were staffed by French-trained Vietnamese clerks. This did not make the Vietnamese popular in these two countries.

So French rule continued till the 1939 war. Tongking (North Vietnam) was poor and overcrowded, exporting her educated young men to make a living in other parts of the region. Cochinchina (South Vietnam) had the riceland of the Mekong delta, but it had little industry. Much of the land was owned by rich landlords; their tenants had no security of tenure, paid high rents, and were heavily in debt. Cambodia and Laos were undeveloped.

Both parts of Vietnam sorely needed a scheme of land reform to improve the lot of the cultivators. With their ancient connections with China, the Vietnamese were interested in the land reform schemes put forward by the Kuomintang in the days when the Kuomintang was young and idealistic. A young man named Ho Chi-Minh took up this question of land reform, and in the 1930s he formed a revolutionary association, with land reform as one of the planks in his platform. His association was banned by the French, and for the time being Ho Chi-Minh could make no headway. But by that time, a high proportion of Vietnamese, even those who had acquired a great deal of French culture, were longing for independence. As a senior French official lamented after the war, 'The people we trusted most, the people who we thought had learned to sympathise with France, even these turned against us'.

During the 1939 war, the whole of French Indo-China was occupied by the Japanese, and in March 1945 the Japanese authorities set up three national states of Vietnam, Laos and Cambodia under puppet governments, with kings in Laos and Cambodia, and with an emperor in Vietnam, named Bao Dai. Ho Chi-Minh spent the war years in China, and while there he organised a Vietnamese national independence movement called Vietminh. It did not take the Vietminh long to gain control of all the rural areas of North Vietnam, and Ho Chi-Minh and Bao Dai quickly came to terms. Ho Chi-Minh recognised Bao Dai as emperor, but outside the two towns of Hanoi and Haiphong, the real power was in Ho Chi-Minh's hands.

In 1946, when the war was over, the French returned. They established themselves in the city of Saigon and came to an agreement with the rulers of Laos and Cambodia, and also with Bao Dai. Outside the cities, the French had very little power; the countryside was in disorder, and the Vietminh were by far the strongest force throughout Vietnam. In March 1946 the French signed an agreement with Ho Chi-Minh, recognising the Vietminh as an independent state within the Indo-Chinese federation. But the details of the agreement were not properly worked out. It was not made clear whether Cochinchina (South Vietnam) was to be included in the Vietminh territory, or exactly how much independence the Vietminh was to have within the federation. As the months went by, it became plain that on these details Ho Chi-Minh and the French had different ideas.

With Ho Chi-Minh and the French pulling different ways, the emperor Bao Dai found his position becoming impossible. Like the French, Bao Dai had no power outside the cities; Ho Chi-Minh and his people controlled the countryside. Ho Chi-Minh kept an eye on China. He had originally been attracted by the Kuomintang's schemes of land reform, but although the Kuomintang talked of reform, they did very little. Mao Tse-Tung and the communists, on the other hand, were doing a great deal to improve the lot of the Chinese villagers, and Ho Chi-Minh was more and more attracted by their example. Bao Dai, like Chiang Kai-Shek in China, decided to throw in his lot with the city folk; he broke with Ho Chi-Minh.

In December 1946 the agreement made in March broke down, and the French and the Vietminh went to war. The French set up what they called the Associated State of Vietnam, including Cochinchina, with Bao Dai as its emperor. Ho Chi-Minh for his part dispensed with the support he had been receiving from non-communist sources. Thus the war, which had begun as a war between the colonial power and a nationalist movement, acquired overtones of a war between a capitalist state and a communist movement; and the French were able to appeal to the Western world for support in their defence of 'freedom' against communism.

From December 1946 to the middle of 1954 the fighting went on, the French struggling in swamp and forest against an elusive and skilful guerrilla enemy. The war went badly for France, and in April 1954 a conference met at Geneva to discuss the problem of Indo-China. Britain and Russia (Eden and Molotov) took the chair alternately; the other parties to the conference were France and the United States, the three states of Indo-China (Vietnam, Laos and Cambodia), and also – to the disgust of the emperor Bao Dai – the Vietminh movement. On 7 May, while the conference was sitting, the French army suffered its heaviest blow with the loss of the fortress of Dien Bien Phu, which had held out heroically even after losing its airstrip and depending on supplies dropped by parachute.

The conference was not a great success: it spent most of its time in 'sparring for position', and was marred by the 'double-talk' which so often hampers communication between communists and non-communists. The Vietminh delegate wanted the conference to admit delegations from the Khmer and Pathet Lao movements in Cambodia and Laos, which he called 'resistance movements'. This was refused; Mr Eden said that these movements drew all their strength from contingents of regular Vietminh troops with heavy artillery and anti-aircraft guns; they could not be described as national resistance movements. France had already recognised the independence of Vietnam, and the governments of Cambodia and Laos had agreed to remain members of the French Union; so the French delegate wanted the Vietminh to withdraw all its troops from all three states. Bao Dai's representative insisted that Vietnam should remain united under the emperor, that free elections should be held under United Nations supervision, and that a representative government should be set up in accordance with the election results.

The conference broke up without reaching agreement on the future of the three states. It is not surprising that although in the last twenty years it has been suggested from time to time that the Geneva conference should be reconvened to try and settle the Indo-China problem, the suggestion has never been received with much enthusiasm. The only result of the conference was a short-term agreement on the way in which the troops should be regrouped and gradually withdrawn. Even this was not reached without a long wrangle on the question which countries should be asked to supply members to the commission which was to supervise these troop movements. Vietnam was divided by an armistice line very close to the traditional dividing line between Tongking and Cochinchina. The French troops were withdrawn south of the line, and the Vietminh at once took over control of North Vietnam, leaving the emperor Bao Dai to rule over South Vietnam alone. There was a hasty migration of Vietnamese refugees across the dividing line: about 900,000 people (most of them Roman Catholics) moved from north to south, and about 100,000 from south to north. All the French forces withdrew from Cambodia, and before the end of 1954 the last rebel leader in Cambodia had submitted to the Cambodian government.

The real problem lay in Vietnam; Cambodia and Laos were left in comparative peace. The Pathet Lao movement in Laos relied largely on the traditional hostility which the poor hillmen felt to the slightly less poor cultivators in the valley; but the movement was certainly much stiffened with Vietminh forces. However, the Pathet Lao leaders regrouped their men in two northern provinces, and in 1957 they came to an agreement with the Laos government, very similar to the 1946 agreement between Bao Dai and Ho Chi Minh. The Pathet Lao recognised the authority of the government and gave up any idea of claiming independence for the two provinces which it controlled; and in return, the government recognised the Pathet Lao as a lawful political organisation. This peaceful arrangement however was too good to last. The Laos government was markedly anti-communist, and the Pathet Lao and its sympathisers were too strong to submit quietly to the authority of such a government. There were quarrels, a military coup, and finally civil war; it was clear that Laos could find no peace either under a communist or an anti-communist government. The situation was cleared up in June 1962, when Prince Souvanna Phouma took power at the head of a coalition government, with a policy of neutrality between East and West. A similar policy was adopted by the Cambodian government, and a new Geneva conference of fourteen nations approved this neutralist policy.

Vietnam remained the serious problem. Everyone agreed that though temporarily divided into two, Vietnam was one country and should be reunited. The difficulty was that Vietnam had now become, like Korea, a border state between the communist and the non-communist worlds, and neither side would agree to its coming under the rule of the other. North Vietnam was more populous than the South, so that if elections were held throughout Vietnam, a Vietminh government would probably be returned. Neither side will trust the other to hold free elections; it is assumed that as a matter of course whoever is supervising the election will rig the results to secure a majority in his favour.

In the view of the United States, the situation in Vietnam was now uncomfortably like that in Korea. Whatever the deficiencies of the government of the emperor Bao Dai, his country of South Vietnam, like South Korea, had now become a bastion of the 'free world', and must be supported against 'communist aggression'. The United States took the lead in organising a South-East Asia Defence Treaty to stabilise the situation in that part of the world. The treaty was signed in 1954 by Australia, France, New Zealand, Pakistan, the Philippines, Thailand, the United Kingdom and the

United States; it came into force in February 1955, and the SEATO states held their first conference at Bangkok in that same month. At that conference the American representative, Mr Dulles, said, 'The greatest problem in South Vietnam is that presented by the communists in the North. Under the armistice they should have removed their forces from the South. Instead, many of their soldiers simply put on civilian clothes and faded into the community as a source of future trouble.'

For the time being, things appeared to be settling down. Politics in South Vietnam developed into a lively contest between Roman Catholics and Buddhists, the Catholics producing an energetic leader, Mr Ngo Dinh-Diem, who was himself a refugee from the North and a member of the French-educated élite. In 1955, as the result of a referendum, the emperor Bao Dai was deposed, and a republic was proclaimed, with Ngo Dinh-Diem as president. He was a strong ruler; he won a handsome majority in the 1956 elections, and the United States hoped that he would govern successfully, easing the hardships of the village cultivators and so building up a strong popular resistance to any communist propaganda. To succeed in this, Diem would have to win over the Buddhist voters, for the Christians (nearly all Roman Catholics) numbered only about one-eighth of the population. But Diem was not successful as a conciliator, and it was not long before his government aroused great resentment among the Buddhists, some of whom expressed it in committing suicide by burning themselves alive.

Although the Christians formed such a small minority of the population in South Vietnam, President Ngo Dinh-Diem appointed Christians to key positions in the armed forces, the police, the civil service, the universities, and even in the trade unions. The discontent among the Buddhists broke out in demonstrations early in 1963, and in May of that year the government forbade the Buddhists to fly their flags on the Buddha's birthday, and forbade the radio to broadcast an account of the day's celebrations. A large crowd collected outside the radio station to protest, and the troops opened fire. The first Buddhist monk committed suicide in June, and others followed his example in succeeding months. Diem declared that the Buddhists were infected with communism and took strong measures against them; many pagodas and monasteries were destroyed by the troops. There was widespread disorder, so serious that in October 1963 the UN General Assembly debated the situation in South Vietnam, and with the reluctant consent of the Saigon government decided to send a fact-finding mission to that country. But at the beginning of November the government of President Ngo Dinh-Diem was overthrown by a military coup and the president himself was killed. The UN mission returned to New York, and the UN decided to leave the matter there.

South Vietnam thus came under military government, but the political situation was unstable. One general replaced another and coup followed coup; between November 1963 and June 1965 the country had eight different governments.

Meanwhile, every government in South Vietnam was faced with the problem of the South Vietnamese communists, called the Viet-Cong. President Ngo Dinh-Diem had taken a strong line. He refused to have any dealings with North Vietnam, and regarded the Viet-Cong as rebels. At different times, Britain, Russia, the United States and France urged him to be more flexible in his attitude, but he would not. The Viet-Cong had genuine grievances. In the beginning, the government adopted a sound type of strategy, the type which the British used in Malaya and Kenya and the French in Algeria. It collected the scattered farmers into villages, which could be fortified and protected by troops; thus it would be harder for communist guerrillas to persuade or compel the people to provide them with food and information. But complaints were soon heard that the people were made to build and fortify the villages for themselves, and that the government troops, instead of protecting the villages, too often stole cattle and extorted money from the villagers they were supposed to defend. A government inquiry was held into these complaints, and in January 1964 it reported that they were justified. It is not surprising that many simple people who cared nothing for communism as a theory came to prefer the Viet-Cong to their own government. Thus the Saigon government lost popular support.

The government in Saigon looked to the United States for help, and the Viet-Cong looked for help to North Vietnam. In 1961 there were 700 American service men advising the Saigon government; by the end of 1963 this number had grown to over 16,000. North Vietnam supplied the Viet-Cong with weapons, and with small bodies of troops; as American aid to the South increased, the North sent more and more battalions and batteries to help the Viet-Cong. The co-chairmen of the Geneva conference, Britain and Russia, discussed the situation. Both sides had broken the cease-fire agreement, but there seemed nothing that Britain or Russia could do to bring about peace.

American policy was set out in an important speech by the Defence Secretary, McNamara. In March 1964 he said that South Vietnam was trying to preserve its independence against communist attack; that South-East Asia as a whole was an area important in the forward defence of the United States; that if communist strategy (encouraging a local communist movement by giving it support from outside) were allowed to succeed in South Vietnam, it would be applied elsewhere; and that North Vietnam was the 'prime aggressor'. He went on to discuss the alternatives facing the United States government. The United States could not withdraw and leave South Vietnam to look after itself; for the region was too important to be ignored. If the whole of Vietnam, North as well as South, could be made a neutral area, that would be the best. But that was out of the question, for North Vietnam was communist and was determined to remain communist; there could be no question of neutralising Ho Chi-Minh's country. The United States was determined to support South Vietnam; it would prefer not to carry the war into the North, but it would not rule this out altogether. We can see here how American thinking was influenced by the experience of the Korean affair of 1950. It is only fair to the Americans to say that they realised that the South Vietnam government had its defects, and that a war against communism could never be won by military means alone. Their large body of 'advisers' included experts on health, agriculture, adult education and rural development of all kinds. But they found, as European colonial powers sometimes found, that the best of advice is not always readily accepted.

The point of view of the North Vietnamese government is easily expressed. To Ho Chi-Minh, the government of South Vietnam did not represent the people. President Ngo Dinh-Diem was a Catholic dictator oppressing the Buddhist majority in South Vietnam; the generals who succeeded him were corrupt and self-seeking, maintained in power by the support they received from the strongest capitalist state in the world. The Viet-Cong were the oppressed people of South Vietnam, fighting for their freedom; the people in the North could not see them crushed by a corrupt government.

Although no war was ever declared, fighting spread over more and more of South Vietnam, and grew more and more bloody and horrible. The United States, with its enormous material resources, believed that it could enable the Saigon government to crush the Viet-Cong by shell-fire, air reconnaissance, and air bombing. As early as January 1962, the United States government admitted that its men were using napalm to burn and chemical sprays to kill the green leaves of the forest, so as to deprive the Viet-Cong of cover. The shells and bombs and napalm sometimes missed their mark, and horrible pictures were seen on the world's television screens of civilian casualties caused by them. In March 1965 the first American combat unit arrived in Vietnam, and from then until 1970 more and more American forces were poured into the fighting. The North Vietnam cities of Hanoi and Haiphong were bombed, the Americans maintaining that they had taken the utmost care to hit only strictly military targets, the North Vietnamese claiming that great damage had been caused to civilian homes and hospitals. There was no ground fighting in North Vietnam. As time went on, it became plain that the American hopes of winning the war by sheer tonnage of metal were not going to be fulfilled. The result of the American methods was that the South Vietnamese army became dependent on air support, the North Vietnamese and the Viet-Cong became accustomed to doing without it. Air support was essential in the Second World War and in Korea, when large bodies of troops and guns and tanks were fighting big battles. It was not nearly so necessary in Vietnam, for the Viet-Cong and their allies usually avoided big battles and fought a guerrilla war with only small bodies of troops in action.

In January 1966, President Johnson told his people in the United States, 'Six years ago North Vietnam decided on conquest; from that day to this, soldiers and supplies have moved from north to south in a swelling stream. . . . We could leave, abandoning South Vietnam to its attackers and to certain conquest, or we could stay and fight beside the people of South Vietnam. We stayed; and we will stay until aggression has stopped.' However, from the beginning there were some Americans who thought it wrong for the United States to become fully involved in the Vietnam war; and as the American casualty lists mounted and the horrors of the fighting were revealed, the anti-war party in the United States grew rapidly. By the middle of 1969 the government decided to reduce the numbers of American troops in Vietnam. Peace negotiations with North Vietnam were long and difficult, but in January 1973 President Nixon announced that a cease-fire agreement had been reached, and that the last American troops would be withdrawn from Vietnam within two months.

The agreement recognised that Vietnam was one country; the armistice line dividing North and South Vietnam was 'only provisional and not a political or territorial boundary'. North and South Vietnam were to discuss and agree on the steps by which the whole country was to be reunited. The two parties in South Vietnam (that is, the Government party and the Viet-Cong) were to come to terms and form a joint national council, one of whose main tasks would be to organise 'free and democratic general elections' in South Vietnam. As in 1954, an international commission was to supervise the military arrangements for the ceasefire and exchange of prisoners; its members were Canada, Hungary, Indonesia and Poland. Laos and Cambodia were recognised as independent, and all foreign troops were to be withdrawn.

The agreement was silent on the question of North Vietnamese troops in the South; it contained no word to suggest that there were any there. Thus any troops hostile to the South Vietnam government could legitimately claim to be South Vietnamese Viet-Cong; and if the whole of Vietnam was one country, a Vietnamese from the North could hardly be regarded in the South as a foreigner. The only provision of the agreement which might hamper North Vietnam was the recognition of Laotian and Cambodian independence; for the so-called Ho Chi-Minh trail, used by North Vietnam as a supply line for its troops (or for the Viet-Cong) in the South, ran through Laos and Cambodia, and was now to be barred to foreign troops, including Vietnamese. Apart from this, the agreement represented an American defeat. Successive American statesmen – Mr Dulles in 1955, Mr McNamara in 1964, and President Johnson in 1966 – had claimed that North Vietnam was invading the South, and had promised that the United States would support the South until this northern aggression was halted. All the enormous American efforts and heavy casualties had failed to get the North to admit that it had ever sent any troops into South Vietnam at all.

INDONESIA

Of all the nation-states of the modern world, Indonesia must surely have one of the biggest difficulties in building up a sense of nationhood among its peoples. Indonesia – the name means the Indian islands – is the East Indies, the true Indies, which Columbus hoped he had found when he stumbled on the West Indies. These are the Spice Islands, as wondering sixteenth-century travellers called them: the lands where nutmeg, cinnamon, clove and pepper grew, spices which were so much prized in hungry medieval Europe, where all winter long people shivered on a diet of rye bread and salt meat.

Indonesia is the largest archipelago in the world, twice the size of the Caribbean. It has some 3,000 islands, two of which are the second and third biggest islands in the world. The archipelago is 2,500 miles long from east to west, and 1,250 miles from north to south. Placed on a map of Europe, the map of Indonesia would cover the area from the Irish Sea to the Caspian, and from the tip of Denmark to the strait of Messina.

The mere size of the area is difficulty enough: the distance from one island to another and the problem of communication. But the difficulty is made greater by the variety of peoples in the area. There are over thirty language groups, with some hundreds of different languages. The islands contain peoples at all levels of civilisation. Some are still in the stage of hunting and food-gathering, with little or no agriculture. Some live by shifting culti-vation in the forest; others are some of the most highly skilled farmers in the world, carrying their irrigated rice-fields on terraces far up the steep mountain sides. Some peoples are Muslim, some Hindu, some Christian, some animist; Buddhism seems to have left little trace here. Some are matrilineal, others patrilineal; there is a great variety of social customs. How is this far-flung mass of diverse peoples to be moulded into a nation?

Like Indo-China, the archipelago was greatly influenced by Indian civilisation during the first thousand years of the Christian era. While the Roman empire in western Europe was crumbling under the barbarian attacks, powerful and highly civilised king-doms, Hindu or Buddhist in religion and culture, arose in Java and Sumatra. With varying success they attempted to gain control over some of the other islands, especially the Moluccas, which were the richest in the valuable spices.

The strategic importance of Indonesia has always lain in the fact that it controls the trade route between China and the West. Long before the Portuguese found their way to the Far East, Arab and Indian and Chinese seamen were sailing to and fro between Chinese ports and the coasts of India and the Persian Gulf; and all of them must sail either through the main gateway of the Straits of Malacca, between Malaya and Sumatra, or else through the side passage of the Sunda Strait, between Sumatra and Java.

The first strong kingdom in Indonesia was that of Sri Vijaya – a Hindu name – which seems to have arisen in Sumatra about the time that St Augustine came to preach Christianity to the people of Kent. Sri Vijaya remained powerful for 400 years, ex-tending its authority over part of Java and of Borneo, and much of the Malay peninsula. About 1250, Sri Vijaya fell into decline, but fifty years later a prince of the royal family, himself named Vijaya, built out of its ruins a new kingdom called Madjapahit.

Madjapahit, like Sri Vijaya, was Indian in its culture; Hinduism and Buddhism had fused into a mixed cult in which both Siva and Buddha were worshipped. Madjapahit had its base in Java, but it obtained authority over some of the eastern islands, and it may have had some influence too in Sumatra and Borneo. It was a strong and brilliant kingdom while it lasted, and it was over-thrown only by the rising of new forces in the archipelago. Neither

Madjapahit nor Sri Vijaya ever ruled anything like the whole of Indonesia.

Madjapahit was at the height of its glory in the fourteenth century, while Robert Bruce was building the kingdom of Scotland and Chaucer and his pilgrims were riding to Canterbury. About the year 1400, the king of Madjapahit was fighting in south Sumatra against a prince of the old royal family of Sri Vijaya. Squeezed between the attacks of Madjapahit from the south and of the Thai people from the north, the Sumatran prince abandoned his country and moved to the other side of the straits; he founded a new town at Malacca, and applied to China for protection. In 1409 the Chinese emperor granted him protection; and since this was at the time when China was a great sea power, the emperor was in a position to make his protection effective. The Chinese admiral held the straits and made any naval attack by Madjapahit impossible. Malacca had time to take root; in 1414 its prince became a Muslim, and this brought him into close connection with the Islamic world of India and Arabia. From about 1450 onwards, Malacca increased in prosperity as an international market, a trading and warehousing centre like a sort of medieval Singapore. It was important also as a focus of Islam, which spread from it along the sea routes through the archipelago. One by one, most of the Hindu states were converted to Islam, Bali alone remaining faithful to Hinduism. With the Islamic religion there spread also a trade language, a simplified form of Malay, much as the Swahili language spread with the Arab traders up and down the trade routes of East Africa. Malacca thus cut away the commercial base of Madjapahit's prosperity, and as Malacca rose, Madjapahit declined.

At the beginning of the sixteenth century, the Portuguese arrived. They found their way round the Cape into the Indian Ocean in 1498; in 1509 they won a naval victory against a mixed Indian and Egyptian fleet; in 1511 they took Malacca. Had the Portuguese arrived a hundred years earlier, they would have met a Chinese admiral in command of the seas, with bigger ships and better seamanship than their own. But China had abandoned her position as a naval power, and there was no Chinese fleet to challenge them.

Portugal is a small country, and the Portuguese were too few to attempt to colonise the vast region which now lay open to their attack. Their strategy was very well devised to make the best use of their scanty manpower. The Portuguese concentrated their strength at the points of commercial importance. They occupied Goa on the west coast of India to serve as their main base and source of food, and they occupied the East African coast to serve as a subsidiary base and to supply naval stores. (East Africa had the additional attraction of supplying ivory and some gold.) Apart from these coastal strips, the Portuguese made no attempt to conquer large areas. They contented themselves with planting fortified trading and customs posts at various points along the trade routes. One was at Macao in China, another at Malacca, a third near the north tip of Sumatra. There were several in the archipelago itself, one at Colombo in Ceylon and several besides Goa on the west coast of India. Lastly, there were three posts placed to control the western outlets from the Indian Ocean: at Ormuz and Muscat for the Persian Gulf, and at Socotra for the Red Sea. There was no Portuguese post at the Cape, for there was no trade there; only a few roaming parties of Bushmen and Hottentots. The Portuguese fleet based at Goa controlled the sea lanes, and no ship could sail from China to India, from the Spice Islands to the Persian Gulf, or from East Africa to Egypt, without passing within range of a Portuguese base and paying dues to the Portuguese authorities.

The Portuguese monopoly was soon challenged by Spain, which was as anxious as Portugal to gain control of the spice trade. In 1494 America was newly discovered, and the Portuguese were busily exploring eastward. If the world was a globe, there was a danger that these two Catholic countries might become rivals on the other side of it, a year's sail away from Cadiz or Lisbon. They wisely asked the Pope at Rome to lay down a guideline for them, and he drew a line west of the Azores at about 40° west longitude. By the Treaty of Tordesillas of 1494, Spain and Portugal accepted this, agreeing that every new discovery east of the line (which included Brazil) should be Portuguese, and everything west of it, Spanish.

In 1521, Spain employed the Portuguese navigator Magellan to explore the Pacific for them. Magellan's expedition penetrated the straits that still bear his name; it discovered the Philippines; and from the Philippines it came south to Tidore in the spice islands, finding the Portuguese already established in the neighbouring island of Ternate. This was the very situation which the Treaty of Tordesillas was designed to provide for. Tidore and Ternate are in 127° east longitude, whereas the treaty line, if produced on the other side of the world, would fall in 140° east. This would put the whole of Indonesia – and for that matter, the Philippines as well – in the Portuguese sphere. But it was too much to expect rival captains, full of patriotic zeal, ambition and greed, and lacking chronometers or any means of fixing their longitude, to refrain from trying to outsmart each other. The rival sultans of Tidore and Ternate were ready to play off Spanish against Portuguese; so there ensued some happy years of rivalry and intrigue. It was not until 1545 that Spain finally acquiesced in the Portuguese claim to the Moluccas, and consoled herself with the Philippines, which she claimed by right of discovery.

Spanish competition was thus removed, but the Portuguese position as a world power was insecure. She had made a magnificent effort, but she had not the manpower to keep all her stations up to strength, and her hold of the Indian Ocean began to weaken. In 1574 the sultan of Ternate was strong enough to eject the Portuguese from his island. And before long the Portuguese were threatened by new competitors, the Dutch.

The first successful Dutch voyage round the Cape was made in 1595, and in the next six years no fewer than sixty-five Dutch ships loaded cargoes of spices in the archipelago. Their usual round was to call at Bantam in Java for pepper and then go on to the Moluccas for cloves, mace and nutmeg. Having no posts of their own in India, and not being influenced (as the Portuguese were) by the traditions of the Arab seamen, who used to cruise up and down on the changing monsoon winds, the Dutch steered straight across from the Cape on the wings of the westerly wind; and they avoided the Portuguese post at Malacca by entering the Java Sea by the 'side door' through the Sunda Strait, between Java and Sumatra. In 1602 the Dutch gained command of the sea by a decisive naval victory over the Portuguese fleet; it was ninety-three years since the Portuguese had won control by their own victory. In that same year, 1602, the Dutch established their East India Company, and a few years later they had set up fifteen trading posts in different parts of the archipelago and had gained complete control of the spice trade. In 1619 the Dutch governor-general, Jan Pieterszoon Coen, established the company's head-quarters at the Javanese town of Djakarta, which he renamed Batavia.[1]

The Dutch did not have things quite their own way. There was an English East India Company, which aspired to share in the spice trade. But as time went on the English company devoted its main attention to India, and allowed the Dutch to squeeze it out of the archipelago. In 1640 the Dutch attacked Ceylon, and completed its conquest in 1656; in 1641 they captured Malacca. After this, the Dutch hold was too strong to be shaken by any European competitor.

[1] The Batavi were the inhabitants of Holland in the days of the Roman empire.

The Dutch East India Company was purely a trading concern. Like its English rival in India, it had no wish to acquire territory; but like the English, it found itself compelled to do so. Its headquarters in Java were threatened with attack, and it had to take control of a good part of the island. There was piracy at sea, and the Dutch had to take and hold the pirate lairs. The Dutch monopoly of the spice production was threatened when people began growing spices in unauthorised islands, and the Dutch had to take control of those islands to stop this illicit production. Thus for one reason or another the Dutch were unable to follow the Portuguese scheme of a cheap commercial empire based on a few strategically placed trading posts; they were forced instead to go in for the more expensive and troublesome kind of colonial empire. But even so, the Dutch restrained themselves as much as they could; to the very end of their time there were large areas in the East Indies in which their authority was very little felt.

During the seventeenth and eighteenth centuries, in spite of the Dutch efforts to restrict production, the supply of spices to Europe increased and the prices fell. In the latter part of the eighteenth century a Frenchman, appropriately named Poivre (pepper), succedeed in smuggling some living spice plants and seeds out of the archipelago and propagating them elsewhere in the tropics, thus breaking the Dutch monopoly. The Dutch replied by taking up coffee and sugar-cane, and encouraging Java to grow these cash crops for export instead of concentrating on marketing and commerce. The Javanese however were not anxious to abandon their tradition of highly skilled rice cultivation; so the Dutch encouraged the immigration of Chinese, as craftsmen, as businessmen, and as workers on the new plantations.

Nevertheless, the financial prospects of the Dutch company were not bright. In growing sugar and coffee, the East Indies were at a disadvantage. They were short of labour, and even with the improved ships of the eighteenth century, they were several months journey from their European market. The Caribbean islands on the other hand were only four or five weeks from Europe, and the African slave trade supplied them with abundant labour. It seemed to the Dutch that a commercial company was no longer suitable for governing the East Indies. In 1798 the company was dissolved, and the Dutch government took over its position in the archipelago.

During the Napoleonic wars, Holland was occupied by French troops and compelled to become an active ally of France. This laid the Dutch possessions open to British attack, and in the course of the wars Britain occupied the Dutch foothold at the

Cape,[1] Ceylon, and everything in the East Indies that was worth occupying. At the peace of 1814, Britain kept Ceylon and the Cape, but gave back to Holland her East Indian possessions. This was a disappointment to Stamford Raffles, who was British governor of Java and had to give up his post; he consoled himself by hoisting the British flag on the island of Singapore. In 1824 Britain made a supplementary treaty with Holland. Ever since 1685 the English had held a post at Bengkahulen on the west coast of Sumatra. It was of little value, but it was a bargaining counter. Britain offered to exchange this post for Malacca, and to throw in an undertaking to make no more island settlements south of Singapore. It was a fair bargain. The Dutch were sensitive to foreign competition in the archipelago, and were glad to have British competition excluded. Britain on the other hand was anxious to find new markets for her manufactures, and wanted to control the trade route to China through the Strait of Malacca. We may observe that the British undertaking was limited to the area south of Singapore. The north coast of Borneo lies north of this line, so Britain was free to make settlements there.

When the Dutch came back to Java, they were not welcomed. There was a widespread revolt, and it took the Dutch five years, from 1825 to 1830, to put it down. In 1830 the Dutch governor-general Johannes van den Bosch introduced a new system of government in Java. In order to increase the island's output of export crops, he compelled the villagers to set aside one-fifth of their land and to hand over the produce to the government as tribute. The villagers regarded this as a heavy burden, but they produced valuable crops of coffee, sugar, indigo, tea and cinchona, which were sold in Holland by a government marketing company. In this way the Dutch quickly accumulated large amounts of capital, much as the British had accumulated capital in the hey-day of the slave-based Caribbean sugar industry. Java became wealthy and extremely populous, but the Javanese villagers hated being compelled to spend so much time growing export crops, and social life in the villages suffered through this system of plantation labour.

Largely for this reason, the Dutch abolished the system after forty years. The new agrarian law of 1870 proclaimed that all unoccupied land belonged to the Dutch state, and could be leased from the state. The Indonesian people were allowed to lease their land to foreigners for limited periods, but not to sell it outright. With Africa in mind, we may wonder whether this concept

[1] Occupied by the Dutch in 1652 as a victualling station for their ships on their long voyage between Holland and the Far East.

L

of unoccupied land was not likely to lead to trouble. But there was plenty of unoccupied land. Java and a few of the smaller islands were densely populated, but even after Indonesian independence, the large islands of Borneo and Sumatra had only eighteen and eighty people to the square mile. This law released the Javanese villagers from their tribute of export crops; it led to a great expansion of capitalist plantation agriculture; but it prevented large-scale alienation of land and the growth of a landless class.

After 1870 mining too was developed: oil was found in Sumatra, tin in the small islands of Bangka and Belitung, and coal in various places. To make land available for mining and plantations, the Dutch government had to extend its political control. Except in Java, the Dutch had not hitherto penetrated far from the coast; but after 1870 they quickly expanded the area under their rule. Even so, much of Sumatra, Borneo, Celebes, and even of the Moluccas (the spice islands themselves) were not brought under control till after 1900. The small island of Bali, next door to Java, was not conquered till 1908. It was not till the 1930s that the Dutch made any serious attempt to establish their power in the western half of New Guinea.

As colonial administrators, the Dutch were in a difficult position. They could not follow a policy of assimilation, for the Indonesians had a civilisation which they regarded as superior to that of their Dutch rulers. Neither could the Dutch follow the French example and give educated Indonesians seats in the parliament at The Hague. These Indonesian leaders would have represented a community of 70 million, demanding equal treatment with the 7 million Dutch. As a modern French statesman said of his own country, Holland would have 'become a colony of her own colonies'. Holland's best course would have been to make up her mind that independence must come. But as the years went by, the Indonesian economy became more and more important to Holland, and the Dutch dared not contemplate letting their empire go. Some people talked of a federation of Holland and Indonesia, but this idea was not seriously put forward until it was too late.

Meanwhile, the Dutch tried to govern through the Indonesian sultans and nobles, and on the other hand they encouraged Chinese immigration. The result was a dual society, the Chinese and Indonesian communities being left as far as possible to run their own affairs under their own leaders. Society soon became still more complicated. Java and some other islands were unhealthy, and were regarded as unsuitable for European women. The Dutch married into the Indonesian community, and there grew up a large group of Eurasians. In 1854 the Dutch legally classed all Eurasians bearing Dutch surnames as Europeans, which meant that they were eligible for 'European appointments', but on the other hand were not allowed to buy land. This led them to concentrate on gaining 'white-collar' jobs, and as the number of such jobs was limited, most of them were held by Eurasians, and the Indonesians were largely excluded from the colonial administration. The administration eventually became very complicated, with separate legal codes for Europeans, Indonesians and 'Foreign Orientals', and with two separate civil services, one for Indonesians and one for non-Indonesians.

At the beginning of this century the Dutch made a gallant attempt to check the disintegration of Indonesian society under the impact of Western and Chinese commercialism. They made a careful study of Indonesian life, laws and customs, and adopted an enlightened policy of trusteeship. They set up some provincial councils and local advisory councils in an attempt to decentralise the administration. But they shrank from setting up a real federal system. The Dutch developed a good system of village education, both for children and adults; but it was conducted in the vernacular, and only a small proportion of primary school children had an opportunity of secondary education. There were no plans for developing higher education or extending self-government. There was a large and growing body of Dutch and Eurasians, living out of contact with Indonesian society, who were making themselves very comfortable in the islands. The Indonesians gained the impression that the Dutch were determined to hold on to their power and to use the resources of Indonesia in the interests of Holland.

Before the 1939 war there was a nationalist movement in Indonesia, led by Dr Sukarno. During the war the islands were occupied by the Japanese; and in August 1945, as soon as the Japanese were defeated, Dr Sukarno proclaimed that Indonesia was an independent republic. The Dutch returned, with allied military support, a few months later. Dr Sukarno moved his headquarters from Batavia and abandoned control of the main coastal cities, but he still held the rural areas of east and central Java. The Dutch set up their headquarters in Celebes, and proposed that the territories which they controlled should be grouped into six administrative units, and that these six units, plus Dr Sukarno's republic, should constitute a federal Commonwealth of Indonesia. But Indonesia was a difficult country for federalism. The island of Java, most of which was under Sukarno, had a population of well over a thousand to the square mile, whereas some of the other proposed units had only twenty or thirty. It is not surprising that Dr Sukarno would not accept the Dutch proposals.

So it came to fighting, and the Dutch sought allies among the Indonesian aristocracy. They had in their favour the fact that the other islands were traditionally jealous of Java; and they hoped also to find many of the aristocracy personally jealous of Dr Sukarno and reluctant to accept him as the national leader. But Sukarno had wealth, numbers, and the central position; and the war went badly for the Dutch. In 1949 they gave up the struggle, and agreed to hand over their powers to a federal republic of the United States of Indonesia. Batavia, resuming its pre-colonial name of Djakarta, was to be the federal capital.

But as we have said, Indonesia is a difficult country for federalism. After the transfer of power, the federation quickly collapsed. By August 1950, all the other units had agreed to join Sukarno's republic, and so on 10 August 1950 Sukarno was able to proclaim the establishment of the Republic of Indonesia as a centralised unitary state.

The new government now had to translate this paper scheme of national unity into fact. The centuries-old jealousy of Javanese dominance was not to be overcome in a day. One wise step that the Sukarno government took was to promote a national language, choosing for the purpose the simplified form of Malay which was already much used as a commercial lingua franca: Bahasa Indonesia, they called it. The government was energetic in carrying out large-scale campaigns for village literacy to spread the use of the new national language.

It was difficult for the government to do anything to lessen the jealousy which the other islands felt for Java; for the government lived in Java, was dependent mainly on Javanese votes, and had the overcrowding and poverty of Java immediately under its eyes. The government's difficulty was increased by party squabbles; no party had an absolute majority, so that the work of government had to be carried on by a series of coalitions.

The strongest of the five main parties was Dr Sukarno's own party, the Nationalists. Though Sukarno himself was a Muslim, his party rejected the idea of a Muslim theocratic state. It was extremely hostile to the Dutch, and was determined to break the Dutch monopoly in trade and finance. The party was solidly based in Java, but was much weaker elsewhere.

Three parties wanted Indonesia to be an officially Muslim state. One of these, the Masjumi Party, ran a close second to the

Nationalists in the 1955 elections; the Masjumi Party was the only one of all the five parties which had any great measure of support outside Java. The communists, who followed the orthodox Moscow line, came fourth in order of strength; they were the party most narrowly restricted to Java. It is understandable that coalition governments should concern themselves mainly with Javanese problems.

But for this they had to pay the price. In December 1956 the military commander in southern Sumatra took control of the administration in his area, saying that he proposed henceforth to send the central government only 30 per cent of his revenue, and to spend the remainder locally on schools, hospitals, roads and irrigation. His example was quickly followed by his colleagues elsewhere in Sumatra, in Borneo, and in the eastern islands. The rebels said they had no wish to secede from the republic; they were protesting against corruption and inefficiency in Java, and they wanted more self-government and more control over their own revenue.

Since Sukarno depended on Javanese support, he could not afford to give up the revenue from the other islands. Partly to divert public attention, partly to compensate for the temporary stoppage of revenue, he whipped up a campaign against the Dutch. He seized all Dutch businesses and plantations, nationalised the Dutch shipping-line which ran all the Indonesian steamship services, cancelled the contract of the Dutch air-line, and expelled all Dutch and Eurasians from Indonesia. Some 120,000 people, many of whom had never seen Holland in their lives, left Indonesia and came as refugees to Holland; their loss was a blow to the Indonesian economy, and it did nothing to reconcile the rebels. In February 1958 the rebel leaders demanded that Sukarno should resign, and should be replaced by the vice-president, Hatta. Sukarno rejected the demand, and civil war followed; but the weight of numbers was on the government's side, and by 1961 Dr Sukarno had reasserted his authority.

Dr Sukarno had certain advantages. He had his personal prestige as the Nationalist leader who had given his country independence. The greater part of the army was loyal to him. Like the majority of his people, he was a Muslim, and the Muslims of Indonesia disliked communism because it was anti-religious and was associated with the Chinese immigrants. Nevertheless, Sukarno's position was insecure. He depended largely on the votes of Java, and the more concessions he made to the other islands, the greater his risk of losing Javanese support. Moreover, Java contained a solid block of communist votes, nearly 3 million of them, and the successes of Mao Tse-Tung and of Ho Chi Minh were causing the Indonesian communists to feel that time was very much on their side. Some of Sukarno's ministers were communists, or suspected of communism; and unless Sukarno could bring prosperity to the island of Java, the communist vote was likely to increase.

The national constitution was still unsettled. So many of the Indonesian people being uneducated, Dr Sukarno put forward a draft constitution based on a principle which he called 'guided democracy'; but in 1959, after a long discussion, the constituent assembly rejected his draft, and he had to fall back on a revised version of the constitution which he had framed for his little republic in Java in 1945.

Thus beset by dangers on every side, Sukarno yielded to the temptation of trying to unite his people by foreign adventure. He conducted an energetic campaign in the United Nations to obtain the cession of Dutch New Guinea, or West Irian as the Indonesians called it. His delegate went so far as to warn the Assembly that if Indonesia did not obtain an Assembly resolution in its favour, she might decide to annex the territory by force.

In 1963, Dr Sukarno saw a still better opportunity for distraction. In September of that year, the Federation of Malaysia was established, to include Malaya, Singapore, and the British territories on the north coast of Borneo. Sukarno decided not to recognise the Federation, his delegate at the United Nations explaining that it was a creation of British imperialism. The statement was literally true, but it implied that the Federation was not genuinely independent. Sukarno may perhaps have sincerely believed that the people of Malaysia wished to be liberated from colonial oppression. In the autumn of 1964 he set out to 'liberate' them. There were border clashes in the Borneo jungle, light naval vessels exchanged shots, Indonesian troops landed on the coasts of the Malayan peninsula, and Indonesian paratroops were dropped in the interior. It was a small affair, with only a few hundred men engaged. The Indonesian paratroop commander was taken prisoner, and explained that his orders were to set up a base for the liberation movement, relying mainly on local support; he was disgusted to find that the villagers regarded him and his men as foreign enemies.

The government of the Federation brought the matter to the United Nations, and it was considered by the Security Council. A Norwegian resolution deploring Indonesia's action obtained nine votes, but was vetoed by the Soviet Union; the Soviet and the Czechoslovak delegates supported the Indonesian view that the

Federation was a sham, erected to conceal the fact of British imperialist power.

Although there was little serious fighting, Sukarno kept up his policy of 'confrontation' with Malaysia for some time longer. The vote in the Security Council showed that only the communist countries supported him, and he found it harder and harder to remain independent of the communist vote. In 1965 there was an unsuccessful military coup. It was widely believed in the country that the coup was communist-inspired; there were serious riots against communists and Chinese, and the army had to be called in to restore order. Early in 1966, Dr Sukarno reshuffled his cabinet, with the effect of strengthening communist influence, and he caused much dismay by dismissing the minister of defence, General Nasution, who was well known to be strongly opposed to communism. At once the country was swept by rioting and disorder on a larger scale than ever before; the cry was for the reinstatement of General Nasution and the dismissal of all ministers with communist sympathies. After three weeks of this disorder, Dr Sukarno gave way, and called on General Suharto, the army chief of staff, to restore order and take control of the government. Suharto did so, and he took the drastic step of banning the communist party.

General Suharto, granted extraordinary powers by Dr Sukarno on 13 March 1966, used them to reverse the government's recent policy. All ministers suspected of communist sympathies were dismissed; three of them, including the foreign minister Dr Subandrio, were taken into 'protective custody'. A new inner cabinet was formed, composed of five deputy prime ministers, all of them strongly opposed to communism. Dr Subandrio's place as foreign minister was taken by Mr Adam Malik. The Suharto government announced that Indonesia would end the 'confrontation' with Malaysia, and at the end of May, Mr Malik went to Bangkok to meet Malaysia's foreign minister, Tun Abdul Razak, and to discuss peace terms. The only point of difficulty was the position of the Borneo territories of Malaysia, namely Sarawak and Sabah. The UN commission of inquiry had satisfied itself that the peoples of Sabah and Sarawak had freely expressed their desire to be part of the Federation of Malaysia, but the Indonesian government under Dr Sukarno had refused to accept the commission's judgement. Some sort of face-saving formula was now needed. No public statement was issued on the result of the Bangkok talks, but it was generally believed that the two ministers had agreed to a cease-fire, to the re-establishment of diplomatic relations, and to some sort of fresh inquiry over Sabah and Sarawak. When Mr Malik returned and reported to General Suharto, the general approved of the proposed outline agreement, but Dr Sukarno (who was still head of state) refused his approval. In a speech on 28 July he repeated that the Federation of Malaysia was what he called a 'Necolim' project, that is, neo-colonialist, colonialist and imperialist; Sukarno had a habit of forming composite words of this kind. The confrontation, he announced, would continue.

In spite of Sukarno's opposition, the definite treaty was signed in Djakarta on 11 August 1966. There was to be an immediate cease-fire, diplomatic relations were to be re-established, and fresh general elections were to be held in Sabah and Sarawak so that the people there could decide whether to remain in Malaysia or to join Indonesia. The treaty was to take effect forthwith. A week later, Dr Sukarno said that he would recognise the treaty, but would not recognise Malaysia until the Sabah and Sarawak election results were known. Seeing that the treaty had already come into effect, the president was being unnecessarily 'difficult'. He went on to say that what he called 'Nasakom' (another of his composite words, meaning nationalism, religion, and communism) was indispensable for rebuilding the Indonesian nation. However, he added, seeing that the Suharto government had banned communism, he was willing to replace communism by socialism. His audience received this speech with jeering, and five Muslim organisations joined in declaring that the speech did not represent the national majority view, and that Dr Sukarno should be dismissed from the presidency.

Dr Sukarno was irrepressible, and he seemed to be losing touch with the people. Though the parliament (the People's Consultative Congress) had passed a resolution outlawing communism and banning the works of Marx, Lenin and others, Sukarno made yet another speech in September. He said that he was a Marxist, and he added (truly enough) that communism would never be destroyed merely by parliamentary resolutions against it. He proposed that Indonesia should intervene in the Vietnam war by attacking the American troops in South Vietnam. This speech was badly received; it provoked the parliament to resolve that the president should stop calling himself a Marxist; he should abandon his idea of 'Nasakom' and join in condemning communism; moreover, he should explain what his own position had been in connection with the abortive 'communist' coup of October 1965. From this time onwards, Sukarno came more and more under attack. In January 1967 it was resolved that his share in the 1965 coup should be investigated by a congressional committee, and next month a demand was made that he should be tried for treason, on the grounds that he had transferred public money to his private bank accounts abroad. On 27 March 1967 he was dismissed from the presidency by a unanimous vote in parliament; General Suharto replaced him as acting president, to hold office until the 1968 elections.

Meanwhile, Dr Subandrio and his two colleagues had been brought to trial on charges of corruption and subversive activities; they were convicted and sentenced to death, though the sentences were commuted to life imprisonment. But nothing was done to investigate the allegations made against Dr Sukarno. It was plain that his health was failing, and after his dismissal he was allowed to live quietly in retirement. He died in June 1970.

Under General Suharto, Indonesia continued its violent recoil from Sukarno's flirtation with communism. The country's new leaders were as hostile to communism as Chiang Kai-Shek in China. In September 1966, Mr Malik estimated that 150,000 communists had already been killed; but even after this date there was much desultory fighting and many more communists were arrested. Gradually the anti-foreign measures introduced by Dr Sukarno were relaxed: foreign banks were allowed to reopen, and foreign businesses which had been confiscated were restored to their owners. The political treaty with Malaysia was supplemented by an agreement for economic co-operation; and Indonesia accepted Western help in such matters as irrigation and hydro-electric schemes. In March 1968 General Suharto was elected president, but he was not granted the far-reaching powers which Dr Sukarno had held: he was made responsible to parliament and was required to govern through responsible cabinet ministers.

MALAYSIA

The Federation of Malaysia is composed of the state of Malaya, the state of Singapore, and a continuous strip of country on the north coast of Borneo, which is divided into the states of Sabah, Brunei, and Sarawak.

Malaya

The Malay peninsula forms the furthest south-east tip of the mainland of Asia; it separates the South China Sea from the Bay of Bengal, and points into the middle of the Indonesian archipelago. The large island of Sumatra lies to the west of it, and between them there flow the tides of the Strait of Malacca, the main seaway between China and the West.

The peninsula is about 200 miles wide at its widest point, and from the narrow isthmus of Kra to the tip it is about 750 miles long, though only the lower half of this length forms part of the Federation, the upper half being part of Siam or Thailand. The peninsula is mountainous, and not specially fertile; even today most of the cultivated land lies in a narrow strip along the western side. It is difficult to cross the mountain ridges from one side of the peninsula to the other. The structure of the country did not encourage the growth of large states. Small independent sultanates – ten of them in an area not much more than half the size of Britain – grew up in the river valleys. Most of the country is thinly peopled. Until fairly recent times, the peninsula served mainly as a bridge across which peoples migrating from Asia passed on their way towards the richer lands of Indonesia. The east coast catches the full force of the north-east monsoon wind, and has no good harbours; during the season of the northern winter, navigation along this coast is dangerous. The west coast on the other hand is sheltered, and the Strait of Malacca is calm; the deep water channel passes close under the Malay shore. The peninsula is well placed to control the ancient trade route between China and India, and about A.D. 1400 the town of Malacca was founded as a commercial centre and a naval power.

By 1511, when Malacca was captured by the Portuguese, it had established its rule over various small states, both in the Malay peninsula and also on the far side of the strait in the island of Sumatra. Malacca was strongly Muslim, and under its influence, all the pagan Malay people of the peninsula accepted Islam by the end of the seventeenth century. Later, when the Dutch took Malacca from the Portuguese, they took no special interest in its political connections. Freed from control by Malacca, the small Malay sultanates drifted apart again. There was a small reverse flow of immigration from the archipelago, and the newcomers carved out two new sultanates, those of Selangor and Negri Sembilan.

During the latter part of the eighteenth century, the kingdom of Siam recovered from a series of disastrous wars with Burma, and began an expansionist policy. It pushed southwards; it took over the whole of the west coast from Tavoy (now part of Burma) to the present frontier of Malaya, and on the east side of the peninsula it annexed the northernmost Malay sultanate, Patani.

The British arrived in the region in 1786. Several times during the eighteenth century there had been naval actions in the Indian Ocean between British and French squadrons. The main British base was at Madras, but for half the year the north-east monsoon made it difficult for sailing ships to leave Madras harbour, and this was a serious handicap to the British fleet. The French fleet had a much more convenient base in the island of Mauritius. For their naval operations, the British badly wanted a base on the windward side of the Bay of Bengal. Moreover, their trade with China was increasing, and they wanted to control the Strait of Malacca. For these two reasons, in 1786 the British occupied the port of Penang. In 1800 they obtained a small piece of land on the mainland coast of the sultanate of Kedah, opposite Penang island; they named it Province Wellesley. About the same time, to help the navy in its fight against the pirates who infested the straits, they occupied a small group of islands called the Dindings, a little south of Penang.

The next British move came after the Napoleonic wars, after Britain had occupied, and then given up again, various Dutch islands in Indonesia. Stamford Raffles had served under the East India Company at Penang, and during the short British occupation of Indonesia he had been governor of Java. When recalled from Java he was reluctant to leave the region, and he had a scheme of establishing a chain of British posts to link British interests in India with the new British world which was being established in Australia. He got permission from the governor-general in Calcutta to set up a British post somewhere beyond Malacca so as to command the southern entrance of the strait. He fixed on Singapore island, and there in 1819, with the agreement of the local ruler, he hoisted the British flag. Five years later, the isolated British post of Bengkahulen on the west coast of Sumatra was handed over to the Dutch in exchange for Malacca.

The British territories of Penang, Province Wellesley, the Dindings, Malacca and Singapore were collectively called the Straits Settlements. They were not settled in the sense that Canada and Australia were settled; they were merely commercial and naval stations. All were controlled at first by the India Office, since they had been occupied in the days of the East India Company. In 1867 the Straits Settlements became a Crown Colony, and came under the control of the Colonial Office.

In the early days of the Straits Settlements, Britain had no special interest in the rest of the Malay peninsula, and had no wish to acquire more territory. But in 1821 Siam was on the move again; she followed up her annexation of the north-eastern state of Patani by occupying the north-western state of Kedah and making its sultan tributary. This brought Siam up against the British in Penang and Province Wellesley, and a British envoy was sent

Map 12. The Malay Peninsula

to the Siamese court to express the hope that Siam would not advance any further.

The situation was changed by the development of tin mining. The Malays had mined small quantities of alluvial tin for many years; but when British rule was established in the Straits Settlements, Chinese immigrants began to arrive and exploit the tin mines further. The tin was easily worked, and there was plenty to be gained without great capital expenditure. In 1848 a large new tin-field was discovered, and there was a great rush of miners to the states of Perak, and Selangor, and Negri Sembilan. There was friction between the Malays and the Chinese; and partly perhaps to oil the bearings, but largely to gain control of the tin-field before the Siamese or the French should claim it, Britain abandoned her policy of leaving the Malay sultanates to themselves. In 1874 a British protectorate was proclaimed over Perak, Selangor and part of Negri Sembilan; Pahang became a protectorate in 1888 and the rest of Negri Sembilan a year later. The four protected states accepted British Residents, whose advice they agreed to follow in all matters apart from Islam and Malay customary law. Chinese immigration continued, and life in these mining states was revolutionised. In 1895 the British grouped the four states together under the title of the Federated Malay States, with Kuala Lumpur as the federal capital.

The four northern states of Kedah, Perlis, Kelantan and Trengganu were left alone and recognised as being in the Siamese sphere of interest. The southernmost state of Johore had no minerals, and attracted few Chinese immigrants; but it had a certain importance as the immediate hinterland of Singapore. In 1885 it accepted a slight degree of British protection, but retained more independence than its colleagues in the Federation.

Till the end of the nineteenth century tin was Malaya's principal product. With the new century came the expansion of the motor industry, and an insatiable world demand for rubber. Rubber was found to thrive even on the relatively poor soil of Malaya, and it replaced tin as the country's main product. The rubber was at first grown on the plantation system, the land being leased by European or Chinese firms; but later on the Malay villagers began to grow a good deal of rubber in small-holdings. The Malays were not greatly attracted by working for wages in the mines or the plantations, so Tamils from India, and again the Chinese, supplied most of the work force.

The wealth of the Malayan tin-field made Britain sensitive to any threat of encroachment from outside. From the 1860s onwards, various schemes were put forward for shortening the journey between India and China by cutting a canal or building a railway across the narrow isthmus of Kra in Siamese territory, thus by-passing Malacca and Singapore. They came to nothing, because the distance saved was too little to dispose shipowners to pay canal dues, and no one would think of unloading a vessel at one end of a railway and loading its cargo into another vessel at the other end, only forty miles away. But Siam was shaking off her old tradition of seclusion; she was developing her railway system, and in 1903 she was considering a German scheme for a long line southward to the Malay border. The line had obvious strategic value if Siam ever resumed her expansionist policy, and Britain took alarm at the idea of her doing so under German influence. In 1909 Britain obtained a treaty with Siam. The Siamese agreed that the proposed southern railway line should be built with British, not German assistance, and that neither the Kra canal nor any other work of strategic importance should be carried out in the peninsula. Moreover, the four northern Malay sultanates of Kedah, Perlis, Kelantan and Trengganu, which had hitherto been under Siamese protection, were transferred to that of Britain, though Patani remained Siamese. The price which Britain paid for these considerable concessions was the surrender of most of her extra-territorial rights in Siam, plus the loan for the railway construction.

The British developed Malaya as a multi-racial state, finding it far from easy to reconcile the interests of the old-world, leisurely, Muslim Malay sultanates with those of the eager, pushing, pig-breeding Chinese. There was a tripartite system of education, with separate schools for Malay, Chinese and Indian children based on the vernacular, and with a few secondary schools using English.

During the 1939 war, all Malaya was occupied by the Japanese, but the forested mountainous country was suitable for guerrilla warfare, and bands of Chinese took to the forest and carried on a resistance movement, as their fellow-countrymen had so long been doing in China itself. When the British returned at the end of the war, they knew that they must give Malaya self-government as soon as possible. Their problem was to rebuild the country and develop some sense of Malayan nationality so as to make self-government possible. The pre-war government system in Malaya had been quite irrational; in this small country, about half the size of Britain, there had been the scattered group of small British-run Straits Settlements, with five unfederated and four federated Malay states, but with no proper representation of Chinese and Indian interests. The tripartite system of education was more effective in keeping alive racial differences than in developing any Malayan nationhood.

The first British proposal was to set up a Malayan Union, to include all the Malay sultanates and the Straits Settlements, but not Singapore, in which three-quarters of the population were Chinese. All people born in Malaya, whatever their race, and all foreign-born people who had spent ten years in Malaya since 1927, were to be eligible for citizenship of the Union. The position of the Malay sultans would be somewhat like that of the princes in India under the British raj.

This Malayan Union scheme of 1946 did not please the Malays. Although they would be the largest single racial group in the Union, they would be outnumbered by the Chinese and the Indians together; and they disapproved strongly of the proposal to reduce the status of their sultans. Without Malay support, the scheme was unworkable, and two years later the British came up with a fresh proposal. This was for a Federation of Malaya, again without Singapore; the Malay sultans were to keep their old position, and the franchise was to be weighted in favour of the Malays. This federal scheme was rejected by the Chinese. It seemed impossible to work out an acceptable constitution as long as the Chinese held all the economic power and the Malays were so frightened of them. Means must be found of building up the economic strength and the confidence of the Malays to the point where they would be ready to admit the Chinese and Indians to equal rights of citizenship. Everything possible must be done to diminish racial cleavages and develop a sense of Malayan nationhood.

This difficult situation was made more difficult by the outbreak of 'the emergency' in 1948. The communist-led Chinese resistance movement, which had given so much trouble to the Japanese, broke out again in the Malayan jungle, directed this time against the British-ruled Federation. The insurgents were almost all Chinese, and the movement was probably more a demonstration of Chinese national feeling than of international communism. The insurgents were able to get food and information from the large numbers of Chinese 'squatters' who had taken to the jungle during the Japanese occupation and settled on the land. The British carried on their campaign against the insurgents in two ways: first, by beating them at their own game of jungle warfare; and second, by rounding up the Chinese squatters and resettling them in new compact villages, where they could be protected, and where the insurgents could not get at them to extort information or supplies. It was a slow business, and it was not until 1960 that the last insurgent band gave up the struggle and retired across the Siamese border.

Difficult though it was, the emergency eased matters for the British in one way. They could not be expected to go on spinning fresh draft constitutions. Unless the insurrection could be crushed, there would be no Malayan state; and even if the insurrection was crushed, no Malayan state would survive unless there were a Malayan nation. To build up a Malayan nation was the immediate task for all civilians, while the soldiers were fighting in the jungle. Much work was done. The old tripartite educational system was abolished; it was replaced by a system of interracial schools, in which Malay, Chinese and Indian pupils learned side by side. The English and Malay languages were developed as the national languages of the Federation. Great efforts were made to build up Malay life by a system of adult education of community development, under an organisation called the Rural and Industrial Development Authority.

The government was agreeably surprised at the success of its policy. Federal elections were planned for 1955. As was to be expected, three racial parties were formed to contest them: the United Malays National Organisation, the Malayan Chinese Association, and the Malayan Indian Congress. But an unexpected thing happened: on the eve of the elections, the three parties formed an alliance, which captured fifty-one out of the fifty-two contested seats. The alliance held together well enough for the new legislative council to accept the offer of an independence constitution which guaranteed certain rights to the Malay people. For example, English and Malay, but not Chinese or any Indian language, might be used in parliament. Malays were promised a considerable share of posts in the civil service, and the land system of the Malay reservations was preserved. Malaya was to be a secular state, but Islam was declared to be the state religion. On this basis, Malaya became independent in August 1957.

Singapore

The island of Singapore had been one of the Straits Settlements, and the city of Singapore had been the biggest commercial centre of Malaya. But the population of Singapore was predominantly Chinese, and it was felt that it would be unwise to include the city in an independent Malaya. Nevertheless, the economic links between Singapore and Malaya were so close that some form of political association was desirable. The problem was how to link the two without arousing the Malays' fears that they might come to be dominated by the Chinese commercial interests of Singapore. Another complication was that Singapore was a British naval base, and although successive British governments after the war could never decide whether there was to be a British fleet to make use of the base, they found it difficult to abandon it.

The British would have preferred to erect Singapore into a separate Crown colony, giving it full internal self-government, but keeping defence and external affairs in British hands. The Singapore leaders wanted full independence; they said that they realised the strategic importance of their city and its close economic links with Malaya, and they would be ready to make appropriate treaties with Britain and with Malaya. But they must do so as completely free agents. In 1956 a constitutional conference in London broke down on this issue; the Singapore leader David Marshall returned home and resigned. At a fresh conference a year later, his successor accepted the British terms; by a face-saving compromise, the post of governor was replaced by that of Head of State, to be occupied by a person born in Malaya. The first elections were held in May 1959, and a new leader, Lee Kuan Yew, won forty-three out of fifty-one seats with his People's Action Party. Singapore is young; half its population is under twenty-five years of age. Its relations with the old-world Muslims of Malaya are bound at times to be difficult.

In September 1963 it seemed as though a permanent solution had been found. Malaya, Singapore, and the British territories in Borneo were combined into a Federation of Malaysia. But in two years, Singapore found her position in the Federation unsatisfactory, and seceded. The Federation as a whole was anti-communist; Malaya itself had spent years in fighting against communist guerrillas, and in 1964 was under attack from Indonesia, whose government appeared to be in danger of falling under communist influence. The Federation government welcomed the South-East Asia Treaty Organisation, and looked to the West for defence against the communist danger in Indonesia and North Vietnam. Singapore on the other hand wanted to trade with Indonesia, North Vietnam and China, and wanted to be neutral ('non-aligned') in the struggle between the communist East and the capitalist West. In August 1965, mainly on account of these differences over foreign policy, Singapore seceded from the Federation.

The Borneo Territories

When Stamford Raffles occupied Singapore in 1819, he alarmed the Dutch; and by the treaty of 1824, Britain promised to make no more settlements in the archipelago to the south of Singapore. Britain was able to give this promise because she had enough to do in India, and at that time had no interest in acquiring more tropical colonies. She was anxious over the economic situation in the West Indies, and it was generally believed in England that sooner or later all colonies would follow the American example and seek independence.

Though not interested in obtaining tropical colonies, Britain was keenly interested in obtaining useful trading posts; and with the coming of steam it was thought important to acquire coaling stations for British naval and merchant steamers. Early steam-engines were inefficient; they needed to be refuelled at frequent intervals, or else their coal-bunkers would be so large as to leave

M

little space for cargo. Singapore was useful as a coaling station, but there was no station beyond it for the China-going steamers until Hong Kong was occupied in 1842. Even when coal became available at Hong Kong, British shipowners felt that another intermediate port would be convenient. The north coast of Borneo seemed a suitable area for the purpose. It had at least one good natural harbour at Labuan, and the whole of this coast lay to the north of Singapore, so that British occupation was not excluded by the 1824 treaty.

Most of the north coast of Borneo had at one time been the dominion of the Sultan of Brunei. Brunei had been a strong state, but during the eighteenth century it lost ground, and by the nineteenth century the western part of the coastal strip paid the sultan only a nominal allegiance. In 1839 an Englishman named James Brooke paid a private visit to the western end of the country. The sultan's local viceroy was in trouble; he was faced with a rising which he could not put down. James Brooke helped him to put it down, and in 1841 the grateful sultan installed him as Rajah of the province of Sarawak, with his capital at Kuching. James Brooke and his son, who succeeded him, set themselves to bring the country into order, and to put down the Chinese pirates who swarmed in the neighbouring seas. In putting down the pirates they received help from the Royal Navy, and in 1846 the island of Labuan was occupied to provide the navy with a coaling station, thus providing also for the needs of merchant shipping.

Putting down the disorder in the sultan's dominions was another matter. This was done gradually; but to do it, the Brookes had to encroach more and more on the sultan's territory, until their province of Sarawak became much larger than the territory remaining directly under the sultan. In 1888, both Sarawak and Brunei became British protectorates, and in 1906 the Sultan of Brunei accepted a position very much like that of one of the sultans in Malaya. After the Second World War, in 1946, Sarawak became a Crown colony, in spite of the protests of the Rajah, Sir Charles Brooke.

While the Brookes were absorbing more and more of Brunei's western territory, others were encroaching on Brunei from the east. Various people laid claim to the north-eastern corner of Borneo. The Dutch of course claimed the whole of the huge island. The Sultan of Brunei said that the north-eastern corner was part of his dominion, but his ancient enemy, the Sultan of Sulu in the Philippines, disputed his claim. The two rival sultans granted concessions to sundry European and American business-men. The Spanish government stepped in, on the grounds that the

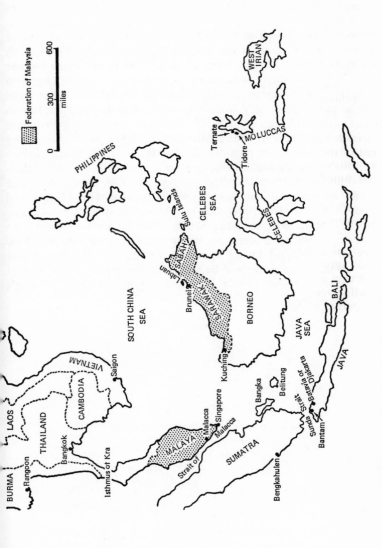

Map 13. South-East Asia and Indonesia

Philippines were a Spanish colony, the Sultan of Sulu a Spanish subject, and any of his territories therefore a dependency of the Philippines. Always ready to fish in troubled waters, the German government put in a claim. Germany had occupied north-eastern New Guinea and sundry Pacific islands, and was interested in China; a coaling station at the tip of Borneo would be very useful to the German navy. In the end, the tangle was cut by the British government. The various concessions held by businessmen became combined into two groups, both held by British firms. One firm held its concessions from the Sultan of Brunei, the other from the Sultan of Sulu; they combined their enterprises and the British North Borneo Company was born. In 1881 the British government gave the company a royal charter, on condition that the company entrusted its foreign relations to Britain. In 1888 North Borneo became a British protectorate, and in 1946 North Borneo, including Labuan, became a British colony. In 1963 the territories of North Borneo and Sarawak were incorporated with Malaya and Singapore into the Federation of Malaysia. On this occasion, North Borneo was renamed Sabah. The Sultan of Brunei also agreed to join the Federation, but at the last minute he withdrew his agreement, and Brunei remained outside. In 1971 Britain and Brunei made an agreement by which Brunei received full internal self-government but Britain remained responsible for the Sultan's external affairs.

11   Israel and the Arabs

Unlike some world problems of today, the Arab-Israeli problem has no long history behind it. The Jews and the Arabs are ancient races; they speak languages which are closely related; in religion and culture they have much in common. In 1919 an Arab leader, the Emir Feisal, told the Versailles peace conference, 'The Jews are very close to the Arabs in blood, and there is no conflict of character between the two races. In principles we are absolutely at one.' The relationships between the two became a problem only as a result of what happened during and after the First World War.

By their own account, recorded in the Bible, the Israelis formed a pair of kingdoms in Palestine which dominated the country, but which lived an uneasy existence between the strong powers of Egypt on one side and Assyria, Babylon or Persia (all of them ruling the modern land of Iraq) on the other. Both kingdoms were eventually destroyed, and many of the people deported to the east. Palestine and Syria eventually became parts of the Roman empire, and under the Roman peace large numbers of Jews became scattered all over the empire.

Six hundred years after Christ, Palestine was conquered by the Arabs, and became a predominantly Muslim Arabic-speaking country. All the Arabic-speaking countries were subsequently conquered by the Turks, so that in 1914 Palestine was an obscure province of the Turkish dominions.

Turkey entered the 1914 war as an ally of Germany, with her possessions in Asia still intact; she held all the land from the Black Sea and the Aegean down to Aden and the Persian Gulf. The total population of Palestine in 1917 is believed to have been about 700,000, of whom fewer than 10 per cent were Jews.

During the 1914 war, one British army conquered the country we now call Iraq, and a second British army under General Allenby conquered Palestine and Syria. Allenby's conquest of Palestine was greatly helped by the Arab revolt against the Turks, a revolt stimulated by T. E. Lawrence. An Arab army manœuvred on Allenby's flank, and though one of the first successes of the campaign was Allenby's capture of Jerusalem, its climax was the Emir Feisal's capture of Damascus.

The Arabs, who had been reluctant subjects of Turkey, thus saw suddenly before them the bright hope of independence. The hope was held out to them not only by their British friend Lawrence, but also by the British High Commissioner in Egypt, Sir Henry McMahon. In 1915 and 1916, McMahon wrote, on behalf of the British government, a series of letters to the Sherif Hussein of Mecca, the guardian of the holiest shrine of the Muslim world. The McMahon letters promised that if Sherif Hussein would rebel against the Turks, Britain would stimulate national independence for the Arabs. The McMahon letters did not promise immediate independence; they made it clear that Britain proposed to set up a series of protectorates and to develop them until they were ripe for independence. Nor did the letters mention Palestine, though their geographical references were so vague that it might reasonably be held that Palestine was one of the areas referred to. Sherif Hussein accepted the British proposals, and his sons Abdullah and Feisal led the successful Arab revolt.

So much for the Arab hopes; what about the Jews? For nearly 2,000 years the Jews had been scattered over the world, suffering much persecution at Christian hands. They had never ceased to look back longingly to the land of Israel and their holy city of Jerusalem. In the nineteenth century the Zionist movement arose, a movement calling on Jews throughout the world to work for the re-establishment of the Jews in their ancient home. In the small land of Palestine, roughly the size of Wales, the Zionist movement wanted to build a Jewish state. There was talk of offering the Jews a national home in East Africa, or in British Guiana, but the Zionists would have none of it. Nothing but the ancient land of Israel would content them.

In November 1917 the British government gave them a chance of obtaining what they wanted. The British foreign secretary was Arthur Balfour, and he wrote to a leading British Jew to convey to him

. . . the following declaration of sympathy with Jewish Zionist aspirations which has been submitted to and approved by the cabinet. His Majesty's government view with favour the establishment in Palestine of a national home for the Jewish people, and will use their best endeavours to facilitate the achievement of this object, it being clearly understood that nothing shall be done which may prejudice the civil and religious rights of the existing non-Jewish communities in Palestine, or the rights and political status enjoyed by Jews in any other country.

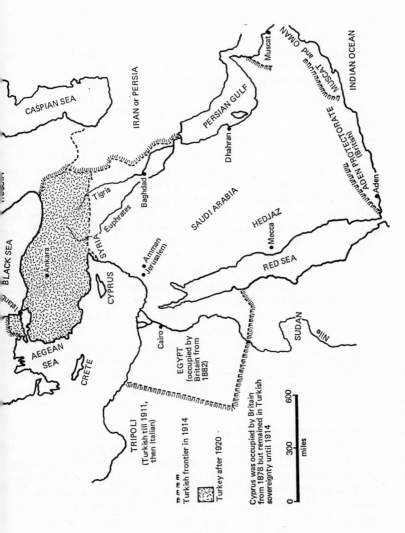

Map 14. The Middle East

This letter is the Balfour Declaration of November 1917, the foundation of British policy with regard to Palestine. It should be noted that the declaration did not promise that the whole of Palestine should become Jewish, but only that some part of it should; the rights of the Arab inhabitants were not to be disturbed. There was at that time no hostility between the small Jewish minority and the Arab majority. There seemed no reason why good administration should not develop the country's resources and enable it to carry a much larger population, so that Arabs and Jews should share in the general prosperity.

No doubt the British government had mixed motives in issuing the declaration: for example, it may well have reflected that it would have a good effect on the powerful Jewish community in the United States, whose support was so important when Britain was fighting for her life. Again, the Zionist leader Dr Weizmann was a distinguished scientist, who had given great service to Britain. But it seems clear that the predominant motive was generosity: Balfour and his colleagues felt that the war was giving Britain an opportunity to do something to atone for the long centuries of oppression which the Jews had suffered.

The British plan was that the new state of Palestine would be placed to begin with under the League of Nations, and governed by some power under a mandate from the League. Balfour and the British government did not want Britain to have the mandate. As foreign secretary, Balfour tried to persuade the United States to accept it. But the United States would have nothing to do with the League, and refused to accept any such responsibility; so Britain reluctantly accepted the mandate, in which the Balfour Declaration was embodied. The British hoped that the two races in Palestine, so closely related, would settle down together, and that an Arab-Jewish state would be stable and prosperous.

Unfortunately, while Lawrence and McMahon were making promises to the Arabs on behalf of the British government, and Balfour on behalf of the same government was making his offer to the Jews, there were other negotiations taking place. All the Arab countries had been conquered from Turkey by British troops and the Arab forces. But Britain's ally, France, had strong interests in Syria, and put in a claim to be granted the mandate for the administration of Syria, which Britain felt unable to oppose. These negotiations for dividing the Middle East into French and British spheres of influence were carried on by Sykes for Britain and Picot for France. The Sykes-Picot agreement was a great blow to the Arabs, especially to the Emir Feisal, who had ridden into Damascus at the head of his victorious troops; especially when it appeared that France had no idea of encouraging Syrian independence. The Arabs felt, and their British friend Lawrence felt also, that they had been betrayed.

Strangely enough, the Arab leaders did not at first feel that the Balfour Declaration too was a betrayal. In January 1918, Sherif Hussein himself told a British representative that he saw no objection to Jewish immigration into Palestine or any other Arab country. Five months later, in June, Hussein's son the Emir Feisal met the Jewish leader Dr Chaim Weizmann. Feisal and Weizmann made a written agreement, which clearly stated that

. . . all necessary measures shall be taken to encourage and stimulate immigration of Jews into Palestine on a large scale, and as quickly as possible to settle Jewish immigrants upon the land through closer settlement and intensive cultivation of the soil. In taking such measures the Arab peasant and tenant farmers shall be protected in their rights, and shall be assisted in forwarding their economic development.

The agreement goes on to provide that the Zionist organisation should send out a commission to survey the economic possibilities of the country and make recommendations for its development. Feisal, as we have seen, was one of the outstanding Arab leaders, and attended the Versailles peace conference as such. At the time of making this agreement, he had hopes of becoming king of a Greater Syria, in which Palestine should be included.

Clearly, the Balfour Declaration in itself did not alarm these Arab leaders. Much would depend on how it was interpreted in practice. The British government hoped that in practice there would be no great difficulties. Some tens of thousands of Jewish immigrants would come to Palestine. Aided by Jewish capital, good British administrators and clever Jewish brains would enable the country to support perhaps four or five times its then population. In due time, Jews and Arabs would sit together in a parliament at Jerusalem and form a cabinet with Jewish and Arab members to govern the country. Englishmen, Scotsmen and Welshmen sat thus together at Westminster; why should the pattern not be repeated in Jerusalem?

This pleasant British dream never came true, and there were two main reasons. One was that the Zionists would never be content with equal partnership with Arabs in a mixed Jewish-Arab state. They were determined to have not merely a national home *in* Palestine, but a Jewish state *of* Palestine. As soon as they had brought in enough Jewish immigrants, the Jews were to become politically dominant. For some time, the British did not realise that nothing less than this Jewish state would content the Jews; and when they did come to realise it, they thought the possibility was remote. It remained to be seen how many Jews would wish to leave Europe or America and go to Palestine; and in accordance with the Balfour Declaration, they expected that the Palestine administration would be able to protect Arab interests by controlling the inflow of Jewish immigrants. In this they were disappointed.

The second reason for the failure of the British dream was the rise of Arab nationalism. Not only the British, but even some of the Arab leaders themselves, men like Emir Feisal, took too little account of this nationalism. There had been little or no Arab nationalist movement against the Turkish government before 1914; the Turkish government dealt very harshly with nationalism among its subjects, and moreover, the Sultan of Turkey was also head of the Islamic world, and it was difficult for a good Muslim to rebel against him. But in the war, not only did the Arab states gain their freedom, but the sultanate itself vanished. The new Turkey was a small secular nation-state, its capital moved from Constantinople (Istanbul) to Ankara, its new leader Mustafa Kemal Ataturk showing himself able to defeat the Greeks and intimidate the British and French. The Turkish example was infectious. The new Arab mandated states became proud of their nationhood.

Here we see the weakness of the Feisal-Weizmann agreement. Feisal came from the Hedjaz, and although he had led the Arab armies into Damascus, the Arabs of Syria and Palestine regarded him as a foreigner. What right had he on their behalf to admit more and more Jews into Palestine?

Thus the British administration in Palestine realised, almost from the beginning, that its task was impossible. By the terms of the Balfour Declaration, if large numbers of Jewish immigrants chose to come to Palestine, it was bound to admit them. At the same time, it was bound to see that the rights of the Arabs were not prejudiced. Palestine was a small country, about 200 miles long and 40 or 50 miles wide, and much of it was mountain or desert. The administration was faced with an active Zionist commission, whose work was to see that the administration carried out its duty of furthering Jewish interests. If the administration allowed too many Jewish immigrants, there were complaints from the Arabs that they were being betrayed. If it tried to regulate the inflow of immigrants, it had the Zionist commissioners on its doorstep accusing it of violating the terms of the Balfour Declaration and of the League's mandate. The officials tried to be fair. But neither Jews nor Arabs wanted fairness; they wanted land and power for themselves.

The first British high commissioner was appointed in July 1920; he was Sir Herbert Samuel, himself a Jew and a friend of the Zionists, but filled with the British desire to hold the balance fairly between Jew and Arab. He had only been a short while in the country when events occurred elsewhere in the Arab world which had important effects on the position in Palestine.

Sherif Hussein was now King of the Hedjaz. His younger son Feisal, who had made the agreement with Dr Weizmann, had now become King of Syria. Feisal had ambitions. Under Turkish rule, the province of Syria had included Lebanon, Palestine, and the lands east of the Jordan; and Feisal aspired to become king of this Greater Syria. But Palestine and Transjordan were under British mandate, Syria and Lebanon under French; and the French had no intention of encouraging Feisal's ambition. It would have needed a more skilful statesman than Feisal to make good his position in these circumstances. The French found him an inconvenience, and the people of Damascus distrusted him as a foreigner who had dealings with the Zionists. In July 1920 the French put down the independence movement in Syria by force and expelled Feisal; and thus the Greater Syria scheme collapsed.

This left a vacuum in Transjordan; the territory was under British mandate, but very little had yet been done to organise its administration. The British had a vague idea that if too many Jewish immigrants arrived in Palestine, some of the Arabs there might agree to exchange their Palestine lands for fresh estates across the river. But they never had a chance to act on this idea. The Emir Abdullah, Feisal's elder brother, gathered an army in the south and began to march through Transjordan with the idea of throwing the French out of Syria and restoring his brother Feisal. The few British administrative officers in the region had no power to resist him; he set up an administration at Amman, and the British government decided to recognise him as King of Transjordan. In return for British financial help and a little political guidance, Abdullah agreed to give up his scheme of making war on the French, the more readily because his brother Feisal was provided for. By somewhat devious means, the British arranged for Feisal to be elected King of Iraq, where he was as much a foreigner as he had been in Syria.

In this way there came into being the kingdom of Transjordan. Now that the land east of the river was no longer under direct British rule, the British no longer had the power to arrange any settlement of Palestinian Arabs in Transjordan. Abdullah dared not, even if he wished, show himself too friendly to the Zionists; Arab nationalism was too strong to allow that.

Although for a few years to come Jewish immigration into Palestine was not large, pressure soon began on Arab land. The Zionist organisation was amply supplied with money from Europe and America. The British administration passed a whole series of ordinances to protect Arab tenants from eviction, but on the whole they were ineffective. From centuries of experience the peasants distrusted all governments and avoided legal documents. Many of them were in debt to money-lenders; much of the land was owned by absentee landlords; there was no proper land registry. It was easy for a wealthy purchaser to make the Arab peasant a generous cash payment to vacate the land. The land being apparently empty, ownership changed hands; and if the new owner were a Zionist, the Arab tenant might find it harder to return to his place than to leave it. Partly by straightforward purchase, partly by such devices as these, large areas of Arab land gradually passed into Jewish control. The ignorant Arab peasants were replaced by eager young Jewish immigrants, well supplied with capital, agricultural skill, and enthusiasm. The land produced much more, but the Arabs had lost their homes.

Unless this pressure on Arab land were eased, the policy of the Balfour Declaration would fail. The tragedy of the situation was that each side had a reasonable case; it was not a plain question of right against wrong. The Jews had been promised a national home in the promised land, and to the Zionists, a national home meant a Jewish state. Palestine was poor, and its agriculture unproductive; but they had the skill and the capital to make the desert blossom as the rose – as indeed they demonstrated on a large scale. To the Arabs on the other hand, Palestine, though poor, was their home. They had no objection to Jews as such, but they objected violently to Zionists, who appeared to them as land-grabbers who cared nothing for Arab rights. The Jews had been oppressed for centuries, but by the Christians of Europe, not by the Arabs of Palestine. Why should the Arabs of Palestine pay for their oppression?

It remained to be seen whether large numbers of Jews would come to Palestine. Fewer than 2,000 came in 1919, but during the next few years the annual figures rose to about 8,000. These figures were not above the country's capacity, but they were enough to alarm the Arabs and to provoke bloodshed. As early as March 1920 there were small-scale Arab attacks on Jewish settlements, and a year later there were more attacks, causing over 300 casualties. The government still hoped that with time, its policy of a joint Arab-Jewish state might succeed; it spoke of limiting Jewish immigration for a while, and of setting up a legislative council in Palestine.

The government's talk of limiting Jewish immigration naturally infuriated the Zionists. The idea of an elected legislative council was unwelcome to the Jews, because at that time they would be in a minority; but they were statesmanlike enough to accept it. The Arabs, who ought in their own interests to have leaped at the offer, rejected it; they refused to have anything to do with a constitution for Palestine unless the Balfour Declaration were revoked and all Jewish immigration stopped. The Zionist leaders were experienced men of the world, who knew how to make the best of their case; the Arabs, whose case was in some ways the stronger, allowed themselves again and again to be outmanœuvred.

The British government too, allowed itself to be placed in a false position. For many years it did not publish the Macmahon correspondence, or the Feisal-Weizmann agreement; and thus it allowed the beliefs to get abroad that Britain had forced the idea of a Jewish national home on the Arab leaders against their will, and that having promised the Arabs of Palestine their independence, Britain broke her promise to please the Jews. Both beliefs were false, but they were widely held, and they were not contradicted. If these beliefs were true, the Arabs argued, the Jews must have paid Britain her price; and the most likely price was that Britain should have the use of Palestine as a military base to protect the Suez Canal in case she ever had difficulty with Egypt. This idea was certainly not in Balfour's mind; if it had been, he would never have pressed the United States to accept the mandate for Palestine. After a time, the British officials in Palestine, plodding along amid the hostility both of Arabs and of Jews, did come to believe that no motive other than securing the Suez Canal could have been strong enough to make the government in London impose this burden upon them. But they were wrong.

In 1925, events in Poland and Russia caused Jewish immigration into Palestine to shoot up to nearly 35,000, over four times the previous annual average. Next year it dropped to 14,000, and for a few years after that, Palestine, like other countries, was affected by the world-wide slump, and the national home became unattractive. But in 1933 Hitler came to power in Germany and the Nazi persecutions began. In that year, over 30,000 Jews entered Palestine; next year, 42,000; in 1935, over 60,000. Figures like these made nonsense of the British government's hope of a peaceful self-governing Arab-Jewish state. In 1935 the government again tried to introduce an elected legislative council, but the proposal was rejected by both sides: by the Jews, because the council would have an Arab majority, by the Arabs, because to elect members to the council would imply accepting the mandate and the Balfour Declaration, and their policy was to reject both as unjust and invalid. Faced with opposition from both sides, the British abandoned their scheme, and no further attempt was made to introduce representative government.

Meanwhile, constitutional progress was being made elsewhere in the Arab world. Lebanon became independent in 1926, Transjordan in 1928, Iraq in 1931, Syria in 1932, Egypt in 1936. Independence was not always complete; many of the Arab states were nervous of the growing power of Saudi Arabia, and were glad at that time to have defence treaties with Britain or France. Still, they were independent enough to be admitted as members of the United Nations, and the Arabs of Palestine were the only Arabs in the Middle East to be left without any measure of self-government.

In 1936 there occurred the first large-scale Arab revolt, directed not only against the Jews but against the British. It ended after a few months, mainly because the rulers of other Arab states had not yet lost their faith in Britain's good intentions. When the government appointed a Royal Commission to inquire into the Palestine situation, four Arab rulers urged the Arab authorities in Palestine to call off their revolt and the general strike which accompanied it.

This Peel Commission of 1937 could not solve the insoluble problem of making the Balfour Declaration workable, of allowing indefinite large-scale Jewish immigration without harming Arab interests. Its chief importance is that it introduced the idea of partition. Since Arabs and Jews could not live peaceably together in one country, let them separate. End the British mandate. Let the Jews have their Jewish state in one part of Palestine, and let the rest of the country be part of King Abdullah's state of Transjordan.

The idea of partition was the last desperate resource. But it would not be a permanent solution. There would have to be an exchange of populations, Jews leaving Arab territory and Arabs leaving Jewish, accompanied with much bitterness and misery. A small Jewish state in one corner of Palestine would never satisfy the Jews, for it would limit immigration; the Jewish state would always be seeking to expand. For such reasons as these, the Peel report was rejected by the Jews. It was rejected also not only by the Arabs of Palestine, but by the Arab states whose rulers had urged the cessation of the Palestinian revolt. Arab nationalism was taking on a new and harder form; no Arab could contemplate giving away another inch of Arab soil.

We need not go in detail through the rest of the British story in Palestine. In 1939, after the utter failure of an Arab-Jewish conference in London, the British government put out a White Paper with its own proposals. There was to be no partition. Palestine was to be developed as a mixed Arab-Jewish state, to become independent in about ten years. Jewish immigration was to be restricted to 75,000 over a period of five years, unless the Arabs agreed to admit more. The high commissioner would issue regulations limiting the Jewish right to buy land from Arabs, and in some areas prohibiting it altogether.

The 1939 White Paper was received by the Jews with horror, by the Arabs without any great outburst of anger, though with protests against the immigration of yet anothei 75,000 Jews. Six months later the Second World War broke out; the Jews wanted to fight against Hitler's Germany, but they did not want to fight for the British, who, they held, had betrayed them. The Palestine administration issued strict regulations limiting Jewish immigration, and applied them strictly. In the early years of the war, the German government rounded up thousands of Jews, and provided them (for heavy payment) with transport to Palestine and with valueless entry permits. These refugee ships, packed with people who had lost everything in the world, arrived in the harbours of the Promised Land, and the British refused to let the people ashore. Some ships were turned back, one or two sank, some were diverted to Mauritius or Cyprus, where the passengers were detained until the end of the war.

In the government's view, this immigration was illegal, being outside the quota permitted by the regulations laid down under the White Paper. Moreover, the government feared that these crowds of refugees might include a few devoted members of the German intelligence service, whose activities might be very dangerous. The Jews on the other hand maintained that the White Paper itself was illegal because contrary to the terms of the League's mandate, and they were supported in this view by the unanimous opinion of the League's permanent mandates commission, the body responsible for supervising the work of mandatory powers.

The refusal of the unimaginative British to consider these despairing refugees from Nazi tyranny in any other light than 'illegal immigrants' turned all Jewish feeling in Palestine against Britain. The Jews came to regard the British administration as cruelly anti-Jewish, as much so as Hitler or Nebuchadnezzar. The older generation of Zionists lost influence, and a more extreme faction came to the fore, a faction which determined that the speedy establishment of a state entirely Jewish and entirely independent was the only hope of saving their people in central Europe. The most fanatical among them began to use terrorism with the object of ending the British administration. From 1944 onwards there were murders and bombings and general sabotage. Jewish terrorism was answered by Arab terrorism; the extremists on both sides seemed agreed in their aim of making civilised life in Palestine impossible.

By the end of the war, it was plain that the situation in Palestine had passed beyond the control of the British authorities in Jerusalem and London. The Jews were now demanding an independent Jewish state with the Jordan river as its eastern boundary, and an annual immigration of 100,000 Jews to populate it. Britain was exhausted; the question now was what line the United States would take. The United States was uncertain. President Roosevelt was disposed on general principles to distrust British 'colonial' administration. There was a strong Zionist movement among American Jews, and many Congressmen thought it wise to curry favour with Zionist voters. On the other hand, a new oil-field had been discovered in 1938 near Dhahran in Saudi Arabia, and the concession for the oil was awarded to the Arabian-American Oil Company. The United States now had large and increasing oil interests in the Arab countries, and the Marshall Plan for reconstructing war-devastated Europe was reckoned to need enormous quantities of Arabian oil, if it was to succeed. Thus there were reasons for American uncertainty over Palestine; the State Department favoured the Arabs, the politicians (thinking of the Jewish vote) supported the Jews. On the whole, both Roosevelt and his successor President Truman favoured the plan for admitting 100,000 Jewish immigrants a year into Palestine.

In October 1945 an Anglo-American committee was formed to investigate the problem of Jewish immigration. It travelled widely among the Jewish camps in central Europe, as well as in Palestine and the neighbouring Arab countries. After six months' work it produced a unanimous report. It rejected partition; it recommended the immediate admission of 100,000 Jews – a number which would cover all the survivors from Hitler's concentration camps; the continuance of the British mandate; and the abandonment of the White Paper's restrictions on Jewish land purchase. The committee's only concession to the Arabs was that Arab labour should not be excluded from Jewish enterprises in Palestine. The report in fact was based on the hope that an Arab-Jewish state might still be possible, even with the balance tilted more and more in favour of the Jews.

The British government rejected the report as impracticably pro-Zionist. President Truman announced his approval of the proposal that the 100,000 Jewish refugees should be immediately admitted to Palestine, though he said that the rest of the committee's recommendations would need study. There was tension between London and Washington. The new British Labour government was negotiating for a badly needed American loan, and the British felt that in publicly supporting the Zionist demand, the president was driving a hard bargain.

The affairs of Palestine were now a matter of concern to the whole world, and the British foreign secretary, Ernest Bevin, felt that they should be considered by the United Nations. The old League had entrusted Britain with the mandate; now its successor should find a solution to the problem.

In May 1947 the UN Assembly discussed Palestine, and appointed a special commission of eleven members to visit the region and report. The commission found the country in much disorder, and its report was not unanimous. The majority report, signed by seven of the eleven members, recommended yet another scheme of partition, which was more attractive to the Jews than any other scheme, because it gave to the Jewish state nearly the whole of the Negev, the southern province stretching down to the Red Sea. Otherwise, the scheme was open to the same objections as earlier schemes of partition. The Arab and Jewish lands were to be so intertwined that without goodwill and co-operation there would be constant friction. In any case, there still remained the fundamental Arab objection to giving up an inch of Arab soil to the insatiable Zionist organisation. The British representative told the UN Assembly that Britain was not prepared to enforce any such scheme in the face of Arab resistance, and that unless Jews and Arabs could agree, Britain would surrender the mandate.

When the leaders on both sides at length came to realise that Britain really did mean to pull out of Palestine, they began to make plans for action. The Arab states were united in an Arab League, founded in 1945; but the League had no effective joint policy. Syria, Iraq and Egypt thought merely of occupying as much land as they could wrench away from the Jews. The chief Arab leader in Palestine, the Mufti of Jerusalem, seemed to want to keep the Arab areas as a sort of petty kingdom. King Abdullah of Jordan had the most sensible plan; he proposed to leave the

Map 15. Palestine 1920–1948

Jewish State as proposed
by the Peel Commission

International mandated area
proposed by the Peel Commission

0   20   50
miles

— · — · — 1949 Armistice line between
Israeli and Arab armies

Jews the lands allotted to them by the UN commission, and to take the Arab areas of Palestine into his own kingdom.

The first problem for the Jews was to secure a supply of arms, which they managed to obtain secretly, though all too slowly, from Czechoslovakia. Their strategic aim was to hold the ports of Haifa and Tel Aviv, with the road from Tel Aviv to Jerusalem; to this they must add the area of their agricultural settlements in the northern province of Galilee. Having secured these essentials, they would gain as much of the rest of the country as they could.

During the early months of 1948, both British and American policy over Palestine wavered to and fro. Meanwhile, fighting between Jews and Arabs grew worse and worse, with terrorist atrocities on both sides. As life became more dangerous and unpleasant, the civilian Arab population began to flee from their homes. Some fled of their own accord, some may have been urged to flee by their local leaders, some were intimidated by Jewish leaders who wanted them out of the way. By the end of 1948 the Arab population of Palestine was reduced to less than a quarter of what it had been a few years before.

On 14 May 1948, Britain surrendered the mandate; the British high commissioner and his staff left the country, and on the same day the Jewish leader Mr Ben Gurion proclaimed the establishment of the new state of Israel. As soon as he heard the news, President Truman announced that the United States would recognise the new state *de facto*.

The new state of Israel was immediately attacked on all sides by the armies of the Arab countries, and heavy fighting followed. By the middle of June, Israeli territory consisted of a good part of Galilee, a narrow strip of land ten to twenty miles wide along the Mediterranean, a narrow corridor connecting the coastal strip with Jerusalem, and the settlements in the Negev; these Negev areas were cut off from the rest of Israel by the enemy armies.

In May, the United Nations gave up the unworkable idea of appointing a commissioner to govern Palestine under the Trusteeship Council. Instead of this, it appointed a mediator, Count Bernadotte of Sweden, with the more limited objective of arranging peace terms. There was as yet no desire for peace, and Count Bernadotte found himself hated by both sides. He succeeded in arranging two temporary truces, and then he was murdered by Israeli terrorists. During the summer fighting the Israelis gained ground, and when the war broke out again in October they attacked in the south and drove the Egyptians before them, linking up once more with the isolated Israeli settlements in the Negev. One of the few Egyptian successes in this campaign was the defence of the village of Faluja by Captain Nasser, afterwards to become head of the Egyptian state. The Israelis pushed south to the Red Sea and established a seaport at Eilat, and in the north they conquered the remainder of Galilee; but they could not throw King Abdullah's troops out of the hill country west of Jordan. When the fighting ended, the state of Israel held a territory of an extraordinary shape: a solid block in Galilee and a much larger solid block in the Negev, connected by a very narrow coastal strip with its projecting corridor to Jerusalem.

The Arabs refused to recognise that the state of Israel existed. Between February and July 1949 the Arab armies one after another made armistice agreements with the Israeli army, arranging a cease-fire and delimiting temporary frontiers. But the Arab governments would have no dealings with the government of Israel. They were burdened with hundreds of thousands of refugees from Palestine; they had not the resources to provide them with homes, food and work; and these unfortunate people in the refugee camps became the responsibility of the United Nations Relief and Rehabilitation Administration. Meanwhile, the flow of Jewish immigrants into Israel continued. The Israeli government passed a law providing that any Jew from any part of the world should be entitled to Israeli citizenship if he chose to settle in Israel. This law has been one of the main obstacles to any peace settlement. The Arabs argue that as long as the law stands, no Israeli frontier can be permanent, for Israel will always demand more territory to accommodate her growing population. What then would be the use of making a peace treaty with a state which must of necessity be expansionist?

The refugees were a problem for Israel also. It could not be denied that they fled from their homes for fear of the Jewish armies and Jewish terrorists. If there were a true peace, Israel might be urged to take them back; but the Jewish state is not desirous of having a large Arab minority. Israelis sometimes suggest that the Arab governments could absorb a good many refugees if they chose, but they prefer to keep them in the refugee camps, because they are useful propaganda material against Israel. No government has a creditable record in this matter; the Arab and Jewish treatment of the refugees has been as inhuman as the British treatment of the 'illegal immigrants' during the last years of the mandate.

With no peace treaty signed, and with these hard and bitter feelings between the Israelis and the Arabs, the armistice of 1949 could not be expected to last very long. Though the regular armies were at peace, irregular Arab forces were soon recruited for the purpose of waging guerrilla war against Israeli settlements. Terrorism, employed both by Jews and Arabs against each other and against the British during the mandate, flared up again. The young men in the refugee camps made good recruits for the terrorist organisations. Apart from this, the eastern frontier was fairly quiet for some years.

The next trouble came from the south. By 1955 Captain Nasser, the gallant defender of Faluja, had become Colonel Nasser, head of the Egyptian state. Without risking large-scale fighting, Colonel Nasser reckoned that he could damage Israel severely by stopping her seaborne trade through the Suez Canal. Although the canal was declared by treaty to be open to the lawful commerce of all nations, Nasser systematically refused to allow Israeli ships to use it, and Israeli protests to Egypt and to the United Nations were ineffective. Nasser then went further. Israel had a seaport at Eilat, at the head of the Gulf of Aqaba. The waters of the gulf were regarded as part of the high seas and open to the ships of all the world, but the gulf was so narrow that it could be swept by gunfire. Nasser planted batteries of guns on the Egyptian shore of the gulf, and announced that any ship using the port of Eilat did so at her peril; in July 1955 one of his shells hit a British steamer. During 1955 and 1956 there were raids and counter-raids over the Egyptian border, and in September and October 1956 these raids became more serious.

No one could expect Israel to submit in silence to having her seaborne trade brought to a standstill. Unfortunately for Israel, when she decided to take action against Egypt, her action coincided with other important events.

During 1955, four countries in the Middle East formed an alliance called the Baghdad Pact; they were Turkey, Iraq, Iran and Pakistan. Turkey and Iran had special reasons for being nervous of Russia, and Iraq was ruled by a statesman named Nuri es-Said, who favoured a pro-Western policy for the countries in that region. Pakistan was a member of the British Commonwealth. The Baghdad Pact thus had the appearance of being an alliance against Russia. It was supported by Britain and the United States, and this in itself led Colonel Nasser to dislike it. Britain and the United States, he thought, were supporters of Israel, and if Iraq were closely linked with them, Iraq would be useless to him in his schemes of overthrowing Israel.

Colonel Nasser's main ambition moreover was to get the British troops out of his country. They had been there since 1882, and although Egypt had been independent since 1936, the British troops continued to occupy the canal zone. True, they did so by virtue of a treaty made by the independent Egyptian government, but Nasser saw no reason why the canal zone should be occupied by British or any other foreign troops. He set himself to negotiate a fresh treaty with Britain, and in October 1954 it was agreed that the last British troops should be out of Egypt by July 1956, though certain civilian technicians should remain for some years longer.

It was unfortunate that all this tension over the canal should be heightened by considerations of the cold war. Nasser wanted large quantities of foreign weapons to build up his military strength for the war against Israel. Knowing why he wanted the weapons, Britain and the United States would not sell him nearly as much as he wanted, so he bought arms from Czechoslovakia. This was unwelcome to the United States, which feared that the deal might bring Egypt under Soviet influence.

These matters of foreign policy were overshadowed for Colonel Nasser by the necessity of finding more land to feed his people, and in Egypt, finding more land means taking more water from the Nile to push back the desert. Colonel Nasser had a plan for building a gigantic dam across the Nile at Aswan. There was already a large dam at Aswan, built by the British; it held enough water to supply the country's irrigation needs for a whole year. But it would be dwarfed by Nasser's proposed new dam, which would hold enough water for five years' supply. It was to be built in stages, the first stage costing £90 million, and Nasser applied to Britain and the United States for financial grants. Late in 1955, the two governments offered him £25 million towards the first stage, and they suggested that the World Bank might provide the rest of the money. But in May 1956 Nasser recognised Mao Tse-Tung's communist government in China. This infuriated the United States, already irritated with Nasser because of his dealings with the communist world and for other reasons. The United States government withdrew its offer of financial help for the Aswan dam project, and both Britain and the World Bank followed the American lead.

Colonel Nasser replied to this in a fighting speech. He declared that the West was trying to stop Egypt from developing; Egypt must have the high dam, and he would take over the Suez Canal and build the dam with the profits which would otherwise go to the Suez Canal Company.

This caused a world-wide outcry. The Suez Canal Company was an international company established by treaty, whose agreement with Egypt did not expire until 1968. All nations disliked the idea that a government should break an agreement which still had twelve years to run; all maritime nations disliked the idea that Egypt might at any time close the canal to their shipping, as she had for some time been closing it to Israeli shipping. They doubted whether Egypt would run the canal efficiently; they feared that she would skimp the maintenance of the canal in order to finance the Aswan dam. Twenty governments met, and agreed to set up an international board to replace the canal company, but they could not agree on what the new board should do. Russia and three others thought that it should be merely advisory to the Egyptian government, and that the running of the canal should be left in Egyptian hands; Britain, America and the fourteen other members thought that the board itself should run the canal on behalf of Egypt. The Egyptian government insisted that it would permit no one to run the canal on its behalf, so the discussions ended in deadlock, and the scheme of an international board was dropped.

However, everyone wanted to see the canal maintained in working order and open to the shipping of the world. In October 1956 the matter came before the United Nations, and discussions there gave some hopes that a workable agreement might be reached. In fact, the broad outlines were agreed on, and it seemed that all that remained was to work out the details.

But while the Security Council was discussing this problem, the news came that Israel, weary of raiding and counter-raiding, and seeing no prospect of reaching any agreement over her seaborne trade, had invaded Egypt in force. The United States proposed a resolution to the Security Council, calling on Israel to withdraw her invading force, and calling on all member states not to use force or to threaten to use force. Britain and France vetoed this resolution; this was the first time that Britain had vetoed any resolution in the Security Council. They did more: they acted together in calling on both the Israeli and the Egyptian armies to keep ten miles away from the banks of the canal, and they threatened that if necessary, British and French troops would land to protect the canal. Israel accepted this ultimatum, Egypt refused it. British and French troops landed at Port Said in the north, and began to fight their way along the line of the canal. Colonel Nasser called on the United Nations for help. Meanwhile, he blocked the canal by sinking ships in it; confiscated British and French civilian property in Egypt; cancelled his 1954 agreement with Britain; and occupied the army base in the canal zone. The Syrian government gave him valuable help by cutting the pipe-line which brought Iraqi oil across the desert to Mediterranean ports for shipment to the West.

The General Assembly of the United Nations took action. It passed resolutions calling on Israel to withdraw her troops, and calling on all member states to refrain from fighting and from sending military equipment into the region. The resolutions called for compliance within twelve hours. They were carried by sixty-four votes to five; only Australia and New Zealand voted with Britain, France and Israel against them, while Canada and South Africa, with four others, abstained. Britain explained that she had acted as she did in order to prevent a general war all over the Middle East, which could easily develop into a third world war. The Assembly found this explanation unconvincing. The three countries gave way, and the last of their troops was out of Egypt again by Christmas. A United Nations force was organised to keep the peace on the Israeli-Egyptian border, and the United Nations undertook the task of clearing the Suez Canal for use once more. The Soviet Union declared that it was unconstitutional for the UN to take peace keeping action of this kind on the basis of a resolution in the General Assembly; the matter should have been dealt with by the Security Council. It refused to pay its share of the expenses, maintaining that the 'aggressors', namely Britain, France and Israel, should be made to pay the whole cost of the operations.

No convincing explanation can yet be given of Britain's action. In his memoirs the prime minister of the day (Mr Anthony Eden, later Lord Avon) makes it clear that he regarded Colonel Nasser as a ruler who, like Hitler and Mussolini, thought peaceful words and reasonable argument a sign of weakness, and would take all he could get. In Mr Eden's view, Hitler and Mussolini might have been stopped if they had been resolutely opposed before they became too strong, and their enemies (notably Britain and France) had made a great mistake in being too timid to take resolute action. Nasser's action over the canal seemed to Mr Eden similar to some of Hitler's early actions, and he was resolved not to repeat the mistake of being too timid in opposing him. Mr Eden claimed that he had reason to hope that the United States would support him, and he blamed the United States for not doing so; if the United States had been firm, matters need never, he thought, have reached the stage of military action.

Colonel Nasser's action was certainly high-handed, and was condemned by many countries. Even so, the Anglo-French invasion of Egypt looked bad. It gave the impression that the British especially were trying to regain military control of the canal, and this at a moment when peaceful negotiations were going on in New York. It also gave the impression that Britain and France were allied to Israel and that the three countries had arranged the affair together. Britain and France could surely have foreseen the blocking of the canal, the cutting of the oil pipeline, and the hostile vote in the UN General Assembly. Britain and France came out of the affair with diminished reputations, Colonel Nasser on the other hand became the hero and leader of the Arab world.

The Suez affair was a defeat for Israel, and after it, matters went on much as before. The Iraqi statesman Nuri es-Said was murdered, and the new Iraqi government abandoned the Baghdad Pact and followed Nasser's lead. Egypt continued to buy arms from communist countries, and Soviet Russia began to give more support to the Arab countries against Israel. The canal was cleared in due course, and Egypt ran it without any international advisory board. Israeli ships were still barred from the canal; Egyptian guns still commanded the Gulf of Aqaba; Arab terrorists and guerrillas still made life in Israel unpleasant and dangerous; the refugees in their camps were still without prospects of resettlement.

In June 1967 Israel acted once more, this time relying on her own strength. In the so-called Six Day War her troops invaded Egypt, Syria and Jordan; they won a complete victory. Israel occupied the whole of the Sinai peninsula and reached the banks of the canal; thus she put out of action the Egyptian batteries in the Gulf of Aqaba. She conquered all the land still held by Jordan to the west of the river, so that the Jordan river became the eastern frontier line of Israel. In Syria, she was content to conquer a narrow strip of high ground near the frontier, where Syrian guns had been planted to shell Israeli villages. Not only did Israel thus gain a good deal of territory, but she gained much more natural and defensible frontiers. On the other hand, with the land taken from Jordan, Israel acquired a large Arab population; she also acquired possession of some of the refugee camps and the responsibility of their unhappy inhabitants.

Egypt again blocked the Suez Canal, and after the fighting ended, ineffectual peace negotiations were begun. The United Nations appointed a new mediator, Dr Jarring, who found, as his predecessors had done, that there was very little will for peace. Six years later the peace negotiations were still continuing, having made very little progress. Meanwhile, Arab terrorism and Israeli reprisals became more violent. The United States continued to support Israel, and the Soviet Union came out openly on the side of the Arab states and sent them large quantities of arms.

In October 1973, Egyptian and Syrian troops attacked Israel in force. After three meetings of the Security Council had ended in deadlock, America and Russia saw the danger of the situation; they held private talks and introduced a joint cease-fire resolution, which the Security Council adopted.

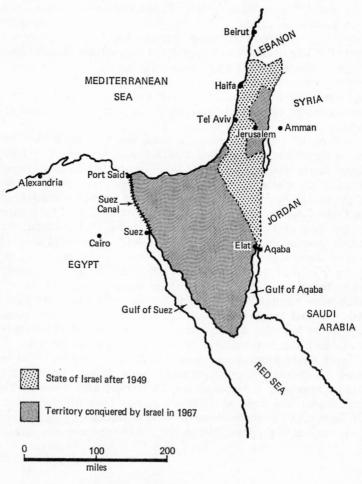

Map 16. Israel since 1948

12   Ireland

It has often been said that the English can never understand the Irish; and many novels have been written describing the bewilderment of the Englishman living in Ireland and facing a people whose ways of thought and behaviour are so different from his own.

Ireland is a picturesque but a poor country: almost devoid of minerals (save for the ubiquitous peat), with great stretches of mountain, moor and bog, and with a damp climate more suited to pasture and root crops than to cereals. When Britain was under Roman rule, Rome never attempted to conquer Ireland. Nevertheless, in the first centuries of the Christian era, Ireland developed an impressive Christian civilisation, and Irish saints and missionaries brought the gospel to northern Britain and many parts of pagan Europe.

The Irish monasteries and cathedrals were wrecked by the Danes; and although the Church survived, Ireland relapsed into tribal disorder, which was made worse rather than better when the English began interfering in Irish affairs. Ireland was the oldest of English colonies, and the most mismanaged. As H. A. L. Fisher put it, she was 'often invaded but never subdued'. The English made repeated efforts to conquer Ireland and – according to their own ideas – to civilise her, but they never finished the job.

The English contact with Ireland goes back to the time of King Henry II, 800 years ago. King Henry himself was not interested in Ireland; he had far too much to do in reorganising the administration of England, in quarrelling with Thomas Becket, and in pursuing ambitious schemes of conquest in France. But a group of his barons asked his permission to go over on a private venture and conquer Irish lands for themselves if they could; and he gave his permission. They found the conquest an easy matter; the Irish were divided by tribal rivalries, and the armoured and disciplined knights had no trouble in dispersing the lightly armed tribal levies. It did not take the English long to capture the principal seaports and a block of country in the east and southeast of Ireland. Gradually there grew up an English colony, owning allegiance to the English king and looking to England for support against the constant border raids by the Irish whom they had dispossessed.

The first result of the English invasion was merely to give Ireland a new aristocracy. Many of the English barons married Irish wives, learned the Irish language and Irish customs, and settled down on the estates they had won, to play the game of Irish tribal politics. But nothing could alter the fact that as more English arrived to make their fortunes at Irish expense, the Irish people had to lose their land. As in Wales, so in Ireland, the English gradually occupied the fertile valleys, and pushed the Celts back into the bogs and mountains.

King Edward I of England (1272–1307), coming to the throne a whole century after the conquest began, did what he could to organise the English settlement in Ireland. He was a great administrator, and under him Ireland made progress both in government and in commercial prosperity; it might have made still more progress if he had been able to give Ireland his full attention instead of spending so much time in hammering away at the Scots and the Welsh. After Edward's death his work was undone. His son Edward II invaded Scotland, to be soundly defeated by Robert Bruce at Bannockburn; and unfortunately for Ireland, Robert Bruce's brother had the bright idea of leading a Scottish army into Ireland to attack the English there and so prevent the English king from coming back to Scotland to avenge his defeat. This led to years of bitter fighting up and down Ireland; the English settlers suffered severely, though neither the Scots nor the Irish could drive them out of the country altogether. The English hung on grimly behind their fortifications. Their settlement, significantly called the Pale, was divided into counties; and they had their own parliament and governed themselves much as their countrymen did in England. Outside the Pale was the mass of tribal Ireland, sullenly and resentfully awaiting its opportunity of revenge. England was too busy, first with the Hundred Years War against France, and afterwards with the Wars of the Roses, to make any serious effort to restore the situation in Ireland.

England's next serious attempt to settle the Irish problem was made in Elizabeth's reign; and by then the problem was made much worse, because England had now become Protestant. The English despised 'the wild Irish' as savages and Papists; the Irish hated the English as brutal conquerors and heretics. In 1580, eight years before the Armada, King Philip of Spain landed a force of troops in Kerry; thinking, like Edward Bruce before him, that he might give England occupation and anxiety in Ire-

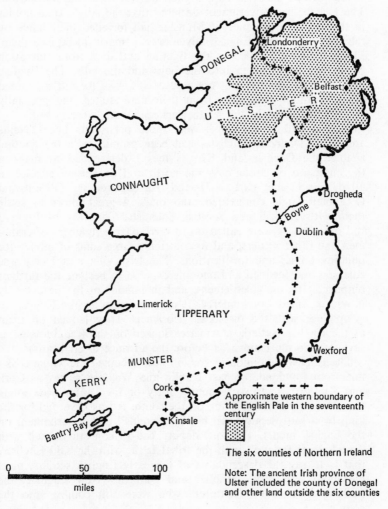

DONEGAL

Londonderry

ULSTER

Belfast

CONNAUGHT

Drogheda

Boyne

Dublin

Limerick

TIPPERARY

Wexford

MUNSTER

KERRY

Cork

– + – + – + –

Approximate western boundary of
the English Pale in the seventeenth
century

Kinsale

Bantry Bay

The six counties of Northern Ireland

Note: The ancient Irish province of
Ulster included the county of Donegal
and other land outside the six counties

0	50	100

miles

Map 17.   Ireland

land and weaken her as an opponent in Europe and in the New World. The Spanish expedition was caught by an English force and destroyed, and a later expedition against Kinsale fared no better; but the Irish kept a guerrilla war flickering on and on. The Elizabethan government declared that the Anglo-Irish nobles in the southern province of Munster had forfeited their lands by rebellion, and fresh English adventurers came in to replace them. Many Irish were killed in the fighting and died from starvation when they were driven into the bogs and the hills. The English plantation of Munster was not a success; few of the settlers gained much profit or enjoyment from their new estates, and gradually the English effort in the south slackened once more.

In the north, the English were more persistent. The O'Neills and the O'Donnells of Ulster had been prominent in the fighting against the English, and King James I determined to make a thorough job of conquering the north and so putting an end to all danger in that part of Ireland. He declared the O'Neill and O'Donnell lands confiscated, and made a great effort to settle them with English and Scottish colonists. The City of London and other towns were called on to recruit large numbers of craftsmen and other settlers, and to contribute large sums of money for building homes and fortifications. The Irish village of Derry was enlarged and fortified at London's expense to become the furthest outpost of the new settlement, and in honour of the parent City it was renamed Londonderry. It did not occur to the English to sympathise with the displaced tribesmen. They looked on them as the English settlers in America looked on the Red Indians, as savages who must move on before the advance of civilisation.

The English dominion in Ireland now occupied the whole coastline from Londonderry past Dublin and Wexford as far as Cork and Kinsale: a strip of country forty or fifty miles wide along the east coast but narrowing on the south. It was governed for the king by a lord deputy, assisted by a council and a parliament on the English model. The lord deputy had to concern himself with the whole of Ireland: with the tribal Irish; with the 'Old English', that is to say the descendants of the early English settlers, most of whom were still Catholic; and with the 'New English', the pushing Protestant adventurers who were still coming into the country.

In Ireland, as in England, Roman Catholics were excluded by law from public life. But in the early seventeenth century the law was less strictly enforced in Ireland than in England. Catholics were well established in local government, and in the first Irish parliament of James I nearly half the members were Catholics, a state of affairs which would have been unthinkable at Westminster. Thus in James's reign the lord deputy presided over an Irish administration which was by no means entirely foreign and hostile to the majority of the Irish people. The question was whether the increasing numbers and influence of the Protestant English settlers would allow a genuine Anglo-Irish society and government to develop. The Catholics in Ireland were clinging to the position they held; many of the new English settlers despised them as uncivilised, and feared them as the allies of Catholic Spain. Men of this kind had no idea of building a mixed society; they erected a social barrier against the Irish Catholics which was as impassable as the most rigid of colour bars in the world today.

This did not prevent Catholic Irishmen from enlisting in large numbers in the royal army, and in King Charles I's day the lord deputy, Strafford, conceived the idea of bringing over an Irish army to fight for the king in England against his rebellious parliament. The idea came to nothing, and Strafford was executed; but from that time onward, the idea of an Irish army under royal control was a danger always present in English minds. After Strafford's death, the Irish rose in despair, and were joined – reluctantly and with much heart-searching – by the Old English. The parliament in England, having won its civil war against the king, replied with Cromwell's short and savage campaign of 1649. All that English statesmanship could think of was to slaughter as many of the Irish 'rebels' as possible and to send over fresh parties of English and Scottish settlers, driving the surviving Irish into the desolate wastes of Connaught. There was no question of inquiring into Irish grievances and trying to remedy them. The population of Ireland was perhaps reduced by as much as a third. Some fled to the Continent, many were sold as slaves to the sugar plantations in the West Indies. Two-thirds of the land of Ireland was taken over by Protestant settlers and land speculators.

When Charles II became king in 1660, he was attracted by Strafford's idea of raising an Irish army which would not be subject to the control of the parliament at Westminster. His successor, James II, who was a Catholic, carried out the scheme with energy. With James's accession, Irish hopes revived: a Catholic king would at least not despise them on account of their religion.

For a time, their hopes were justified; but unfortunately for the Irish, James II had but a short run. He became king in 1685 and lost his throne in 1688, the fear of being invaded by an army of Irish Catholics being one of the causes which drove England into rebellion. King James fled to France and became the pensioner of the French king. He was succeeded by his daughter Mary and her husband, the Dutchman William of Orange, who reigned jointly. William at once set himself to organise Protestant England into a principal member of the European coalition which he was building against the power of France.

During his short reign, James had energetically remodelled the government of Ireland in the interests of his fellow-Catholics. Judges and magistrates, mayors and councillors, army officers, government officials of all kinds were now Irish Catholics. Thousands of English settlers fled from Ireland back to England; those who remained were the tough ones who would rather fight than surrender. In March 1689 the Irish rose for King James; they gleefully despoiled the English, looting and burning houses, slaughtering livestock, and turning the country into a desert. When King James's army set out from Dublin to conquer Ulster, the surviving Protestants abandoned and destroyed their homes, broke down the bridges and sank the ferry-boats, and took refuge in Londonderry.

The rumour spread that on a certain day in December 1688 all surviving Protestants in Ireland were to be massacred. Shortly before that day, a detachment of Irish troops presented themselves at the gates of Londonderry with a warrant requiring the corporation to provide them with quarters in the city. The corporation had been remodelled by King James, and except for one English Catholic, was composed entirely of Irishmen. They were disposed to obey the royal warrant. But a group of thirteen apprentices took matters into their own hands: they shut the gate in the face of the King's officers and called their fellow-Protestants to arms. The royal troops were too few to besiege the city, and retired. This bold action by the apprentice boys of Derry is still commemorated every year.

A few weeks later King James came to Ireland, with a force of French troops to stiffen the half-trained Irish levies. The city of Londonderry was closely besieged for over three months, but was relieved in the nick of time by an English force landed from the sea. In 1690 William III came to Ireland with a strong Anglo-Dutch army, and on 1 July he defeated his rival at the battle of the Boyne. The anniversary of William's victory is still commemorated by the Protestants of Northern Ireland, where 'King Billy on his white horse' is a hero to this day. King James fled back to France; and his Irish troops, even with French help, could not resist the advance of the English. The campaign ended with the surrender to the English of the town of Limerick, in which the last hopes of the Irish had been fixed. When, after a gallant resistance, the garrison capitulated, they received the honours of war. All who preferred to go to France and enlist in French service were allowed to do so, and some thousands went. This 'Flight of the Wild Geese' took from Ireland many of its choicest spirits; they scattered over Europe, and found in foreign service scope for the talents and energy which the English refused them in their own country. In the nineteenth century a Macmahon was a marshal of France, and an O'Donnell prime minister of Spain.

The military capitulation of Limerick was supplemented by a civil treaty, the first clause of which promised that Catholics in Ireland should be as free to practise their religion as they had been in the time of Charles II, who had died six years earlier. But as early as 1697 the restored Protestant parliament in Dublin broke this clause of the treaty by imposing harsher restrictions on the Catholics. Throughout the greater part of the eighteenth century a Catholic in Ireland had no vote and could hold no public office. He could not attend a university, and was forbidden to send his children abroad for their education. He could not teach in a school or practise in law or medicine. He might lease land, but not buy it. If he already owned land, it must be equally divided at his death among his sons; he could not bequeath it by his will. It was not made illegal for him to attend Mass, or for the priest to celebrate it. The Irish parliament did not attempt the impossible task of suppressing Catholicism by force. The object of these penal laws was to ensure that Catholics should remain politically powerless and socially inferior; and that as much land as possible should remain available for Protestant settlers. During the eighteenth century, six-sevenths of the land of Ireland was owned by Protestants, many of whom were Englishmen who lived in England and employed professional agents to collect their rents for them. The absentee landlord became one of the most hated symbols of English oppression. The eighteenth century was not a good period in the history of the Church of England, and in Ireland there were not only absentee landlords but also absentee Protestant clergy, who drew their stipends from the enforced contributions of their Catholic parishioners.

For nearly a century, the English settlement in Ireland enjoyed a modest prosperity, though its trade was closely restricted in the interests of its competitors in England, and many Ulster Protestants emigrated to America. The Irish however lay in utter despair; their best leaders were in exile, making their careers in foreign service.

Irish hopes began to revive during the war of American Independence, when England was hard pressed in fighting not only the American colonists but also the combined forces of France and Spain. The Dublin parliament threw up a real statesman, Henry Grattan, who succeeded in obtaining some concessions from Westminster. Some of the restrictions on Irish trade were abolished; the Westminster parliament gave up its right to control the proceedings of the parliament in Dublin; and some of the penal laws were eased; in particular, Catholics were at last permitted to buy land. Grattan wished to go much further: 'The Irish Protestant', he said, 'can never be free while the Irish Catholic is a slave.' But far-reaching reforms needed long years of campaigning, and Grattan was not given time; the French revolution broke out, and England was too frightened to make the concessions that would have saved Ireland.

Grattan had given Ireland new hope, and a political society calling itself the United Irishmen set out to continue his work. Political life in Ireland was reserved for members of the Anglican Church, the Church of Ireland; until 1780 the Presbyterians of Ulster, like the Catholics, were excluded from it. The United Irishmen combined Catholics and Presbyterians against the English oligarchy and the parliament in Dublin. There was at that time no religious bitterness in the north; there were no Orange lodges, and the Catholic priests had not yet turned to politics. The United Irishmen hoped for a self-governing Ireland based on the ideals of the American and French revolutions, but owning allegiance to the Crown.

In 1793 the government went so far as to allow Catholics to vote, though it still debarred them from sitting in the Dublin parliament. Two years later the Viceroy, Lord Fitzwilliam, gave the United Irishmen grounds for hoping that the penal laws would be further relaxed, if not altogether repealed; but the government at Westminster said that Lord Fitzwilliam had exceeded his instructions, and recalled him.

This was a bitter disappointment to the United Irishmen. Next year, only bad weather prevented a strong French invasion force from landing in Bantry Bay; and the United Irishmen, feeling that nothing more was to be hoped for from England, made the fateful decision to turn to violence and look for help to France. The government, having no disciplined troops available in Ireland, tried to forestall rebellion by using the undisciplined Protestant yeomanry to disarm the Catholics, with the result that the frail comradeship between the Catholics and the Ulster Presbyterians broke down. The government had plenty of grounds in past history for fearing a Catholic Irish rising; and it no doubt reckoned that in such an emergency the Presbyterians would rally to their fellow-Protestants rather than make common cause with with the Irish rebels. The government's policy of breaking up the alliance between Catholics and Presbyterians succeeded: the Catholics formed defence associations, and the Presbyterians formed Orange lodges, so called in honour of William of Orange, their hero 'King Billy'. The hope of a united Ireland disappeared, and in 1798 the Catholics, now led by their priests, rose in rebellion. The bitterness that today divides Protestants from Catholics in Northern Ireland arose in those days when the United Irishmen felt themselves betrayed.

The rebellion of Ninety-Eight was easily put down, and Pitt's government in England then threw away another chance of making a peaceful settlement in Ireland. Pitt was a great statesman and would have preferred to follow Grattan's policy. Having already given Irish Catholics the vote, he proposed to allow them to sit in parliament; to abolish the Dublin parliament and make Ireland part of the United Kingdom, with adequate Irish representation at Westminster; and to recognise the Catholic Church in Ireland and give it financial support. This programme would leave the land question untouched, but it would have done a great deal to win Irish loyalty. Pitt however was leader of the Tory party, and was unable to carry his party with him. In 1800 he managed to abolish the Dublin parliament: the Catholics voted for the abolition because they trusted Pitt to carry out the rest of his scheme, and the wealthy owners of pocket boroughs were compensated for their loss. But King George III and the Tory Party refused to consider Catholic emancipation. As for paying 'Popish priests', the idea was unthinkable in evangelical, No-Popery England. Pitt had made promises which he could not fulfil; he resigned, and Ireland once again felt betrayed.

Meanwhile, the economic condition of Ireland went from bad to worse, and the Westminster parliament of landowners, even though strengthened in both Houses by the Irish members, did nothing to remedy matters. The population increased to eight million, twice today's figure. Farms were more and more subdivided. No improvement was possible in agricultural methods. Nothing was done to lighten the burden of rent or to improve the position of the poor tenant farmer. In 1846 and 1847 the potato crop failed; over half a million people died of starvation and disease, and in the next four years another million emigrated to America, there to prosper both in business and in politics, and to keep burning a steady flame of hatred for England.

The policy of admitting Catholics to sit in parliament and to take part in public life generally, which Pitt had failed to carry through in 1800, was at last carried through in 1829. Ireland had found a new leader, Daniel O'Connell, who saw that the Catholic majority vote, if properly organised, could be a more powerful weapon against the alien government than unorganised terrorism and agrarian crime. He formed his Catholic Association, in which the parish priests were officers, to control the way in which the Catholic vote was used. Protestant candidates, even those who were well known and personally popular, were defeated in the elections by Catholics, who by law were ineligible to take their seats in parliament. The Duke of Wellington was at the head of the ministry in England. He recognised the force of discipline; he realised that the discipline which O'Connell had used to defy the electoral law might equally well be used to set Ireland in flames from end to end. As he told the House of Lords, Wellington had passed his life in war, and a great part of it in civil war; and he was not prepared to face large-scale civil war in Ireland. He split the Tory party; but he carried through Catholic emancipation; and O'Connell himself and some of his Catholic followers entered the House of Commons at Westminster. Wellington is not the only English party leader to split his party over the Irish question; nor is he the only British general to be of Irish origin.

Disraeli summed up the problem of Ireland as being 'a starving people, an alien Church, and an absentee aristocracy'. It was Disraeli's rival Gladstone who said, on first becoming prime minister in 1868, 'My mission is to pacify Ireland'. He began at once by disestablishing the 'alien Church'; the Anglican Church in Ireland was set up as a self-governing corporation, with about half its old revenue paid to it and the other half kept in hand for charitable purposes.

In 1870 Gladstone carried the first of a long series of laws for improving the Irish land system. The long campaign over Irish land was fought by Gladstone and his successors against the English landowning interest and the House of Lords, and by the Irish themselves against the landlords and their agents. Burning, cattle-maiming and murder were the weapons used by the Irish peasantry, and their treatment of the unlucky agent Captain Boycott has given a new word to the English language. In his novel *The Eustace Diamonds*, published in 1876, Trollope describes the melancholy and ineffective politician Lord Fawn as having an income of £5,000 a year (a good round sum in those days) from his Irish estate in Tipperary, 'not at all a desirable country to live in'; the two villages on the estate are named Kill-lord and Kill-agent. Eventually, at the beginning of the twentieth century, the absentee landlords were bought out and agricultural co-operative societies were launched. With these reforms, and with the introduction of effective local government, the settlement of the Irish land problem was at last placed in Irish hands.

But Gladstone knew that Ireland would not be pacified by the settlement of the two problems of the absentee aristocracy and the alien Church. In 1873 an Irish leader formed the Home Rule League, and Home Rule became the ultimate object for which all Irish politicians campaigned. The idea of Home Rule at once raised the question of Ulster, where the Protestants were opposed to the idea of being governed by a predominantly Catholic government in Dublin. Gladstone introduced Irish Home Rule bills in 1886 and 1892, but he split his party in doing so and failed to carry either bill through parliament.

In 1914, after scenes of bitter parliamentary disorder, Gladstone's disciple Asquith succeeded in placing his Home Rule Act on the statute book. But the Ulstermen formed a militant organisation to resist Home Rule; the Irish nationalists formed a counter-organisation; there was drilling and gun-running; and some of the British army officers stationed in Ireland embarrassed the government by saying that they would resign their commissions rather than go into action against the Ulster volunteers. Ireland seemed on the brink of civil war; but at this moment the First World War broke out and the Home Rule Act was temporarily suspended.

It was generally expected that the question would be taken up again at the end of the war; but the extreme wing of the Irish nationalist party, which called itself Sinn Fein, 'Ourselves Alone', would not wait till then. As in 1688 and 1798, it seemed to them that England's danger was Ireland's opportunity. At Easter 1916 they began an armed revolt in Dublin and proclaimed the establishment of the Irish republic; they elected a parliament, the Dail, and set up their own administration. In spite of being fully engaged in the war against Germany, the British government was able to put down the open rebellion; but it could not put down the guerrilla warfare and miscellaneous terrorism which followed it.

When the German war was over, the British government came back to the Irish question. It decided that Ulster's refusal to be governed from Dublin as one province of a united Ireland was a fact which must be accepted. The Home Rule Act of 1914 was replaced by the Government of Ireland (Partition) Act of 1920. Six counties of Northern Ireland were separated from the rest of the country; they became a self-governing province in local affairs, but continued to send members to the parliament at Westminster.

Sinn Fein of course would not accept this arrangement; like their forefathers of Ninety-Eight, they stood for a united Ireland. The guerrilla war went on. The British government recruited a force of auxiliary troops, whom the Irish nicknamed (from the colour of their uniforms) 'the Black-and-Tans'; and horrible excesses were committed on both sides.

After a year of this bloodshed, the British government, under the Welsh prime minister Lloyd George, realised that it must choose between putting out its full strength not only to conquer southern Ireland but thereafter to hold it down indefinitely – or else negotiating with the men it called terrorists and rebels. It chose to negotiate, and there ensued weeks and months of delicate diplomacy. The Irish were divided: the party led by Cosgrave and O'Higgins was prepared to accept dominion status and membership of the Commonwealth, while the party of De Valera insisted on preserving the independence of the republic which had been set up in 1916. In the end, the moderates won, and in December 1921 they signed the Treaty of London, which set up a new dominion called the Irish Free State, consisting of twenty-six counties, while the remaining six counties of Ireland composed the self-governing province of Northern Ireland, as proposed by the Act of 1920.

De Valera and his party immediately denounced the Treaty men as traitors to their country. They formed the Irish Republican Army, and for more than a year they waged civil war against the Free State authorities, this being an Irish affair in which the British took no part. In 1923, elections were held for the Irish parliament, the Dail, Cosgrave winning sixty-three seats and De Valera forty-four. In that year the government forces had so much gained the upper hand that De Valera ordered the IRA to cease fire, though the members of his party still refused to take an oath of allegiance to the king as head of the Commonwealth, or to occupy their seats in the Dail.

However, a silent boycott of parliament is a profitless policy for a strong opposition party; political parties exist to obtain power. When the next elections were held in 1927, De Valera's party increased its representation to fifty-seven seats, Cosgrave winning sixty-one. De Valera then decided to recognise the Treaty and become leader of the constitutional opposition in the Dail. Five years later he had his reward: his party won the elections and he became prime minister.

Having attained power, De Valera naturally set himself to

achieve by peaceful means what he had failed to achieve by war. Between 1932 and 1936 he carried through legislation which abolished the Irish senate; abolished the office of governor-general; abolished the right of appeal from the Irish courts to the judicial committee of the privy council; deprived Irishmen of their status as British subjects ; and replaced the king's prerogative position as head of the Commonwealth by a statutory authority to act in that capacity on behalf of the Irish Free State. De Valera had thus transformed the Free State into a republic within the Commonwealth, recognising the king only as far as it might suit Irish convenience to do so. In 1937 he completed his constitutional work by promulgating a new republican constitution, in which the governor-general was replaced by a president.

These changes were not carried out without a certain amount of heat and difficulty. Like any other politician, De Valera had to win support from blocks of voters whose allegiance was doubtful. He set himself to win the vote of the Irish farmers, and he appealed to them by attacking the long-standing arrangement by which the landlords had been bought out. In 1903 the British government had transferred the land from the landlords to the tenants, and instead of paying rent for ever, the tenants were to pay 'land annuities' for a period of sixty-three years. The annuities were paid to the British government, which created land stock for the benefit of the former landlords and used the annuities to finance the interest payments. De Valera won the farmers' vote by promising to cease paying the annuities to the British government and retain them in Ireland. When he carried out his promise, there was trouble. The British government put a heavy duty on imports from the Free State so as to compensate it for the loss of the annuities: the Free State retaliated; and for more than three years the two countries carried on a trade war, from which the Irish dairy farmers and cattle-breeders suffered severely. To make up for the loss of British manufactures, the De Valera government set itself to develop Irish manufacturing industry.

In 1938, the two countries came to an understanding. De Valera agreed to pay £10 million in final settlement of the annuities. The trade war, with its heavy penal duties and its restrictions on imports, was ended. The last relic of British rule was abolished: the three naval bases which the 1921 treaty had left in British hands were handed over to Irish control, the Irish government merely promising that it would never allow them to be used by Britain's enemies. The final step towards independence was taken in 1949, when the Republic of Ireland left the Commonwealth. The high commissioners in Dublin and London were replaced by ambassadors. The Irish, being no longer citizens of a Commonwealth country, became foreigners in Britain; but it was agreed that though foreign, they should not be deemed to be foreign.

There remained only the question of Ulster, or more strictly, the question of the United Kingdom province of Northern Ireland, which did not correspond exactly with the ancient Irish province of Ulster. The Orangemen were still determined not to submit to being governed from Dublin: even more determined now that the republic was headed by the Sinn Fein leader of 1916. De Valera was content for the time being to leave the matter open. Perhaps in the course of a generation or two, Catholic immigrants into Ulster might come to outvote the Orangemen, and then Ulster might vote itself peacefully into a united Ireland. But the Orangemen were just as alive to this possibility as the republican government; and the more Catholics came into the six counties, the greater became the Protestant fears. Protestants and Catholics in Northern Ireland lived in separate communities, almost like whites and blacks in South Africa. There were Protestant streets and Catholic streets, Protestant schools and Catholic schools, Protestant firms and Catholic firms; it was possible for a child to be born into one community and grow into middle age without having any effective social contact with members of the other community.

So matters remained for another twenty years. No government in Dublin could formally abandon the claim for a united Ireland, and there were plenty of Irish-American orators to make St Patrick's Day speeches in protest against the existence of Northern Ireland as a province 'supported on British bayonets'. But the matter was not pressed, and the British and Irish governments remained on friendly terms.

Then, at the close of the 1960s, trouble broke out in Northern Ireland. Marches and demonstrations were held in Belfast, Londonderry and elsewhere to protest against what was described as unfair treatment of the Catholics in Northern Ireland by the provincial government, which was overwhelmingly Protestant. These 'civil rights' demonstrations provoked counter-demonstrations by the Orangemen. Annual events like the Protestant commemoration of the Boyne and the Derry apprentices became occasions of disorder. The British government, fearing that Protestants and Catholics in Northern Ireland might soon be at one another's throats, sent over strong forces of British troops to assist the police in keeping the peace. The Irish Republican Army seized on the arrival of the troops as an opportunity to stir up ancient hatreds. It began a terrorist campaign, aimed not only at shooting down the 'enemy troops' and murdering those suspected of sympathising with them, but at making civilised life impossible in Northern Ireland by bombing hotels, shops, cinemas and restaurants, with great loss of life among civilians. The British government suspended the government of Northern Ireland and placed the country under a special secretary of state, responsible directly to the cabinet in London.

Thus the unhappy features of Irish history were seen yet again, on the smaller scale of the six counties. The Orangemen demanded that there should be no surrender to terrorism and that the Protestant majority in Northern Ireland should not be handed over to Catholic rule. The IRA hoped to wear down the British patience, and meanwhile to gain international sympathy for conducting a war of liberation against colonial oppression. The government in Dublin was in an embarrassing position. It dared not outrage public opinion by supporting the British against the IRA, and yet it doubted whether the IRA, if victorious, would be content to disband itself and retire to a peaceful life. It seemed more likely that the leaders of the IRA hoped for an Ireland that would be united under their own leadership, not under that of the moderate statesmen then in power in Dublin.

The British government felt that the civil rights demonstrators had some justification for claiming that the government in Northern Ireland was unfair to its Catholic citizens. Feeling this, it had the difficult task of deciding what concessions and reforms should be made; how the Protestant majority in Northern Ireland could be persuaded to make them; how to stop the terrorism in the shortest time without too much bloodshed; how to satisfy the moderate men among Catholics and Protestants alike without being deterred by the violence of the extremists; and how to resist the murmurings among its supporters in Britain, some of whom demanded ruthless action against the IRA terrorists, while others asked why British troops should suffer in an Irish quarrel, and why the Irish could not be left to fight it out among themselves.

It is not surprising if the Englishman does not understand the Irishman. Apart from any differences in temperament between Celt and Saxon, the two races have had very different experiences since the days when both suffered the incursions of the Danes. The English slowly developed a national unity; the Irish lost their national unity and sank into tribal disorder. The English were disciplined by a centralised Church and by the Norman Conquest; the Celtic Church was not centralised, and Ireland never came under the direct rule of such a strong king as William the Conqueror, Henry II, or Henry VII. All through the history of Anglo-

Irish relations, the English have been the many, the rich, the strong, the business-like, the attackers; the Irish have been few, poor, weak, disunited, on the defensive. The English have had their schemes and their ambitions; the Irish have been left with little but their dreams. But Ireland has always had a great power of attracting and absorbing her attackers. Many of Ireland's leaders in her long fight against England have been men of English origin.

The story of the English in Ireland is a sad tale of misunderstandings and mismanagement. Ireland was too close to England to be suitable as a place for those who wished to escape from royal misgovernment. The English who wanted to live in freedom went to Virginia or New England; those who wanted to make money went to India or the Caribbean. Comparatively few went to Ireland: enough to provoke, but – except for the seventeenth-century plantation of Ulster – not enough to conquer. The English government was too much influenced by the Englishmen who had estates in Ireland; but for their opposition, Pitt and Grattan might have made a deal with the United Irishmen before the Orange lodges were founded in Ulster, and Gladstone might have settled the land question without need for the miserable violence that marred Ireland in his later days. At no time did English statesmen before Gladstone ever sit down to consider seriously how Ireland differed from England and how best to develop it in the interests of the Irish. They always assumed that the Irish must be made to conform to English ways, and that Ireland was to be exploited for the benefit of England.

Bibliography

In addition to standard histories of Britain and of Europe, I have consulted the following specialist works:

Stephen King-Hall, *Our Own Times 1913–1938* (Nicholson & Watson, 1938).

Maurice Waters, *The United Nations* (Collier-Macmillan, 1967).

J. D. Clarkson, *A History of Russia From the Ninth Century* (Longmans, 1969).

Louis Fischer, *The Life of Lenin* (Weidenfeld & Nicolson, 1965).

George Lichtheim, *Marxism, a Critical and Historical Study* (Routledge, 1964).

Stefan D. Possony, *Lenin, the Compulsive Revolutionary* (Allen & Unwin, 1966).

Bertram D. Wolfe, *Three Who Made a Revolution* (Penguin, 1966).

Victor Purcell, *China* (Benn, 1962).

John Robottom, *Twentieth-Century China* (Wayland, 1971).

C. A. Fisher, *South-East Asia* (Methuen, 1964).

Denis Warner, *Reporting South-East Asia* (Angus & Robertson, 1966).

Jon Kimche, *The Second Arab Awakening* (Thames & Hudson, 1970).

Tom Little, *Egypt* (Benn, 1958).

John Marlowe, *The Seat of Pilate* (Barrie & Jenkins, 1959).

Terence Robertson, *Crisis* (Hutchinson, 1965). The crisis referred to is the Suez affair, 1956.

Christopher Sykes, *Cross-Roads to Israel* (Collins, 1965).

J. C. Beckett, *The Making of Modern Ireland 1603–1923* (Faber, 1969).

I have drawn much information on recent events from the press digests in Keesing's Contemporary Archives.

Index